Praise for The *Self*

"An inspiring read for anyone grappl ....
or self-esteem. What often holds people back is not skill or education or network, but their sense of self-worth. Filled with wisdom and practical tools, this is a timely read in today's world."

KRISTIN ENGVIG founder and CEO of WIN and WINconference, a global platform for women's leadership since 1997

"John gets to the heart of the deep lack of worth that afflicts so many people, even those who are unaware of the affliction. As a CEO coach, I often work with leaders who feel a relentless need to prove themselves and gain external validation. They oscillate between soaring self-esteem when the going is good, and sinking imposter syndrome when something is not going to plan. The greatest leaders operate from an innate sense of self-worth which enable them to focus on making betting choices and being of service rather than on the flashy deals or grand moves which, at their roots, are really more about ego than value."

GEORGINA WOUDSTRA founder and lead trainer of Coach Executive Studio and co-author of "Coaching Global Top Teams" in *Leadership Coaching: Working with Leaders to Develop Elite Performance*

"John's deep insights about value have brought tangible rewards to our sales team: at least $4 million in the first three years. Self-worth enables sales professionals to achieve more."

THOMAS MOLNAR VP global sales, TOMRA Sorting Food

"Lord Chesterfield advised, 'A man had better overvalue than undervalue himself... Whatever real merit you have, other people will discover; and people always magnify their own discoveries, as they lessen those of others.' In *The Self-Worth Safari*, John Niland beautifully expands on this sage advice. This is a compelling and action-oriented guide on learning to befriend and value oneself. Peppered with humor and story, this is a must-read for anyone struggling with how to value themselves or live up to their own expectations, creating a reputation with themselves of which they can be proud."

RONALD J. BAKER host of *The Soul of Enterprise* radio show and author of the bestselling *Implementing Value Pricing: A Radical Business Model for Professional Firms*

"*The Self-Worth Safari* shows you how to stop being a slave to your own self-doubt and anxiety, and ultimately discover more joy by becoming your own best friend."

MARSHALL GOLDSMITH *New York Times* #1–bestselling author of *Triggers, Mojo,* and *What Got You Here Won't Get You There*

"A fresh perspective on how self-worth is fundamental, at the core of every human being's ability to be impactful."

MONIKA MAJVALDOVA Head+Heart® Leadership, Prague, the Czech Republic's most established leadership program, running since 2007

The
Self-Worth
Safari

VCO
ACADEMY

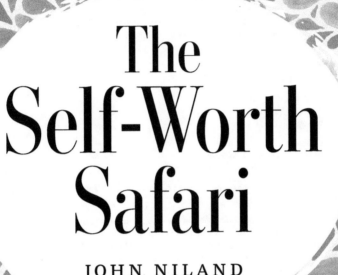

The Self-Worth Safari

JOHN NILAND

Valuing Your Life and Your Work

ISBN 978-1-5272-3548-9 (paperback)
ISBN 978-1-5272-3549-6 (ebook)

Published by VCO Academy Ltd.
Produced by Page Two
www.pagetwo.com

Cover design by Teresa Bubela
Interior design by Peter Cocking
Cover and interior illustrations by sofiacolor

Every reasonable effort has been made to contact the copyright holders for work reproduced in this book.

A special thanks to Dónall Dempsey for his kind permission to use the poem "ARTIST AT WORK." Also to Carcanet Press Limited for permission to quote Robert Graves' poem "On Giving." We acknowledge "Love After Love" from *THE POETRY OF DEREK WALCOTT 1948–2013* by Derek Walcott, selected by Glyn Maxwell. Copyright © 2014 by Derek Walcott. Reprinted by permission of Farrar, Straus and Giroux, for territories outside the UK and British Commonwealth. For UK and British Commonwealth countries, we acknowledge Faber and Faber Ltd. to quote "Love After Love" from *The Poetry of Derek Walcott 1948–2013*, published by Faber and Faber Ltd. For David Whyte's "Everything is waiting for you," we acknowledge permission from Many Rivers Press, www.davidwhyte.com, David Whyte, *Everything Is Waiting for You*, together with © 2003 Many Rivers Press, Langley, WA USA. For the poem "Calls" from *THE COMPLETE POEMS OF CARL SANDBURG*, Revised and Expanded Edition. Copyright © 1970, 1969 by Lilian Steichen Sandburg, Trustee. Reprinted by Permission of Houghton Mifflin Harcourt Publishing Company. All rights reserved.

Some names and identifying details have been changed to protect the privacy of individuals.

The Self-Worth Academy has chosen to follow American spelling and style for this publication.

SelfWorthAcademy.com

This book is dedicated to my mother, Annie:
a role model of unconditional love.
Ar dheis Dé go raibh a hanam dílis.

"And the end of all our exploring
Will be to arrive where we started
And know the place for the first time."

T.S. ELIOT, *FOUR QUARTETS*

Contents

Introduction

THIS IS A book about being happy, but more than that it's about enhancing your capacity to act in the world. It's not a book about staring into space, mindfully contemplating your navel. Or your selfie.

Its subject is how we value ourselves. When a person's sense of value is deeply rooted in real self-worth, they feel more secure from day to day. They are no longer a hostage to the ups and downs of their nebulous reputation with themselves. Even if today they don't meet their own expectations, they can resume life tomorrow without a loss of identity or energy. They contribute more because they are not constantly seeking validation.

For decades, however, we have been educated in a culture of conditional *self-esteem*—not intrinsic *self-worth*. As a result, there is mounting evidence that we are nurturing narcissism and an ever-present anxiety about not living up to one's full potential. While self-esteem often motivates action, it also writes a blank check for depression, insecurity, self-preoccupation, self-obsession and an insatiable craving for attention and validation. Welcome to twenty-first-century living.

How did I learn this? The hard way: from the University of Life. Over a two-year period, a succession of losses forced me to reexamine how I'd been living life up to that point. I'd always assumed I had a reasonable relationship with myself: neither too confident on the one hand, nor too self-abasing on the other. However, that series of setbacks showed me with brutal clarity that my self-esteem was *contingent* and vulnerable: very dependent on the ups and downs of life. My friendship with myself depended on how I was doing at the "game of living."

When business was going well and I was happily in love, I felt good about myself. But when I suffered a burnout, the loss of a relationship, the death of my mother, and a succession of business disappointments, my reputation with myself also suffered. I developed compensation habits, such as overeating (particularly when traveling), and gained more pounds than I wanted to be wearing. I had difficulties making decisions. Despite reasonable reserves of willpower, my usual resources and determination seemed to be deserting me.

Looking back, I now see that I was a typical product of "self-esteem thinking": driven by performance, striving for potential, in a constant quest for my own approval. As I began to share my experience with others, I found that I was not alone in this. As one conversation followed another during my meanders around the world, some key distinctions began to emerge from the mists around me. Week by week, the "Self-Worth Safari" was conceived and eventually born, with a gestation period roughly that of a black rhinoceros. This short adventure can be taken today in the form of a coaching journey, or a series of online or in-person workshops, usually over a six-week period. You will find more about the Self-Worth Safari at the end of the book.

Why call this journey a "safari"? The thrill of discovering an unexpected new friendship with myself was incredible: a bit like breaking through into a sunlit valley that I never before knew was there. Some fellow adventurers have joined me along the way, and most of them also found the self-worth journey to be a novel exploration. It's the beginning of a new friendship with oneself, a new loyalty to one's own being.

I travel a lot: mainly to speak at conferences and events. I've left some of my own geography in the writing of this book out of a deep respect for the places where key insights about self-worth occurred to me. But the real reason for calling this program the Self-Worth Safari is not my own geographical wanderings but the unexpected thrill of a new inner adventure, an excursion that takes us to fresh pastures and horizons.

I felt it was important to test these new shifts of perspective: in particular, I was curious if they would work across cultures. So in the first couple of years while the Safari was still being constructed, we ran pilots with about 120 people across five countries to validate the shifts. In a real sense, we were building a bridge while we were walking on it: crossing from an old, limiting bank of self-esteem toward a new perspective, a radically different relationship with ourselves.

A few people confessed that, for them, this happy state of intrinsic, unconditional self-worthiness was a dream, a distant horizon. I recall one woman denying that such a utopia even existed: she flatly declared that she could never befriend herself unconditionally. Yet after only a week, she was rocked by an unjustified complaint from a friend and discovered that an intrinsic friendship with herself was just around the corner. In the space of that incident, her roots grasped new soil.

The purpose of this book is to provide a navigation guide for that very excursion and to bring that distant dream closer to present-day reality for more people. However, just as a guidebook is not a safari, *this book is not the adventure.* There is a world of difference between having an intellectual grasp of self-worth and living the experience of self-worth as part of life's journey. Self-worth is like good food: it has to be enjoyed in the belly, not just in the brain.

The book is divided into two parts. The first distinguishes self-worth from self-esteem and illustrates how this distinction can really empower a person in life and work. In this section, we look at how to build self-worth via a series of seven shifts across six "terrains": the body, relationships, career, money, friendship, and leisure. In the second part, I address some of the issues that have come up during Safari groups, ranging from typical setbacks, leadership challenges, saying yes and no, dealing with negotiation, and the phenomenon of imposter syndrome.

Whether you feel you need a better relationship with yourself, wish to nurture the self-worth you already have, or want to support others with these issues, I hope these pages will encourage you to embark on this exploration. Perhaps you are not starting with any great optimism. If so, don't worry: many others who took part in the early Safari groups have felt the same. Others were outwardly successful people, yet their external sense of confidence gave no clue about the insecurity that often lurked within.

Struggling with this issue of self-worth is not just philosophical or abstract; it's very real and can be very painful. Many people suffer from constant insecurity. Nevertheless, we will try to bring a light touch to this adventure. As Robert Frost reputedly said, "If we couldn't laugh, we would all go insane." Living lightly is an integral part of the Safari, dropping a lot of unnecessary burdens as we travel.

One Safari participant, Marie, put it this way: "I've discovered that I am enough, I do enough, and I have enough. Furthermore, I found that all of this was true for years before I found out. At last, I can give myself permission to enjoy it."

More about the Safari groups can be found at the end of this book. The stories included are real, drawn from Safari voyagers as well as from my coaching clients. I trust that details are disguised sufficiently to protect identities: any resemblance to any living person is therefore either accidental or coincidental.

Some Safari groups focus on specific issues: work, relationships, money, business development, the body, or friendship. Whether you join a group or not, I hope this book will give you some fresh awareness, so that you can make a good beginning on the adventure of a new friendship with yourself.

"Childlike, I danced in a dream;
Blessings emblazoned that day;
Everything glowed with a gleam;
Yet we were looking away!"

**THOMAS HARDY,
"THE SELF-UNSEEING"**

Part I
Discovering Self-Worth

. . . .

(1)

Why Self-Worth?

"To love yourself is the beginning
of a lifelong romance."

OSCAR WILDE

TO ALL OUTWARD appearances, Sam is a confident, friendly, and talented career woman. Now in her mid-thirties, she has broken through several layers of male-dominated management at the global media company where she works and has won respect everywhere for her ability to perform and deliver. Everyone speaks highly of Sam.

Unbeknownst to her work colleagues, however, Sam is on the verge of a breakdown. Behind the facade of confidence, she has spent a decade in a state of constant anxiety. Sometimes, she forgets to eat or just pretends to do so. When she comes home, she is often in a state of near collapse from exhaustion.

Skilled in the subtle art of how to present herself, she is adept at hiding her inner turmoil. If you met Sam, you would find no bitten nails, no fleeting eye contact, no visible clues about the unrest within. You might detect a slight tightness in her voice and in her laugh, which you would only hear if you listened very, very carefully.

Sam's friends know nothing about her anxiety. She is careful to share with them her frustrations about work or relationships or life issues, but she keeps her deepest fears a closely guarded secret. Even from herself.

Sam is constantly in motion: traveling, going to and from the yoga studio, social events, cocktails, the cinema. Even on holiday, Sam is moving: climbing, diving, sailing. She starts each day in a tornado of activity... even on weekends. When her last boyfriend moved out, one of his comments was "I just cannot live at your pace."

Once or twice, a well-meaning friend has asked, "Why the hurry?" Sam's response has always been one of irritation. To her, life is about achievement, excellence, living the dream. She dismisses both Zen and Xanax as cop-outs, despising both meditation and medication as the consolations of the dispossessed. Life for Sam is about "living large": having an impact on the world. Not just contemplating sunsets.

However, this ever-present anxiety is now starting to take its toll. With the collapse of her last relationship, the additional responsibilities of her latest promotion, and a recurring sleep problem, Sam is wondering how long she can hold all this together. Inside, she feels a hollow sense of failure, a gnawing suspicion that she has been an imposter all along. She constantly questions herself. If she stops, will it all come crashing down? How then will she live with herself? Who indeed will she be?

Sam is operating on self-esteem. To some extent, she is looking for validation from others, too. But mostly she wants her *own* approval. This is hardly surprising: Sam is doing exactly what her education (and upbringing and peer group) has taught her to do. Her level of satisfaction with herself is based on certain *conditions*. As a result, her sense of self is rooted in shallow soil. Sam is in a constant state of anxiety, even when she sleeps.

Sam's high self-awareness—which for so long has been an asset—somehow appears to have become a liability. The incessant self-questioning is draining her energy. Her capacity to act is weakened. The very self-esteem that drove her early success and achievement now seems to be eating itself from within.

Seduced by Self-Esteem

Thousands of books have been written about relationships. From *How to Win Friends and Influence People* to finding love to impacting others, our relationships have long preoccupied our minds. Our relationship with ourselves, too, has come under close scrutiny, particularly in the Anglo-American world of personal development, where the self often sits center stage. The perennial pursuit of self-esteem has filled countless courses and therapy rooms, as well as been front of mind for at least two generations of educators. Let's be honest: an entire personal development industry is eager for you to knock on its door, to share any issues you may have with your self-esteem and so be a candidate for their services.

But is self-esteem really the ultimate goal? There is mounting evidence that self-esteem—long regarded as the holy grail of personal development—is not delivering on its promise. Instead, the widespread pursuit of self-esteem seems to be nurturing narcissism, addiction to praise, and ever-present anxiety about not living up to one's full potential. Far from producing generations of self-assured adults, we seem to be cultivating even more self-preoccupation, anxiety, and depression than ever before. According to the World Health Organization, more than 300 million people are now living with depression, an increase of more than 18 per cent between 2005 and 2015.

In my business-coaching work, I see the consequences of self-preoccupation every day. The incessant question "How am I doing?" is a recipe for weaker negotiators, narcissistic managers, and insecure professionals. In every walk of life, self-preoccupation is a malaise that often weakens real job effectiveness. If you are a manager of people, you probably see this every day. When it's your turn to buy a service, don't you want a professional who is focused on *your* needs, not his or her ratings or performance? Self-obsession usually diminishes a person's capacity to bounce back from setbacks, because every disappointment is a reflection on *them*.

One evening in London some years ago, this was summed up for me by an intelligent young man who was prey to a host of insecurities. In one sentence, he summarized his constant anxiety with the exclamation: "I'm not much... but I'm all I think about."

The philosopher Alan Watts once labeled this the "law of reverse effect." As Watts put it, "Insecurity is the result of trying to be secure." In the pursuit of self-esteem, we often become increasingly aware of that which we lack. For example, when you are finally able to run a half-marathon, you want to run a full marathon. When you move into that dream home, you start thinking about a yacht. Or a new lover. Or both.

The result is a vicious cycle of self-preoccupation. In the pursuit of self-esteem, we keep moving our aspirations one step further, and the end of the rainbow moves ahead of us however close we get to it.

Self-esteem can hold you back and limit your happiness in three ways. First of all, it's a hungry ghost: an insatiable craving for endless approval from the Self. Second, while self-esteem can initially boost performance (in our desire to impress ourselves and others), it ultimately limits our effectiveness and resilience. (This is illustrated in chapter 5.) Third, it's a recipe for narcissism, anxiety, and depression.

Unlike self-esteem, self-worth is a loyal companion, not contingent on meeting expectations—neither those of others nor of ourselves. Self-worth is independent of our performance; it's

"I'm not much . . . but I'm all I think about."

a fundamental, *unconditional* friendship with ourselves. Unlike the fickle friendship of self-esteem, self-worth is a faithful ally in the most challenging of times, on those gray days when we most need to be a friend to ourselves. We can have self-worth even when we skip the yoga class, eat a bag of chips, or get rejected.

No matter where we go, we take ourselves with us. So we might as well be friends. No matter how illusory a psychologist may claim a self-concept to be, what possible joy can we have in any relationship or accomplishment if we go home to be miserable with ourselves?

Benefits of Self-Worth

When you possess real self-worth, you are not obsessed with proving yourself. An unconditional sense of your own value gives you a new lease on happiness and freedom. You develop energy and stamina. You recover quickly from setbacks and gain confidence that you can develop and grow. You are not afraid of people or situations, because you trust your power to deal with them. Being able to say yes and no, you negotiate with new clarity and confidence. Your relationships improve. You tackle hitherto difficult tasks with fresh energy, lightness, and purpose. No longer a hostage to prolonged spells of anxiety, frustration, envy, or guilt, you have an enhanced capacity to act. You are therefore more valued as a colleague, advisor, or partner at work. And your self-esteem grows, too, precisely when you are no longer chasing it.

You might imagine that such profound changes take time. While self-esteem certainly does take time to build, a powerful inner foundation of self-worth can be built in a relatively short time via a new awareness of clear distinctions coupled with a few focused affirmative actions. Welcome to the Self-Worth Safari.

For many of us, this was an unexpected, new adventure. Self-esteem is a bit like walking down the street as if you owned it. Self-worth is walking down the street and not caring who owns it. Self-worth is an intrinsic sense of your own value as a person, independent of what's going on around you.

It's worth noting that this is *not* how we have been taught to think ... in the Western world, at least. For several decades now, we have been indoctrinated with a self-esteem mindset. "If you want self-esteem, do esteeming things" goes the mantra of achievement. So we are constantly exhorted to prove ourselves—in school, in higher education, in sports, in physique ... —by setting goals and achieving them. By the time we

Self-esteem is a bit like walking down the street as if you owned it. Self-worth is walking down the street and not caring who owns it.

reach the workplace—if we achieve that goal at all—we have been fully indoctrinated and feel we must somehow prove ourselves at every turn of the road.

The problem, however, is this "prove yourself" religion is a surefire recipe for insecurity. Self-esteem thinking writes a blank check for anxiety, a check that Big Pharma is ready and willing to cash. In the United States, prescription rates for Xanax have been climbing at an average 9 per cent annual rate since 2008. The number of Xanax prescriptions has risen from 29.9 million to 37.5 million between 2010 and 2015.

By cultivating self-worth, you nurture a rich soil in which real achievement can grow. When setbacks happen, your sense of self is not undermined but is strengthened. You go into meetings and presentations with a new attitude. Self-care comes easily, as a natural consequence of your friendship with yourself. You enjoy a new level of energy and happiness. Your capacity to have an impact in the workplace and in the world is increased. In the words of Irene—an experienced yoga teacher who participated in the Safari—"Self-worth just comes from the belly... and lifts you from the ground."

From Words to Reality

"A man cannot be comfortable without his own approval."

MARK TWAIN

Sounds plausible, doesn't it? Particularly when attributed to Mark Twain. But we are going to expose the fallacy behind the Twain quote above, as well as questioning a few other clichés along the way.

If someone always needs their own approval, then they are destined to have many uncomfortable days, indeed. Worse still, they may spend a lifetime in a state of "undeserving." Approval has to be earned, right? If approval has to be granted, it can just as easily be withdrawn.

We begin with a distinction between self-worth and self-esteem. This is not just a semantic, intellectual difference. To get the full significance of this distinction, it is necessary to live it. Intellectually, I understood the distinction for at least two years before I began to live it. I hope you find it more easily.

To fully benefit from the Self-Worth Safari, it's necessary to get clear not just about certain words but about the reality behind the words. Let's start with a few basic descriptions.

Other-Esteem

Other-esteem is chasing recognition and affirmation of your value from an external source, often a person or group.

Until I was in my mid-thirties, my confidence in myself was low. In one way or another, I seemed to always be chasing a rainbow. No matter how much I succeeded in college, in jobs, or in society, there always remained a sense of hollowness inside, coupled with an insecurity that sooner or later I would be "found out." When, later in life, my colleague at the Self-Worth Academy Claudia Vettore told me about imposter syndrome, I readily related to the phenomenon, which is discussed in depth in chapter 15.

Outwardly, I could wear the mask of confidence, even as a student. In my first project-management roles, for example, I did my best to "act the part," at least on good days. Confidence (defined here as how we present ourselves to the world) can be faked and I had a master's degree in pretending.

Because my self-esteem was low, as was my confidence, I did a lot of things to win the approval of others and of myself. Like many a young person, at work I pursued promotions, solved difficult problems, and volunteered to take on responsibilities (occasionally working all night); I was friendly so that I'd be liked, told jokes to make people laugh; I bought property and a bigger car... You get the picture.

From the surveys done by my colleague Alison Spackman at the Self-Worth Academy, we see a similar pattern. Other-esteem seems to climb steadily during the twenties and peak in the early thirties. Winning the approval of other people is a key motivator in early professional life.

All the time, I was chasing other-esteem in a vain attempt to fill the hollow within. I was like an Easter egg in search of more chocolate. Because my self-esteem was low, my need for approval from others was high. Hence, I expended a lot of energy on the behaviors noted above. The unconscious rationale was that if other people thought well of me, I would eventually feel good about myself.

Self-Esteem

Self-esteem is the reputation that we have with ourselves... even when nobody is watching.

During the time I spent chasing approval from others, I was also trying to build a reputation with myself. When I worked all day and night to solve a difficult problem at work, I was not just trying to get approval from my boss, I was trying to prove something to the guy in the mirror. Sometimes this was fun: it was a game I played, competing against myself. But it still absorbed a lot of my energy and attention.

The need for self-esteem starts very early in life. In pursuit of self-esteem, we can aim for high marks, weight loss, awards, qualifications, romance, children, charitable giving, appearance, cars, houses, financial security, personal fitness, better/more sex, or a different career. Naturally, we tell ourselves that we are *choosing* to do these things—that we are doing them for ourselves, not for anyone else. Or we convince ourselves we are having fun doing so. To be fair, sometimes we are.

Indeed, are we not educated to think this way? From a very early age, we are encouraged to develop exactly this sort of inner motivation. We are often expressly taught that this quality of self-esteem is precisely what differentiates successful people from the broad mass of average achievers. The catechism of twenty-first-century secular belief begins with self-belief and the liturgy of self-esteem is by now an extensive one. A recent example of this is the rise of "your optimized self": a myriad of apps tracking your every move, exhorting you to set goals and be the best you can be. The implication being that you are not already okay.

Having a value of excellence from early days, I totally bought into the self-esteem credo. Five years in an Irish boarding school ensured I had the survivor's dubious gift of self-reliance. By the time I left college, I believed in total freedom and responsibility . . . even before I read Sartre's writing on the subject.

With self-esteem as the new credo, its litany is made up of affirmations. Day by day, we try to affirm that we are smart, beautiful, successful, whatever it takes to establish that chimerical relationship with the Self. "Fake it 'til you make it" is expressly taught in Confidence School, along with power stances and the absolute imperative of self-belief. The slightest deviation from the path of positive self-regard is pounced upon and corrected. Like a Catholic nun might have reproached your venial sins a half-century earlier, lapses of "self-limiting beliefs" are now exposed and shamed in the orthodoxy of self-esteem.

But while believing in self-esteem is one thing, possessing it is something else. It was to be another decade before I gained any real measure of self-esteem. As fast as I met my own self-imposed conditions for self-esteem, new conditions appeared. Self-esteem is a hungry tyrant: the more you feed him, the more he expects. So it was not enough to get a job, get married, and have kids, I also had to emigrate, support my family of origin, go on foreign holidays, buy property, start my own business . . . and still the monster was forever hungry. So I was never really happy with myself.

Drawing on the results of Alison Spackman's research at the Self-Worth Academy, we see that in the early thirties, self-esteem seems to take over from other-esteem as a key driver. Our reputation with ourselves now begins to assume more importance. So, without knowing this at the time, I guess I was part of the general pattern.

Both other-esteem and self-esteem have one characteristic in common: they are contingent. Only the source is different. When we are operating in esteem mode, it hardly matters what the source is. Whether we are getting that validation from inside or outside, the level will always be variable and based on achievement. We pursue each new validation with all the earnestness of a dog chasing a car.

Self-Worth

Self-worth is a deep belief in your inherent value as a person, from a position of unconditional friendship with yourself. You don't earn self-worth by doing worthy things: you already have it.

Like many people, I used to equate self-worth and self-esteem, assuming they were synonyms. It took a succession of losses in my fifties to teach me this vital distinction.

When you are in love, or your career is booming, you feel good about yourself. In those halcyon days, self-worth and self-esteem both seem to be on the rise. The distinction will appear merely semantic, drowned out in the happy song of love or success. The soft whisper of self-worth is hard to hear when an orchestra of romance or success is playing its full crescendo. But when life is tough, or you fail to live up to your own expectations, the difference between self-worth and self-esteem suddenly becomes very real.

Self-worth is *intrinsic*, not extrinsic. It comes from within, not from your behavior or your performance. It's about you, not your actions or even your feelings. It's already there within; you just need to find it. It's a belly-level sense of being on your own side. It has nothing to do with whether you are eating a bag of chips while you are thinking about it.

Self-worth is not contingent. In other words, you always have it. There are no conditions to be fulfilled. You don't even have to feel it or believe in it; it's yours by the very fact of your existence. Even if you have not found it yet.

Self-worth is a primal belief in your own value as a person. It is not variable based on your deeds, possessions, or whether you go to the gym. It's about you; not your behavior, your current state, or your achievements. For all these reasons, self-worth is the strongest possible foundation for self-esteem, confidence, and general happiness.

How do you know that self-worth is "real"? Unlike self-esteem, which you can readily feel—whether by its presence or absence—self-worth speaks in a softer voice. So you have to listen carefully. People can access their self-worth in a range of different ways. Over the course of this book, we will consider many of these.

Based on our initial Self-Worth Academy research, conducted by Alison Spackman, the group that seems to be most motivated by self-worth is self-employed women. By contrast, self-employed men show up as overwhelmingly driven by self-esteem. Women in employment also share the self-esteem driver. Indeed, the profile of self-employed men looks remarkably similar to employed women.

Interestingly, to date, our survey work at the Self-Worth Academy has not uncovered that legendary "self-esteem gap" between men and women. Levels of self-esteem were broadly similar across genders. However, the responses obtained suggest that women may be more driven by self-worth, while men are motivated by a blend of self-esteem and other-esteem. This may throw an interesting spanner into the works of a lot of self-esteem literature: is it possible that the "self-esteem gap" has arisen because we have been measuring conditional, performance-based self-esteem, as opposed to intrinsic, unconditional self-worth? More work remains to be done here.

One thing, however, is clear. The softer voice of self-worth has been largely ignored in the clamor for self-esteem. In pursuit of the holy grail represented by a positive evaluation of ourselves, we have generally neglected the truth that we've been standing on all the time: the possibility of an unconditional loyalty to one's own worth.

Self-Compassion and Self-Love

There are two other terms commonly used in connection with self-worth. The meaning of each is very close but subtly different.

Self-compassion has been extensively written about in recent years, notably by authors like Kristin Neff and Christopher Germer. Self-compassion is being kind and understanding toward oneself, particularly when confronted with personal shortcomings. The practices of self-compassion described by both of these writers fit very well with self-worth—as long as you believe that you are worth it, of course! For many people, this is the crux of the problem: they do not believe that they *deserve* self-compassion. Their friendship toward themselves often takes second place to their sense of responsibility toward others. This book focuses on your sense of *deserving*. The books by Kristin Neff and Christopher Germer are certainly recommended reading; the practices of self-compassion usually flow easily as an expression of self-worth.

Self-love is a broad term, used in different ways by different people. Some people think of it as an attitude; others focus

"Roots are not in landscape
or a country, or a people,
they are inside you."

ISABEL ALLENDE

more on the action of taking care of oneself. I have even seen it used as an excuse, for example by people invoking "self-love" when they want to avoid keeping promises or when they cancel appointments at the last minute . . . an excuse that others are naturally expected to understand! Because of this vagueness—and perhaps even misuse—I have generally avoided using the term "self-love" in this book, opting instead to use words with more specific meaning.

Working Definitions

Summing up the descriptions above, I am using the following definitions of confidence, other-esteem, self-esteem, self-worth, and self-compassion.

Confidence: This is how we present ourselves to the world. Confidence can be real or faked.

Other-esteem: This is our reputation with others, which can be established by popularity, positive feedback, people-pleasing, making people laugh, "likes" on social media, and a host of other ways by which we register "social impact."

Self-esteem: Using Nathaniel Branden's definition, self-esteem is our reputation with ourselves. Self-esteem is how we perceive we "measure up" to our own standards. Therefore, it fluctuates according to how we perform and how we judge ourselves.

Self-worth: This is our intrinsic sense of worth as a person. It comes from within, not from our behavior or our performance. The strongest foundation for self-esteem, self-compassion, and confidence.

Self-compassion: Being kind and understanding to oneself, particularly when dealing with "failure" or setbacks.

Perennial Roots

You can think of self-worth as the roots and self-esteem as the stem and the branches of a plant. Like roots below the ground, self-worth is unseen. What we see is the plant, the branches and leaves, which may be flowering or not, depending on the season of the year. Indeed, self-esteem goes through its seasons, albeit more unpredictably than the climatic seasons. At times, it is spring and self-esteem grows, particularly when we feel we are progressing in life. Perhaps we are doing well at work or we've fallen in love or lost weight or gained in fitness. At these times, the self-esteem "plant" thrives.

In the soil, the roots exist throughout the seasons. Even in autumn, when the leaves are falling or the flowers fading, the roots are still alive. Much the same is true of self-worth. So when we are *not* doing so well at work or we've lost a loved one or we've fallen off our planned diet, the roots of self-worth are as present as ever. Indeed, it's precisely when the plant is in its autumn or winter that the roots are most important, protecting the future of the plant. In much the same way, self-worth provides a perennial foundation for self-esteem—an idea also expressed in a poem by Tolkien:

> *All that is gold does not glitter,*
> *Not all those who wander are lost;*
> *The old that is strong does not wither,*
> *Deep roots are not reached by the frost.*

Shame and Guilt

There are many opposites to self-esteem. These range from self-doubt, self-deprecation, self-loathing, shyness, timidity, diffidence, even self-disgust. You can probably add a few more of your own.

So what is the opposite of self-worth? If there is one word that keeps cropping up in nearly everything I've read or experienced, it's *shame*. This short word seems to capture that deep sense of undeserving or unworthiness, which anyone who has struggled with self-worth will probably recognize immediately. So let's unashamedly talk about that.

As humans, we have the capacity to reflect on what we have done, or not done. This produces two closely related feelings, both of which will be all too familiar to many readers: guilt and shame. Using Brené Brown's very accessible definitions, let's first distinguish between these two corrosive cousins.

Guilt: I've done something I shouldn't have: the act was bad. Guilt is about the *action*.

Shame: I've done something I shouldn't have (or not done something I should have). *I am bad.* Shame is about *me*, not the action (or inaction).

In this context, we can regard shame as the opposite of self-worth. A person with high self-worth can still experience guilt, but somehow it does not impinge on *who* they are. They can make amends (or not) and move on. But for the person with low self-worth, a sense of shame constantly withers their inner roots. Even when there is no specific act to feel guilty about, they can feel ashamed of who or what they are *not*.

According to Brené Brown, shame has been correlated with "a wide range of mental and public health issues including self-esteem/concept issues, depression, addiction, eating disorders, bullying, suicide, family violence, and sexual assault." In extreme forms, shame can lead to social withdrawal and isolation. It's easy to see why: the inner void constantly craves fulfillment.

Shame is a deeply pervasive emotion: "the swampland of the soul," as Jung once described it. Deep feelings of shame may relate to early life experiences (abuse, chaotic household, violence, bullying, etc.) and, as such, are matters for therapeutic help, well beyond the scope of this book. But many people who have no such trauma in their upbringing also experience shame. Brené Brown believes that the experience of feeling unworthy is universal.

Even without the therapeutic extremes, it seems that most human beings get to grapple with some shame-related issues at some point of their lives. For example:

- "I am a failure with money/in bed/at love/at work."
- "I am unattractive."
- "I am a failure as a parent/family member."
- "I am defective/wrong."
- "I am stupid/useless/easily fooled."

For many people suffering from shame-related issues, just grasping the distinction between self-esteem and self-worth can be enlightening—even transformative. One Safari participant who had suffered real trauma in early life found that she could somehow hold on to self-worth in those foggy days when otherwise her reputation with herself lay in tatters. Today, she is working full-time for the first time in years.

The Self-Worth Quiz

The distinction between self-worth and self-esteem is a vital one to understand. It's a new distinction for many people, which can take time to grasp. So before going much further, may I ask you to examine each of these statements and consider whether it's one of self-worth or self-esteem?

Please take the time to write down your answers. When you have considered your answers, you can turn to Appendix A (page 309) for comments and explanations. Be prepared for some surprises! And please note that your self-worth does not depend on getting the "right" answer. The questions are here to illuminate the distinction, not to declare anyone right or wrong. Not even me!

1. If I could only find meaningful work, I would feel so much better about myself.
2. I am grateful for my good health.
3. I deserve to be happy.
4. I am so proud of my children.
5. I believe in always doing my best.
6. I want to be a good friend to myself.
7. A healthy lifestyle is essential to a good relationship with myself.
8. I have value because I am loved by God. (Or, the Universe supports me.)
9. I choose to take responsibility for my own well-being.
10. Good time-management is essential for self-care.
11. I live for my family.
12. One of the benefits of a new relationship with myself is the freedom to contribute.
13. I must live with integrity. It's essential that I can trust myself.
14. I must remove all negativity from my life.
15. I sometimes feel very lonely.

Making Space for Learning

When I do this quiz at Self-Worth Safari workshops, or individually with clients, interesting discussions usually follow. Most of these are healthy discussions that deepen understanding and guide participants toward a fresh perspective of unconditional friendship with themselves. As is normal in any development environment, we sometimes disagree about certain questions and responses. Furthermore, there is a huge cultural inheritance of self-esteem with which to deal. The net result is that it takes *time* to digest these distinctions.

There are, however, a number of less helpful narratives that can easily block that digestion process. I call these the Self-Worth Hijacks because of the tendency for such discussions to commandeer the Safari. I include three of the most common ones here, addressing any readers who may be reacting to the quiz above in one of the following ways.

The Academic Hijack

Intellectuals and lawyers love debate and there is enough material here to keep them busy for months. Furthermore, self-worth (unlike self-esteem) has not as yet been much researched, so it's an easy target. When we add all the nuances of language and culture, it's easy to bury that precious friendship with ourselves under a truckload of linguistic rubble.

The problem with the academic hijack is twofold. First, it's often a classic power play of self-esteem in action, particularly in group settings, where people try to prove how clever they are. Second, the academic hijack can also be used as a form of "sophisticated procrastination," forever postponing discovery of self-worth in an endless cycle of learning and intellectual preconditions.

The Spiritual Hijack

Some readers may be familiar with the term "spiritual bypassing": the tendency to use spiritual ideas and practices to avoid facing unresolved emotional issues or psychological wounds. The term was introduced in the early 1980s by John Welwood, himself a Buddhist teacher and psychotherapist. In the context of self-worth, this often surfaces as a rejection of the mind and of understanding, replacing that with a perennial cycle of chasing "experiences" or "states," which will somehow confer self-worth by magic.

There are many spiritual approaches that support intrinsic self-worth and enhance a person's capacity to act and have impact in the world. But there are also many spiritual ecosystems full of vulnerable people with low self-worth, often at the mercy of self-appointed "gurus" and "teachers" claiming an innate right to download some very questionable truth and tell others how to live their lives. But the problem is that you cannot fix low self-worth with astrology or divination. That just postpones the issue. The route proposed in this book may at times be arduous and tedious: it certainly lacks the psychedelic effects of an ayahuasca trip in Peru. So, while it's easy to be seduced by the allure of a charismatic guru, perhaps the most reliable guru is that friend in the mirror.

The "I've Done It All" Hijack

For some people, self-worth is a topic for others to learn from, but it's not new for them. I recall a long email from a friend who reacted to a workshop invitation in exactly this way. She claimed to be secure and confident in her career and development journey. But equally she was angry at those "others" who needed it.

I do not doubt for a moment that many people possess a calm self-assurance. A lucky few seem to be born that way. Others develop it as part of life's experience. Yet I have little doubt that my accomplished friend who emailed me is still living her life based on self-esteem, not self-worth. I see this in her drive for recognition, in her tendency to judge others, in her frustration with the world around her, and in her constant need to impress and be right.

The Name-Your-Own Hijack

There are many other hijacks: the Culture Hijack that relativizes self-worth or the Gender Hijack that makes it an issue of gender and society. There is the Generation Hijack, the Status/Success Hijack, and the Life Is Awesome Hijack. There are so many settled people who want to stop others from going on the Safari.

Whatever way this grabs you, I invite you to make space for learning in this adventure. You don't have to agree with my language or my beliefs. You don't even need to like what I'm saying. In the end, there is only one thing that counts: your friendship with yourself.

Being Loyal to Yourself

As you work through the following chapters, you will hear a constant refrain about being loyal to yourself. Loyalty is a vital ingredient of self-worth. Isn't it strange that we hear so much about loyalty to others (such as employers, colleagues, friends, a life partner)—yet so little is said about being loyal to yourself? Why? Are you not worth it?

Being loyal to yourself means staying on your own side, even when (perhaps *especially* when) you are disappointing yourself and not living up to your own expectations. It means not berating yourself when others don't like you and equally not berating yourself when you don't like aspects of yourself. It means extending the same hand of supportive compassion to oneself that we would willingly extend to a friend.

Australian nurse Bronnie Ware wrote about her many years of working in palliative care in *The Top Five Regrets of the Dying*, and the most common regret of all was "I wish I'd had the courage to live a life true to myself, not the life others expected of me." I've heard the same sentiment expressed many times in my coaching work, particularly when people look back on their work experience. I've never heard anyone tortured by the idea of not spending more hours at work ten years ago, not going that extra mile for the team. I've heard many, many people express regret that they tried so hard with that difficult client or boss.

Why do so many people find it hard to be loyal to themselves and their deepest needs? The answer to this question is sure to be complex, involving factors of culture, generation, gender, and a host of individual phenomena. It would be far too simplistic to say that low self-worth was the only reason. However, one thing is certain. It's very unlikely that anyone can live a life true to themselves if they do not believe they are worth it.

Being *worth it* is not something you earn. That's just more self-esteem talk. You are worth it already, whether you recognize it or not. So let's start discovering that truth.

About the Exercises and Practices

You will get more value from this book if you take time to do the exercises and practices . . . #justsaying!

There are suggested exercises at the end of each chapter that follows in part I. However, you don't have to do all the exercises at once: I suggest you choose two or three that most appeal to you from each chapter. Some of the exercises are reflective, particularly at the beginning, in order to promote understanding. As we progress on the Safari, the exercises become more action-focused in order to build self-worth.

On the Resources page of SelfWorthAcademy.com, there are downloadable documents to support you on your own Safari. Before the adventure begins, would you like to check your self-worth, as it is today, before you read further in this book? At the beginning of the Safari, the first question on many people's minds is "Where is my self-worth now?" If you wish to establish this baseline, you can download the Self-Worth Stocktake. We have also created an online guide to create your own (totally confidential) Self-Worth Journey that includes occasional checkpoints to review how your self-worth is growing. You are also welcome to design your own.

Practices are sprinkled throughout the book. I suggest you incorporate these into your daily routine as soon as possible, in order to gain an experience of self-worth. In particular, I suggest you create your Self-Worth Check-In: a scheduled moment in your agenda when you consciously turn your attention to your friendship with yourself. Ideally this should be daily, at the very least weekly.

You can use your Self-Worth Check-In to do the exercises, to reflect and/or journal about what you are reading, or to complete the online Self-Worth Journey. Or, if you prefer, you can simply go for a walk in your own company.

Exercises for Understanding Self-Worth

In order to better understand the dynamics of self-worth and self-esteem in your life, I invite you to reflect on some or all of the following points, recording your answers in a journal.

1. List some things that you have done to win the approval of others (other-esteem).

2. List some things that you have done to gain a good reputation with yourself (self-esteem). What have these cost you, financially or otherwise?

3. Can you identify some events or external influences in early life that gave you a sense of shame? (For example, poverty,

bullying, religious teaching, abuse, trauma, or a chaotic household. Please note that some of these issues may require therapeutic help, which is beyond the scope of this book.)

4. What have you learned by doing the self-worth quiz? Can you identify a belief that you currently hold that might be camouflaging your sense of self-worth (such as the need to sacrifice your well-being for loved ones)?

5. Do you have any recurring patterns of negative self-talk? (For example, "I'm an idiot!" or "How could anyone want me?")

6. Chart a personal life history of where/how you have been brought up on self-esteem rather than self-worth. Consider the influence of teachers, parents, stories, religion, heroes, first experiences of college and/or the workplace, and early relationships. In what key moments did you learn you needed to "prove yourself"?

(2)

The Seven Safari Shifts

"The curious paradox is that when
I accept myself as I am, then I can change."

CARL ROGERS

AT THE CORE of the Safari program is a series of seven shifts, which take us from a mindset of self-esteem to one of self-worth. The shifts can be practiced in most areas of life (career, family, relationships, money, and so on). I call these areas "terrains," and the following chapters are each dedicated to one of six terrains. I illustrate one or two shifts per terrain, but each shift can (indeed should) be applied in all areas. The practices and exercises in each chapter are to help with that. Even so, it usually takes a bit of thought to apply each shift to each terrain. The seven shifts are:

- Shift #1: from assessing to asserting
- Shift #2: from condition to expression
- Shift #3: from self-reproach to self-acceptance
- Shift #4: from self-evaluation to usefulness
- Shift #5: from "should" to "could"
- Shift #6: from "proving oneself" to "valuing oneself"
- Shift #7: from "being interesting" to "being interested"

Before we examine these in depth, let's consider Pete's story to understand how the shifts and self-worth work in action.

Pete's Story

Pete came to the Self-Worth Safari after a succession of business failures. After enjoying a meteoric rise in his early career, he was both shocked and shaken to find himself in financial trouble in his early fifties. The prospect of divulging to his wife and two teenage daughters that the days of private schools and ski holidays might be about to end caused Pete to feel that he had made a total mess of his life, that he was a failure as a man, husband, and father. If Pete's self-esteem could be measured by a thermometer, it would have read several degrees below freezing.

Above all, Pete wanted practical help. Though open about his sense of failure, he wanted to focus on things he could do, as opposed to, as he said, "revisiting my childhood or wallowing in the awfulness of the mess." One of the conditions of our work together was an agreement that we would address two dimensions: the problem and how Pete felt about the problem.

When I meet people like Pete—professionals who have enjoyed early life success but then suffered upheaval—I feel their sense of puzzlement and shock. They never imagined they would end up where they are and hence feel totally unprepared for the experience. Those of us who struggle earlier in life are probably more fortunate. Perhaps our expectations are not as high, or we treat any success as an unexpected bonus. Or maybe it's easier for a starving kitten to adjust to a kind, caring home than it is for a cozy domestic cat to be chucked into the cold to survive alone in the wilderness.

In Pete's case, the effect on his self-esteem was devastating. He had lost all confidence to set up meetings with prospective customers. Even when he did so, his performance and credibility was far below what he knew it could be. He slept dreadfully, often waking in the early hours in a cold sweat of fear. His ability to concentrate and make decisions was dissipating fast. In an effort to hide what was happening from his family, he increasingly withdrew, which was damaging his marriage.

Pete blamed himself incessantly for his failure. He berated himself for decisions that should have been made sooner, for misplaced trust in business partners, for getting caught in snares of cash flow and regulation. Each time he met a friend or former business associate, he felt diminished because they all seemed to be doing so much better than he was.

Worst of all, his predicament was all-consuming. For months, Pete had been unable to think of anything else—even in his sleep. His former pleasures in golf or sailing were gone; even a simple walk by the river would become another wallow in the awfulness of his impending failure.

Critical Voices

Pete readily recognized the crowd of self-critical voices that lived in his head. It seems they had always been there—even during his early years of success and indeed all the way back to his student days. His mother, a teacher, had been hypervigilant during his studies, constantly checking his homework and urging him gently but firmly to achieve his full potential. Pete's father had been largely absent during his childhood, so Pete became the "young man of the house" at an early age. Long before he entered the workplace, Pete was an achiever.

Indeed, he avoided any activities at which he didn't excel. As a student, he played the piano well but was mediocre at sports. Being a bit small for his age, it was simply easier for Pete to practice scales and arpeggios than to be outperformed on the sports field. He enjoyed progressing through school and music grades, usually excelling at everything he chose to do. Or more accurately, choosing those activities at which he excelled.

Critical voices are not always harsh or negative. When Pete's mother supervised his homework, she was gentle and encouraging. When Pete continued this habit of self-appraisal in his early years at work, he often congratulated himself on how he was achieving. The experience of self-assessment is not always a negative one.

Subtle Tyranny

When times are good and you are happy with your performance, the critical voices may well have a positive sound. This was perfectly illustrated in Pete's early life: success at school, excellence at university, and early opportunities in the workplace. By the time he was thirty, Pete's trajectory seemed assured, at least as far as career and achievement were concerned.

Without being aware of it, Pete was, however, already a hostage to the subtle tyranny of self-esteem. His relationship with himself was totally conditional on his performance. Pete was proving himself in work, in his hobbies of golf and sailing, in his ambitious acquisition of a country house, and in his eventual capacity to support his mother. He found comfort in an intact sense of self-esteem just by thinking about his achievements and plans for the future. But his relationship with himself was contingent on how he felt he was doing at this game called life.

The problem with this tyranny is fourfold. First, it takes a lot of effort to keep proving things to ourselves. In Pete's case, this brought its share of benefits, but it always takes a lot of energy.

The second problem is that this tyranny often limits our horizons. Pete often didn't do things at which he did not excel. He avoided sports as an adolescent, not necessarily because he didn't enjoy them but because he wasn't outstanding at them. The inability to do things at which we don't optimally "perform" is a limiting side-effect of the tyranny of self-esteem.

The third problem is that when performance fluctuates, self-esteem also fluctuates. Unfortunately, it's precisely when our performance is suffering that we need self-esteem the most. This creates some really unfortunate timing, just as Pete was experiencing when he joined the Safari. We most need a deeply rooted relationship with ourselves when we've had a succession of "failures." When the winter is frosty, the tree needs deep roots.

The fourth problem relates to energy, stamina, and the capacity to act. Proving ourselves to ourselves consumes energy and when self-esteem is low, energy tends to slump. This results in a diminished capacity to act, which drags energy even lower. Resilience (the capacity to bounce back) is adversely affected. So the smallest setback becomes yet another proof of a growing suspicion that deep down, somehow, we are not worth it. In this state, if we manage to recall our earlier successes at all, we quickly dismiss them as luck. Perhaps we were just imposters all along.

Making the Shift

Pete felt like an abject failure and a complete imposter. By the time he arrived to do the Safari, he was also totally exhausted, in need of medical attention, and some self-worth rehabilitation. His effectiveness was clouded by the Four Plagues, the unintended by-products of self-esteem thinking.

1. **Anxiety:** about the future and how he would cope
2. **Shame:** about where he now found himself and the effects on his family
3. **Envy:** of others who seemed to be doing so much better than he was
4. **Frustration:** that none of his initiatives were working

Pete used the seven shifts to reverse his negative spiral, but the first crucial shift in awareness he made was understanding the distinction between self-worth and self-esteem. In one sense, it was easy for Pete to digest. Given that he felt like a total failure, he couldn't comprehend how any effort to restore his self-esteem would work. So when he described how his self-esteem was in tatters, and I replied, "Then let it be," he heaved an audible sigh of relief.

For Pete, we reduced the seven shifts of the Safari program to seven specific micro-practices that Pete agreed to do repeatedly, until his self-worth grew from the legs up rather than from the head down. Pete didn't begin all these in a single week; he phased them in over a six-week period.

- **Shift #1: from assessing to asserting.** Each time he caught himself having a critical thought, Pete would take a sip of water. Pete drank a lot of water in the first few weeks of the Safari. Along with this, Pete found at least three moments of pleasure every day, no matter how short-lived or fleeting these might be—as a conscious *assertion* of his right to exist.

- **Shift #2: from condition to expression.** Pete stopped all self-improvement initiatives, including attempts to diet or exercise. He replaced these initiatives with a conscious statement: "Because I'm worth it." He used this mantra every time that he did something healthy or pleasurable. Not that Pete believed this mantra—at least at first—but he accepted the challenge nevertheless. In whatever activity he did, he focused his attention on a self-worth-based intention.

- **Shift #3: from self-reproach to self-acceptance.** Pete accepted that his self-esteem was in tatters but that, even so, he was still alive and functioning, albeit just. This meant that Pete had to accept the reality of everything about his current situation but learn to do so without self-reproach.

- **Shift #4: from self-evaluation to usefulness.** In work-related meetings or in any form of conversation, Pete eliminated all forms of self-presentation or promotion, focusing instead on what would be most useful even if he would not be the person to provide it. He allowed others to define what was useful.

- **Shift #5: from "should" to "could."** Over the course of several weeks, Pete cut out the words "should," "must," and "need to" from his speech and writing.

- **Shift #6: from "proving oneself" to "valuing oneself."** Each time Pete caught himself trying to prove himself at something, he changed his intention to valuing himself and then did one of the previous shifts to express this, such as enjoying a good cup of coffee or another symbolic act of pleasure.

- **Shift #7: from "being interesting" to "being interested."** When socializing or meeting people at work, Pete focused on being interested in others rather than trying to position himself or to attract attention.

Pete was somewhat surprised by how these micro-practices allowed him to access a new experience of himself, the beginnings of an unconditional relationship. Many of these steps— such as the sipping of water and the moments of pleasure— started out as purely symbolic acts, but he soon began to acquire a physical sensation of them in his body. As the cool water trickled down his throat, Pete felt that he was not just hydrating but was consciously reviving a long-forgotten friendship with himself.

Applying the Seven Shifts

Let's now look at each of the shifts in a bit more detail.

Once you grasp the concept behind each shift, the key to success is making each specific and concrete for you, via specific actions. This is where the exercises in each chapter are vitally important. But it's equally important to understand the shifts in our mindset that we need to make in order to build self-worth. If we take action without deeply understanding each shift, it's easy to slip back into self-esteem thinking, for example, by going for a run in order to lose weight. Many of the "self-improvement" tasks that people burden themselves with reinforce the imperative of self-esteem as the master of their universe.

However, if you confine your grasp of each shift to an intellectual understanding—without taking any action—then reading this book will have little permanent effect. As we saw in Pete's story, it was only when he lived the shifts, via specific actions, that a change took place. It's not enough to think self-worth thoughts, you need to feel self-worth in your belly, too. Just letting your eyes glide across the page will not build self-worth.

Shift #1: From Assessing to Asserting

Shift #1 asks us to break the habit of constantly assessing ourselves based on our performance and to replace that with choices and actions that express our unconditional relationship with ourselves. As we saw in Pete's early life, self-evaluation does not always take the form of harsh criticism. However, it's a habit that must be broken if we are ever to enjoy a real sense of friendship with ourselves.

It's hard to stop doing anything unless we start doing something else at the same time. One of the best ways to experience the self is in action, or in assertion. Moving from assessment to assertion can take several forms. In Pete's case, he simply replaced assessment with sipping water. Your shift could be from thoughts of assessment to voicing a mantra, standing up or sitting down, going for a brief walk, making a call, writing something down, or indeed any other experience of action.

Although it's easiest to demonstrate this shift through the terrain of the body, it can be applied to any area, for example:

- at work, when overwhelmed by negative self-assessments, we can simply remind ourselves that "nobody will die" and to go get a coffee. (Okay, please ignore this if you are a surgeon or nuclear physicist.)

- in relationships, when drawn into a drama in which you feel you are being manipulated or dumped upon, you can simply touch your heart and remind yourself that you are enough, you do enough, and you have enough.

- when choosing a holiday or leisure pursuit, it may be helpful to assert that you do not have to prove anything to anyone, even to yourself.

Shift #1 is more fully explored in chapter 3 on the body (the first terrain).

Shift #2: From Condition to Expression

The Safari is a program of action, not just of reflection. Though fresh awareness is part of the journey, this consciousness will have little permanent effect unless it's accompanied by the capacity to act on a new foundation of self-worth. That's why Shift #2 consciously shifts the intention behind our actions from one that is conditional (for example, "I'll read that article because I should, to impress my boss") to one that is imbued with the principles of self-worth ("I'll read that article because I want to"). Therefore, whatever we do becomes an expression of the intrinsic value we hold for ourselves.

The expressions of our worth can be small (for example, eating a delicious chocolate) or large (treating ourselves to a holiday). They can pertain to work, such as taking a quarter-hour each day to do something for our future; or to friendship, such as texting a friend to ask how her birthday party went. From time to time, the actions will be saying no to something, such as refusing a slice of chocolate cake or turning down an invitation to an event that we do not wish to attend.

The *intention* behind the action matters more than the action itself. For this reason, Safari participants are asked to create a mantra, a reminder that they say to themselves. Pete's was quite simple: "Because I'm worth it." This served him equally well whether he decided to enjoy a chocolate or to refuse one, whether he went for a run or took a rest, whether he made a call that demanded some courage or decided to prepare for it first. In all cases, the intention behind the action was the affirming of self-worth.

With this shift, you are not creating a new condition for your relationship with yourself. This is a pitfall into which many of us can easily fall. In pursuit of self-worth (as opposed to self-esteem), you can enjoy a chocolate or go to the gym: both are valid expressions of self-worth.

In the Safari groups in Brussels and in Prague, this shift generated a somewhat controversial debate. One woman exclaimed, "Then surely I will just stay on the couch all day eating chocolate?" Perhaps she will, at least on some days. If someone has spent a lifetime shackled to the chains of self-esteem, they can indeed run a bit wild when unchained from these conditions. But, sooner or later, most people who are genuinely pursuing self-worth will hear an inner voice suggesting that it's time to get off the couch. If they can do so voluntarily— as a free expression of what they want to do, rather than an imposition of another "should," "must," or "need to"—then there is a much greater likelihood that they can sustain their chosen actions.

Shift #3: From Self-Reproach to Self-Acceptance

Shift #3 moves us from a place of self-reproach (for example, beating ourselves up for a messy situation) to one of self-acceptance (acknowledging the situation and embracing the incumbent feelings about it). For someone like Pete, accustomed to a lifetime of self-assessment, self-reproach is the inevitable consequence. Pete constantly blamed himself not only for his situation but also for how he felt about his situation. He believed that he could—and should—be doing better. He resented himself.

Thinking of Pete and others, I notice that sometimes this can be the effect of critical parenting. But not always. Sometimes, it's the effect of "helicopter parenting," where the parent is always hovering over the child, watching their progress at every step. There are many reasons why young people may internalize a permanent state of self-assessment.

Self-reproach means blaming yourself or rebuking yourself for a situation you are in, for who you are or are not. One of the worst effects of self-reproach is the destructive effect it has on energy. Precisely when we most need our capacity to act and perform, we are often smitten by a bout of self-reproach, which can be as sapping of energy as a bout of the flu.

In my work with Pete, I started by suggesting that he simply accept that his self-esteem was in tatters. This was easy enough for Pete to do, because his self-esteem really was in tatters; it was just the honest acknowledgment of a reality. One of the first fruits of that acknowledgment was a sense of relief and, with that, a small uplift in energy.

In this book, this third shift is described more fully in chapter 4, on relationships and family, for the simple reason that this terrain is where we most frequently have to practice self-acceptance. Other areas where it can be applied include:

- at work, when feeling rejected or ignored. We can acknowledge this to ourselves and give ourselves permission to feel "down" about that.

- in our financial situation, when confronting difficulties. We can honestly acknowledge these problems, without running away or hiding from them, and affirm our right to feel depressed or anxious about them.

- in our bodies. For example, we can honestly face the inconvenient truth that our physique might not be the ideal we want and we can learn to accept that uncomfortable reality without self-reproach (nor creating a negative "story" about other people).

Some Safari voyagers have found it easiest to think of self-acceptance in terms of "permission." So, for example, "accepting the need to rest" might become "giving myself permission to rest." In whatever way you look at it, self-acceptance or permission means you honestly acknowledge reality. It also means putting down the stick that we've been using to beat ourselves. In this way, the pain lessens and our capacity to act is enhanced.

Shift #4: From Self-Evaluation to Usefulness

Shift #4 asks us to move from an inward-looking state of self-evaluation to an outward focus on others and how we can be useful to them. Pete constantly evaluated himself and came up short, and so all of his actions were motivated by his need to measure up to his own standards. When, like Pete, we feel worthless and full of self-reproach, there are two common pitfalls. The first is shrinking into isolation, where setting up any meeting (even with friends) can take superhuman effort. The second is talking too much about ourselves, often out of desperation for validation or to fill the void inside.

In working with Pete, I suggested a temporary embargo on all forms of self-presentation. Instead, his task was to become curious about others: their challenges, their priorities, their risks, their constraints, their opportunities. This shift is very effective for several reasons. First and foremost, it provides a degree of mental relief from the vicious cycle of self-preoccupation that often afflicts people with low self-worth. Remember the guy who said, "I'm not much . . . but I'm all I think about"?

Our opportunities in life lie in how we are useful. In other words, our value in the marketplace or the world stems not primarily from our intrinsic qualities (such as strengths, talents, passions, interests, and so on) but from the extrinsic context in which these are needed (such as other people's risks, issues, and opportunities). Put simply, it doesn't matter how talented you are at something if nobody needs or wants it.

This came as a bit of a revelation to Pete. Like many people, he had been searching inside himself for something that would make him valuable. The self-worth approach is different: you recognize that you are worthy and that there is nothing to be proved. Then you get out into the world (or marketplace) to find opportunities to provide something of value to others. As with Shift #2, you do so as an expression of your self-worth, not as a condition of your self-esteem.

Safari participants implemented this shift by:

- encouraging others to talk for the first few minutes of any meeting, whether at work or with friends;

- changing the format of typical "self-appraisals" to enquiries about *usefulness*. For example, asking "What was most useful?" rather than "What did you think of the meeting?"

- not reacting when criticized, contesting the adjectives or going deeply into the drama of self-justification, but instead asking, "What would have been more useful?"

- instead of chasing prospects, reaching out with questions about usefulness, for example, "What challenges do you anticipate next year?"

Pete found this kind of approach very liberating. It gave him some relief from self-preoccupation. From a practical standpoint, it also allowed him to be curious, to set up meetings that perhaps he would not have otherwise. When we are focused on usefulness, this often unleashes a new sense of creativity and inquisitiveness. We think more clearly about issues when we are not trying to prove ourselves.

Shift #5: From "Should" to "Could"

One of the core problems for many people on the Self-Worth Safari is the never-ending imperative of the word "should." Many describe this as a nonstop tyranny in their heads since their earliest years. Some trace it back to early childhood: many find that it was well established at around the age of ten. Shift #5 takes the word "should" out of our vocabularies and replaces it with "could." We cease to act out of obligation to the invisible authorities in our own heads and instead choose what we'll do based on an array of possibilities.

Behind the word "should" lies an incessant need to prove something to ourselves. Why? Usually because we don't feel good enough. As soon as we accomplish something, we are thinking about the next thing we "should" do. This does not appear in our minds as a "want to" or "can do": it shows up as "I must" or "I need to" or "I have to."

In Pete's case, this pattern was well established. I noticed that he used the word "must" a lot: "I must get more meetings," "I must get up earlier," "I must get out of this stupor." He readily agreed that this was an accurate reflection of how he thought. Initially skeptical, he became quite excited at the idea of eliminating the words "should," "must," and "need to" from his speech and writing.

For Pete, this was closely linked with Shift #2. Each time he corrected a "should" to a "could," he did so consciously as an expression of self-worth, moving away from yet another condition for self-esteem. One of the early benefits of this practice was a new sense of lightness and humor that brought fresh energy into Pete's days.

Nevertheless, it wasn't always easy. The habits of "should" and "must" had been formed over the course of his lifetime, all the way back to his relationship with his mother, who used the vocabulary of "should" all the time. Pete became very frustrated when he caught himself living on the basis of this constant imperative. At other times, he found it funny and began to invent cartoon characters to go with the voices in his head. Some spoke like mother hens and others more like Nazi generals.

Shift #6: From "Proving Oneself" to "Valuing Oneself"

Shift #6 is about taking the focus off the idea that we need to prove ourselves to others (or to ourselves) and moving to the ways in which we value ourselves. There are many ways in which we can do so.

- In the terrain of the body, we can exercise with an intention of valuing the physical self, rather than proving anything to ourselves.

- In the terrain of relationships, we can date from a perspective of fulfillment (and therefore value ourselves and what we wish to share) rather than a perspective of hunger (and therefore seek to prove ourselves via the attention of another).

- In the terrain of friendship, we can choose to hang out with friends who nurture us rather than to spend time with people in order to prove we belong.

For Pete, behind the voices of mother hens and Nazi generals lay a lifelong need to prove himself. This need lurked in practically every "should" and "must" in his head. He also found it linked with nearly every act of self-reproach.

Of course, it's one thing to recognize a need; it's entirely another thing to change it. Pete found that mental activity alone was not enough to switch from proving himself to valuing himself. However, the actions of the previous shifts, when coupled with the intention of valuing himself, began to make an impact.

This was particularly important when Pete decided to make research calls. At that point, valuing himself was little more than an intention. But he went ahead and set up the meetings, not to prove anything but simply as an expression of self-worth. Freed from that imperative, Pete discovered that he was blessed with an innate sense of curiosity, his "secret weapon" as he started to call it. Like a sword removed from its sheath, the secret weapon of curiosity was unleashed and Pete began to formulate better questions. More importantly, he began to enjoy the process.

Over the years, I've worked with many clients who have equally benefited from a spirit of curiosity. Being curious is your innate right: you don't have to earn it. Just watch a child of four asking all those "why" questions. They have not yet learned the need to prove themselves, so they inhabit a state of constant, unfettered curiosity as they explore the world. As adults, many of us benefit enormously from recapturing that spirit of enquiry... without trying to explain it or justify it.

Shift #7: From "Being Interesting" to "Being Interested"

Because of his driving need to succeed, Pete readily recognized that he was always striving to be interesting, to get attention. Whether he was socializing or meeting people for work purposes, he wanted to be well thought of. Even when silent, he often longed to be the star of the show. So, as many people do, when he asked a question or told a story, his intention was to "be interesting." Shift #7 asks us to let go of that need to be fascinating to others and instead to pay attention to what's interesting about them.

On the Safari, Pete was expressly asked to change his focus from "being interesting" to "being interested." He found this distinction to be quite novel and refreshing. It wasn't hard for him to be interested, as long as he gave himself permission to be so and didn't slip back into his storytelling habits to attract attention. "Being interested" works well in many terrains, for example:

- with friends, showing that you care instead of seeking attention;

- with colleagues, noticing their contribution instead of striving to be seen;

- in relationships, showing you are really listening; and

- when new activities or sources of pleasure come along, being willing to try them instead of rejecting the unfamiliar.

As with so many people who have practiced this distinction, Pete quickly found that it deepened his conversations. He learned more and built trust more quickly. Other people seem to have a sixth sense about whether another person is really interested in them. Pete also found that this shift helped to liberate him from the constant need to prove himself, so this practice went very nicely with Shift #6.

An immediate benefit was that conversations became less tiring and required less energy. It takes a lot of energy to "be interesting" all of the time. "Being interested" is so much easier; it's much more fun to find something in which both parties are interested and let the sharing conversation flow.

Pete: After the Shifts

After making the shifts, it took a while for Pete's economic fortunes to be revived. However, with a newfound sense of self came an almost immediate admission that he was hiding the full extent of his financial difficulty from his wife, largely because he feared her loss of faith in him. But Pete now realized that he would have to depend on himself for validation, not someone else, not even his spouse.

Pete came clean with his wife about the impending economic calamity. The discussion was quite emotional, albeit not for the reasons Pete had anticipated. After coping with his increased withdrawal over the course of several months, Pete's wife was sick with worry that he might be hiding either an affair or a life-threatening illness. She knew that the financial situation was fragile but was far more worried that there might be something else that he was hiding from her. To discover that the problems were purely financial was a huge relief for her. As is so often the case, so many of the problems that we have occur in the absence of a vital conversation.

While Pete continued to suffer moments of apprehension about the situation, his anxiety about his ability to *cope* began to diminish. As he accessed a clearer sense of unconditional self-worth—which was not dependent on his financial status—Pete began to see how much of his anxiety was not so much about his situation but about how he would handle it (and be perceived). This distinction helped Pete reduce his anxiety and free up his energy to tackle the real issues.

Tackling the Problem

Though Pete's financial problems remained, he enjoyed a happy Christmas with his family, even if he and his wife were fearful about what lay ahead in the new year. Pete's energy enjoyed a revival—not just from good food and the sipping of water but from a lot less self-reproach and a huge emotional boost from the love of his family. He was no longer beating himself up every minute, and he actually managed to laugh for the first time in many months.

As the new year dawned, Pete was tempted to start another promotional campaign for his struggling business. In our conversations, I persuaded him not to do so for both personal and commercial reasons. I was concerned that Pete's growing sense of self-worth might easily wither in the face of repeated rejection. Furthermore, I've frequently observed how promotional conversations (and messaging) limit conversations that might otherwise generate opportunity.

Instead, we worked out a strategy that had Pete engaging in "research mode" rather than in "selling mode." His task was to have as many January coffees as he could to gather information, not to sell. It is not easy to do this when the wolf is howling at the door. Pete needed every ounce of his fledgling self-worth to get through that long month. However, toward the end of the month, he had a meeting that by good fortune coincided with a resignation of a key employee from a prospect company. The temporary position would give him some breathing space. Though the role was a bit low for his self-esteem, his newfound sense of self-worth gave him a degree of choice that he would not have had even six months earlier.

Ripples of Benefit

Pete's story is not over. His situation is far from ideal, but he has won a reprieve from financial ruin. He still wants to revive his business, perhaps with a new approach that he is still engineering.

Nevertheless, he has a new lightness and sense of freedom. He discovered that he can be a friend to himself in all circumstances, whether anyone approves or not. Though he still has moments of self-reproach, these moments are short-lived. Pete has discovered that it's relatively easy to banish the poltergeists of self-criticism with a simple sip of water or a five-minute walk in the open air. His joy in his family life is more wholehearted than ever.

By discovering unconditional self-worth—and subsequently shifting from self-esteem to self-worth as a basis of life and work—Pete has significantly freed himself from the Four Plagues of anxiety, frustration, shame, and envy. While he still experiences moments of apprehension about the future, he is no longer paralyzed by anxiety. Focusing on usefulness has significantly reduced his frustration, as he is no longer pushing any message (or service) to his customers. Possessing a new sense of friendship with himself, guilt has almost entirely evaporated—as has envy of others because he no longer needs to compare himself with anyone in order to prove himself.

Pete has also discovered that he is not alone: he has met several people in a similar situation. Looking at their lives and businesses, he sees that there is no intrinsic link between economic fortune and self-worth. Through the worst of times, he has found he can still be a friend to himself.

Furthermore, Pete is thrilled by the thought that this new friendship with himself never has to end. Whatever his state of finance or health, whether he gains or loses weight, even whether he is admired by his children or not, Pete now knows that he can always be happy in his own company. For him, this is a whole new adventure. In a real sense, he has come home to himself.

Opportunity is everywhere around us, if only we give ourselves permission to see it. The blinders that prevent opportunity from being seen are not just the product of upbringing and society, they are often fashioned by our own need to prove ourselves, an insight articulated centuries ago by the Persian poet Rumi:

> *There is a basket of fresh bread on your head,*
> *yet you go door to door asking for crusts.*

> *Knock on the inner door. No other.*
> *Sloshing knee-deep in clear stream water,*
> *you keep wanting a drink from other people's waterbags.*

> *Water is everywhere around you,*
> *but you see only barriers that keep you from water.*

> *Mad with thirst, he cannot drink from the stream*
> *running so close by his face.*

> *He is like a pearl on the deep bottom*
> *wondering, inside the shell, Where is the ocean?*

(3)

First Terrain:
The Body

"Take care of your body.
It's the only place you have to live."

JIM ROHN

WE BEGIN RIGHT at the heart of the pain. For many people with low self-worth, a casual glance in the mirror is enough to spoil a happy day. In a matter of nanoseconds, they frown at the shape or size or lines or color or style or appearance or age of the person looking back at them. Or they soon will, a few years from now, when the first wrinkles appear.

My bum is too big/too small. My hair looks awful. Those glasses have to go. Why am I so short/tall/fat/thin—insert your own adjective.

You by now appreciate that this is all self-esteem talk. But the problem remains. It can still hurt, right? Particularly on days when a person is tired, disappointed, or otherwise feeling low.

Big Business

It's probably impossible to determine the percentage of gross world product derived from all the combined industries that profit from our inadequate physical self-esteem. In the United States alone, the personal development sector is estimated at $9.6 billion and rising. When you add in the businesses of dieting, fitness centers, cosmetics, clothes, surgery, advertising, and a host of so-called healthcare services, you are really looking at a staggering multibillion-dollar vested interest in your dissatisfaction with yourself.

By contrast, no business invests money to encourage you to be *satisfied* with your own image. Even the personal development industry profits from your dissatisfaction with your life, your circumstances, or your self-image. That's the size of what you are up against. (No pun intended.)

Our Self-Worth Safari is indeed heading straight into an overgrown jungle. Most of us are only vaguely aware of the subliminal messages beamed at us by the thousands every day, which cultivate our dissatisfaction. Think of the contestants chosen for reality TV shows, the millions spent on careful product-placements in movies, the complexity of social media algorithms targeting your vulnerabilities more carefully than any of your colleagues ever could. Every year, millions are invested in fostering your dissatisfaction with yourself and your appearance.

We all have ideas about how we should look. Let's allow for a moment that some of these ideas might occasionally be healthy and/or even good for self-esteem. For example, Tom might want to weigh a few pounds less. So far, so good. It might be good for his health. No problem. In pursuit of this noble objective, Tom might do some esteeming things, like avoiding doughnuts or going for a run. Wonderful!

If Tom has reasonable self-worth to start with, he will indeed be quite likely to do these things. He will walk past the temptation of the bakery window or run after work, even when it's drizzling. However, if Tom's sense of self-worth is low, how likely is it that he will be able to sustain his motivation? Indeed, he may never get started in the first place.

Erosion of Self-Worth

Though I have no way of proving this (yet), I am convinced that the current emphasis on self-esteem (as contingent and extrinsic) is eroding self-worth (unconditional and intrinsic). In a famous experiment conducted by Mark Lepper and David Greene in the early 1970s, two groups of children—both of which liked drawing—were studied and compared. One group was given rewards; the other group was allowed to draw without rewards. Not surprisingly, perhaps, the effect of the rewards was to distract from the creativity of the first group. They spent more time squabbling over the rewards than enjoying the activity of drawing.

Even more perniciously, when the rewards stopped, those kids who were previously rewarded stopped drawing. However, the second group, who had never received rewards, continued to draw. The psychologists concluded that extrinsic rewards have a negative effect on intrinsic motivation.

Could something similar be happening with self-esteem and self-worth? What if our emphasis on, for example, physical self-esteem is actually eroding intrinsic self-worth? This might at least help explain why, for all the emphasis on physical wellbeing, Western countries still have the highest levels of obesity ever. By focusing on appearance, we seem to be ignoring the widening black hole inside: an emptiness that craves fulfillment.

You can conduct your own research. I have personally discovered (albeit by accident) that I can lose more weight with an approach based on self-worth than I ever did while dieting or following an exercise plan. Furthermore, the pounds stay off. You do not need to join an expensive health club or follow any specific diet. Nor do you need to keep an eye on the scale. There is no need for targets, goals, or incentives. When faced with temptation, your only thought needs to be "Because I'm worth it" (or whatever you decide for your own personal declaration).

While a few people's personal experience does not exactly constitute an empirical study, I'm absolutely convinced that the key to better physical health and appearance is to stop pursuing this objective as a condition of self-esteem. Instead, it's far more exciting to approach physical well-being as an expression of self-worth. We are celebrating something that already exists, rather than trying to create it.

Self-Acceptance

What we resist persists. The more you rail against any aspect of your identity, the more it will rule you.

Any approach to self-worth must therefore begin in the fertile soil of self-acceptance. This means accepting and loving yourself as you are, right now, today. You cannot practice self-worth but still resent your age, your height, your shape, or any aspect of your physical appearance.

Does this mean that you have to permanently reconcile yourself to an unhealthy weight? Perhaps it does. It's quite likely that some things will change later on, as part of your Safari, but these benefits will be forever postponed if your adventure is not firmly grounded in acceptance of yourself, exactly as you are to start with. If you cannot love and accept the person that you are—even with those extra pounds or "bad" eating habits—you can be sure that they will stay there. The emptiness within will continue to sabotage any behavioral regime of diet or exercise.

How often have we tried to get around this truth? Usually we fake acceptance as a necessary starting point, while hurrying on to the next steps of change. It seems we are always impatient to get to the promised land as soon as possible. Even self-esteem proponents, such as Nathaniel Branden, are swift to qualify acceptance as applying to today's reality: that acceptance of today does not imply that you have to accept tomorrow.

We ought to be wary of watering down self-acceptance. The addiction to self-esteem will swiftly re-enter by the back door and soon we will again be proving something in order to feel good about ourselves. On the Self-Worth Safari, we ask you to make your self-acceptance as radical as possible. Which takes us to our first shift in the Safari program.

Shift #1: Stop Assessing, Start Asserting

In the terrain of the body, the first shift is about quitting those lifetime habits of self-assessment. It really does not matter whether the results of these assessments are good or bad: both have the power to make your relationship with yourself conditional on performance. We want the roots of self-worth to be firmly planted in the rich soil of unconditional friendship with ourselves, not subject to the vagaries of assessments.

Therefore, this is not about replacing "negative" assessments with "positive" ones; it's about stopping the self-assessment habit entirely. This often comes as a bit of a surprise to Safari participants. They expect to be taught things like how to make ten positive self-assessments every day (for example, "I am beautiful") in the hope that these will eventually drown out the negative ones (such as "I am ugly"). Unfortunately, what often happens is yet more time lost staring at "mirror, mirror, on the wall," hoping for better answers, while making even more judgments about the self.

To ensure that you are not pursuing self-esteem by another name, I also ask you to stop assessing your progress, especially in this terrain, by weighing yourself or setting goals and the like. For many professionals addicted to the treadmill of SMART goals (specific, measurable, attainable, relevant, and timely), this may come as a surprise. Let me put forward a short explanation.

There is nothing wrong with goal-oriented motivation. It works in many parts of life, particularly in business and in sports. Not surprisingly, these are the domains from which most of the legends of motivation come.

However, if you continue to assess yourself, you will invariably end up back on the self-esteem treadmill. Now, how well has that been working for you? We can all remember times when we managed that diet or exercise regime for a couple of weeks or months, but could you honestly say that assessments have helped to sustain any desired lifestyle change for any lengthy period of time?

As the foundation of all progress with self-worth is *acceptance*, we build self-worth by *asserting* our value, not *assessing* it. *Self-worth is a declaration, not an evaluation.* There are no scales, no points, no scores out of a hundred, no preconditions. There is but a single assertion: "Because I'm worth it" or your own equivalent.

It's important to make that assertion into a physical action, as well as one of mental awareness. For example, along with your "because I'm worth it," you may:

- take a sip of water;
- stand up or sit down;
- go for a brief walk, for example, to the water cooler;
- call a supportive friend;
- make a note in your journal (but not a self-assessment!);
- make a plan or a decision;
- remind yourself of your resources (sticking to facts, not judgments);
- recall what your purpose is;

- take a few mindful moments;
- glance at your favorite symbolic object or picture; or
- eat a piece of fruit.

Each of these actions is a real-world assertion, rather than yet another mental assessment of yourself. Isn't it incredible that the images that usually torment us are just that—images in our minds? Let's take an example. You are on your way to the shops. A light rain is falling, but otherwise it is a warm spring day. The birds are singing. Just ahead of you, you notice a person who has the physique that you would ideally love to have. You think of how your life to date might have been different, if only you looked like that. You contrast their (imagined) lifestyle and opportunities with yours. Perhaps you drift into remorse about your eating or exercise habits or into resolutions about what you are going to do in the future.

How much of this is real? Surely only the light rain, the birdsong, and the sound of your footsteps as you walk to the shops. Everything else is just a series of flickering images across your mind, like an old black-and-white reel-to-reel movie. Usually what torments us is just a series of imaginings, most of all those negative self-assessments. The first step of the Self-Worth Safari is to quit watching out-of-date, depressing movies and to step outside into the spring sunshine.

Hooked on Self-Assessment?

Why this necessity to drop *all* assessments? Why not keep the positive ones, particularly if they work?

I recall a young woman who once challenged me by making exactly this point. She was a devout follower of positive thinking and pointed to the outstanding results this had recently brought about in her life. Having just had a breakthrough in her career (which she attributed directly to her discovery of positive think-ing), she was almost offended at my suggestion that positive assessments could have their shadow side.

On that occasion, I confess, I did not press the point. She was on a high at the end of a successful year, and I had no wish to rain on her parade. Without doubt, her self-belief had grown signifi-cantly and, by her own account, she was enjoying a breakthrough following several dull and uninspiring years. In terms of self-belief, positive thinking clearly brought abundant benefits her way.

My concern with positive assessments is twofold. First of all, positive self-assessments do not always produce positive results. Life is life, and sometimes life is hard and unfair. Sometimes, people are just unlucky. Legends tend to be constructed only from happy endings; nobody tells you about those thousands of positive affirmations that only ended in frustration, disappoint-ment, or loss of hope. Worse still, some hard-core devotees of positive thinking will even suggest that if the happy ending did not materialize, then this must somehow relate to your failure to "manifest" or "attract" it. (Hopefully, they keep a safe distance when saying so, less they manifest the swollen nose that such utterances could risk attracting.)

But my biggest concern with positive affirmations is not so much whether they work or not, but that they reinforce this tyrannical imperative of positive thinking (and self-esteem). In this kingdom of positivity, there is no room for down days. When my friend cannot be positive, will she be even harder on herself? That's the problem with positive thinking: it's a plant with shal-low roots. We need deep roots to sustain us through prolonged harsh conditions. Hence the insistence on planting self-worth in deep soil, below the shallow layer of all assessments.

Some Safari participants have struggled with the sheer simplic-ity of assertion. The idea that self-worth is a basic declaration—not a syllogism from Euclid—seems too easy somehow. Perhaps they expect to be taught a new way of self-assessing that will magically replace the old negative way. Or a new bodywork practice. Others are looking for a sophisticated narrative that they can insert into their heads as a new story to somehow bestow self-worth as a happy ending. Not surprisingly, most of these people will say (initially) that a simple declaration is just not enough.

What usually happens? In practice, life often delivers the learning. Quite of few people report that in the days or weeks that follow the Safari, something happens that provokes the very declaration that they had been resisting. One man had a running injury, forcing him to separate his physical self-esteem from his exercise plan and to declare (or assert), "I'm good enough as I am." Another participant suffered a painful barrage of criticism from a friend but, in the midst of her tears, realized that she didn't have to descend into self-blame. The declaration "I am a good friend" flowed naturally between her sobs and she suddenly discovered the simple power of assertion.

Shift #2: From Condition to Expression

Shift #2 flows naturally from Shift #1 in the terrain of the body. With this shift, you stop dwelling on *conditions* and instead start doing things, day by day, as an *expression* of self-worth. To do so, you simply need to create your own mantra, similar to Pete's "because I'm worth it."

Participants in the Safari program have had a lot of fun with mantras. It's important that the mantra is a statement of fact or belief and not a self-assessment. It can (and perhaps should) be a declaration. Here are some examples:

- "I'm worth it."
- "I am enough, I do enough, and I have enough."

- "I am a friend to myself, no matter what."
- "I am loyal to myself, so I take care of myself and my energy."

Let's apply these two shifts to the age-old problem of diet and exercise. You decide to drop all self-assessments (Shift #1) and you replace these with an assertion/declaration, enshrined in the mantra "I take care of myself." You now start doing things like walking or eating fruit instead of potato chips for a snack, as a conscious expression of self-worth not as a condition of self-esteem. In this way, there is no blaming of the self if you forget or "slip": you just naturally resume with the new practice.

My experience is that this approach is so joyful and freeing that you will soon weave it into everyday life. Not only did I find myself avoiding doughnuts, I also ran upstairs instead of taking escalators. I went for a walk for the sheer pleasure of doing so. When I jogged, I enjoyed the springtime, the waves, or the sunshine, rather than obsessing about my pace or my target for the week.

Conditions are like a thousand little threads that tie us down, just like Gulliver in the land of Lilliput in Jonathan Swift's classic tale. Conditions do exactly the same to our self-worth: they bind us by a thousand little strands, one by one. When we stop assessing and start asserting, when we shift from proving our self-worth to asserting our self-worth, we systematically cut the cords that tie us down.

Asserting requires action. Self-worth is an active process, not a passive state. When we start asserting our worth, we do healthy things like eat well, exercise, and conciously choose people and activities that are good for us. We do a couple of things each day to improve our lives—because we are already worth it.

Drinking water can be a particularly effective gesture of expressing self-worth. Many of our symptoms of fatigue are really symptoms of dehydration. In our air-conditioned offices

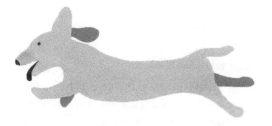

"I run for me, not for a weight-loss plan."

and public buildings, many people are dehydrated without knowing it, particularly if they consume caffeinated drinks, which further dehydrate our bodies. As we saw with Pete in the previous chapter, drinking water as a gesture of self-worth is therefore a particularly effective expression at many levels, particularly when tired or feeling low. With that intention, we are literally watering our own self-worth.

In doing such actions, we uncover a new level of loyalty to ourselves. Instead of pursuing an idealized self-image, we learn to be a loyal friend to the person that we are today. We stop making those remarks to the mirror that we would never make to a good friend. We look on ourselves with a new kindness and nourish ourselves accordingly.

This spirit of loyalty to oneself has captured the hearts of many Safari participants. We often think of loyalty in terms of others or causes or countries. We talk of being loyal to a spouse or a friend. But what about being loyal to ourselves? One participant spent his life being loyal to what his family wanted. When asked what he wanted for himself, he could not answer the question. For him, the very idea of loyalty to himself was totally new and it took him several weeks to begin to get his head around it.

During one of the online 2018 Safaris, a participant, Jacinta, summed up Shift #2 really well:

> My biggest takeaway from the Safari is that we can look at how we view ourselves in a completely different way. Many of our thoughts are habitual and there is one great big habit to change: that of being nice to ourselves and feeling good about ourselves only when we do something like exercise, or withhold things we like and indulge in. It takes constant readjustment to practice and embed new behaviors, but this shift is really worth the effort.

Practice: Self-Worth Morning Routine

As soon as we wake up, our minds often turn to what we need to do today: preparation, tasks, problems, meetings. As a result, it's easy to get into a state of hurry or anxiety or of "not being enough." Even while outwardly sipping that perfect coffee or going for a run, the mind can easily be elsewhere, rehearsing the hours that lie ahead.

This morning practice is designed to take no time at all but will bring conscious awareness of self-worth into your morning routines. To build a solid habit, it's recommended to do this seven days a week, not just on working days.

1. Before you get out of bed, consciously affirm your mantra (for example, "I am more than okay" or "because I'm worth it"). No matter what happens today, this is a truth to hold. Even if you have a hangover, feel tired, or are otherwise unwell. Especially then.

2. As your feet touch the floor, take three deep breaths. As you do so, feel the ground under your feet and, in that moment,

bring your attention just to the little chores of the next thirty minutes (for example, waking the kids, making breakfast, doing yoga, or going for a walk). Decide that this next half-hour is for you to *take care of you* (and your loved ones) as an *expression* of self-care, not to meet expectations or any condition of self-esteem.

3. When you're in the bathroom, look at yourself in the mirror. Using your hands, physically brush away any harsh judgments or anxieties that come to mind. Yesterday's calamities didn't happen, you cannot even remember last week's. Repeat your mantra. You can deal with whatever comes your way today.

4. If you take a morning shower, feel the water running over different parts of your body. Bring your attention to each part, in a conscious act of care. (If you like a poem or a song that expresses this, recite or sing it.) Vary the shower temperature so that you feel your whole body and don't disappear into your mental preparation for the day ahead. You have the rest of the day to deal with that.

Feel free to adapt these points to your own routines, but make sure to focus on your activities as an expression of your worth. Just beware of two common pitfalls:

1. creating new conditions for self-esteem (for example, stepping on the scale or setting exercise goals); and

2. attempting something so convoluted and ambitious that you "fail" and end up feeling worse about yourself.

Keep your routine simple. What matters is that the first thirty minutes of your day be as unconditionally happy as possible. Because you are worth it.

Subtle Saboteurs (The Body)
....

The Self-Worth Safari is a program of action, not just of gazing in the mirror pondering the self. By now you are probably becoming quite fluent in the language of self-worth. Nevertheless, most of us have found that old habits die hard and that those self-critical voices easily resurrect themselves. I call these the voices of the "self-worth saboteurs." Notice how some of these voices sound cunningly optimistic and positive but are all the time capable of undermining your relationship with yourself.

Note the voices below that you recognize. Because we are focusing on the terrain of the body, we'll look at voices related to physical appearance.

- "By my birthday [or wedding, or other future occasion], I will feel really proud of how I look." (Future-planning for relationship with self.)

- "I feel good about myself when I dress up, visit the hairdresser, etc." (Creating conditions for relationship with self. No problem feeling particularly good when you look good, but why not feel good about yourself even when you don't?)

- "I envy those who are attractive; their lives are so much easier." (Two problems with this. First, it's factually incorrect. Many attractive people have lives that are wracked with fear and insecurity. Second, what are you really saying about yourself?)

- "I have a plan to get to my ideal weight." (Good, as long as your self-worth does not depend on that outcome.)

- "I guess I will just have to accept these wrinkles/gray hair, etc." (These things will happen whether you accept them or not. Either way, why should your relationship with yourself be dependent on things like hair color? The challenge here is self-acceptance, not resignation.)

- "I feel good about myself when I go to the gym." (Then what happens when you don't? How about feeling good about yourself all the time and going to the gym out of exuberance?)

- "Compared to others my age, I'm lucky to enjoy good health, fitness, etc." (While this sounds positive—and is clearly self-esteeming—its conditions potentially create a future trap for self-worth.)

- "Thanks to being still reasonably attractive, I can always find a partner." (Even if this were to be true, are you establishing your self-worth based on how others esteem you? Or your ability to find a partner? These are all notoriously sandy foundations.)

When it comes to self-worth, it pays to watch out for sabotaging voices, particularly those masquerading behind "positive" affirmations or conditional gratitude. Real self-worth—the type that stands the test of time—is built by decoupling our relationship with ourselves from all conditions. While your health or physical appearance may influence what you have—or even what you do—there is no intrinsic reason for it to shape who you *are*.

Though it may take a lifetime to fully grasp this distinction, the fundamental truth can be grasped in a matter of weeks. If you have not already done so, why not decide today to cut all those ties that end up sabotaging your self-worth?

The Body as Home

You can change careers, friends, and even partners, but the body always comes with you. You cannot emigrate from your body. Cosmetic surgery may be capable of removing the pockets from under the eyes—at least for a few years. It is certainly capable of emptying your pockets in other ways, too.

The body is the house that we always reside in. I look at my hands as I type this paragraph. These hands have been with me even since before my school days, even before I learned the alphabet. These hands are as much a part of me as my head or my heart. When we talk about self-worth, we are not just referring to some inner "ghost in the machine." We include hands, feet, legs, belly, chest, and shoulders. Whatever age these parts of us may be, whether they are too big or too small, too long or too short, even healthy or sick, when can we make peace with each vital part of ourselves and recognize its intrinsic value?

The vast majority of us do not conform to ideal shape and size, as defined by fashion or conventional norms of glamour. This is particularly true for women: the current ideal is achievable by less than 5 per cent of the female population, and that's just in terms of weight and shape. To make matters worse, standards of female beauty are getting more stringent. In 1917, society's definition of the physically perfect woman was about five-foot-four and weighed nearly 140 pounds. Even twenty-five years ago, top models and beauty queens weighed only 8 per cent less than the average woman, now they weigh 23 per cent less. Furthermore, the pursuit of "beauty" is a losing game; the gap inevitably widens as the body gets older.

Nor do men escape obsessions with ideal shape and size. When a US-based magazine surveyed women about the height and body type of the guy they want to date, 73 per cent of ladies said they preferred a guy taller than five-foot-nine. Attractive people of all genders have many well-documented advantages when it comes to jobs, relationships, credibility, and social attention. They even get shorter prison sentences! So do they also enjoy higher self-worth?

A study entitled "Happiness and Despair on the Catwalk: Need Satisfaction, Well-Being, and Personality Adjustment among Fashion Models" concluded that attractive models who made a living from being beautiful suffered lower well-being and greater personality maladjustment than non-models. The authors of this study (based at City University, London; Sheffield Hallam University, UK; and University of Texas at Austin, USA) found that these beautiful people also suffered from a host of problematic personality traits, such as being more suspicious, intensely emotional, interpersonally alienated, eccentric, and self-centered. So much for the life of "beautiful people."

The problem with all these assessments is that people frequently judge themselves for what they are *not*. If society puts the majority of people on the wrong side of the attractiveness line—and seems even more likely to do so in the future—then your friendship with yourself becomes more vital than ever. If self-esteem is conditional upon feeling good about your looks, you are planting your relationship with yourself in shallow soil, in ground that is destined to be eroded even further in the years ahead.

I once imagined that younger people on the Safari may not wish to heed the warning about linking self-worth to appearance, particularly when the seductions of attractiveness are ever-present and available. I was initially surprised to learn how many attractive people have deep issues with self-worth. As one former model described it, "I'm fed up of being valued for the packaging and not for my mind or who I really am. I feel I constantly have to prove myself."

For all these reasons, the invitation of the Self-Worth Safari is to abandon *all* the assessments and *all* the conditions that relate to ideal size or shape and to become a friend to your own "bone-house" exactly as it is. Even for the tiny minority who may (temporarily) possess society's desired physical characteristics, there is no evidence that satisfaction with physique is working when it comes to self-worth. On the contrary, there is abundant evidence that it produces a host of other issues, such as an internal hollowness, a fear of loss and abandonment, a constant striving to be really seen (as opposed to being seen for the "packaging"), and hence the need to prove oneself in other ways.

I look back at the hands that have typed the above paragraphs. I see the spots and veins and lines that are the marks of our years together. We are old friends. I would not swap them for any other.

The Bone House

Yesterday I went shopping and
As I queued for the changing room
I was surrounded by all those mirrors
Mouthing silent words of doom

The adjectives kept coming
As the queue just shuffled along
A wave of critical voices that
Left me feeling low and wrong

When the wait was over
And I finally got inside
To try on those bloody trousers
I just wanted to hide

Yet at last the ordeal was finished
And I joined another queue to pay
Thinking "now I deserve a coffee
A nice cake to save the day"

But then I got a funny text
From one of my good friends
And suddenly remembered
My power to change the lens

That those voices in the mirror
Were just images and ghosts
While the man that stood to pay the bill
Was real and his own host

Those images could not buy a treat
Would never make me tea
Unlike real people of flesh and blood
True friends and family

So I laughed off the illusions
And even skipped the pastry
If my friends thought I was worth it
I could too be a friend to me

Instead I chose to walk home
In fresh air to give a head start
To this tiny act of friendship
Towards the bone house of the heart

Exercises for the Terrain of the Body

As usual, some exercises will appeal to you more than others. Please choose at least three, and I highly recommend number 5. That mantra may be very important in the weeks ahead.

1. Look in the mirror for thirty seconds. What goes through your mind? How do you feel? Write down the phrases or feelings that come up.

2. What conditions about your appearance do you place on self-esteem? Please identify at least three. (Examples might include weight loss, appearance, style.)

3. What effort have you expended in pursuit of these objectives? What costs (time and/or money) have you incurred?

4. What could you learn to accept about yourself? Take your time with this question. The more you can deeply accept, the more you can change later on. (But please avoid the pitfall of superficial acceptance as a tactic of change. It simply doesn't work!)

5. Please choose your "because I'm worth it" mantra (or use that one). Your mantra is your rallying point when doubts and insecurities arise. As we saw with Pete, the mantra also helps articulate your intent, particularly when practicing Shift #2. Write down your mantra and place it where you can see it regularly.

6. Are there particular times when your (physical) self-worth is vulnerable? When you feel tired or disappointed? When you see beautiful or athletic people? In changing rooms or on the beach? What truth do you wish to hold onto in those vulnerable moments? Record your truth somewhere you'll see it regularly.

7. Create your physical self-worth ritual: drinking a glass of freshly squeezed orange juice, taking a warm bath or a walk, getting into the sunshine, taking a short rest or doing a meditation, anything that accompanies your mantra. What action can you take daily to express your friendship with yourself?

8. Construct a self-worth gratitude list. This is not as easy as it sounds. Most of the time, we list good things that have happened to us or things we are proud of having done. However, that is self-esteem yet again, not self-worth. Try to find the things you unconditionally like about yourself. An example might be "being kind to myself even though I broke my diet."

9. Consciously do the exercise you most enjoy as an expression of self-worth rather than as a condition of self-esteem.

If the "Self-Worth Approach to Weight Loss" is of interest, see the Resources section at SelfWorthAcademy.com. No diets, no calorie-counting, no starvation. Instead, we get down to the emotional conditions that drive eating habits in the first place. Using an approach based on self-worth, we find other ways to "fill the emptiness" inside.

(4)

Second Terrain: Relationships and Family

"Loneliness is not the experience of missing another person.
Loneliness is the experience of missing yourself."

JEFF FOSTER

IN THIS CHAPTER, we focus on the role of self-worth in personal relationships and family settings. As with physical appearance, this topic touches wounded places for many people. Whether you are single or in a relationship, whether you have children or not, whether you are gay or straight or other, whether you have siblings or living parents or not, there is usually much more to these states than a "relationship status." Each relationship carries its own emotional load, often heavy with judgment about the self.

Our relationship with ourselves significantly affects how we interact with other people. Our self-esteem frequently depends on how we feel we are "doing" at relationships. Given that this fluctuates, so does our self-esteem. Intellectually, we may tell ourselves that it shouldn't, but when have emotions ever obeyed the intellect?

Before plowing into this chapter, a caveat: this book does not offer any form of relationship advice or any recipe to find love. Our purpose is simply to start understanding (and perhaps disentangling) self-worth issues from relationship issues. In this way, we can at least learn to love ourselves, a foundation that will hopefully serve us well in our dealings with others.

Penalty Points

Let's take a simple example: imagine you forget to do the shopping on the way home from work, despite having promised your partner that you would buy some essential groceries. You arrive home, and there is nothing for dinner. Your partner is annoyed and some angry words get flung around, phrases that probably contain words like "always" and "never." Many of us have experienced this sort of situation, whether from one side of the argument or the other.

If your self-worth is high, you will be able to withstand some criticism. After all, it was your mistake, and your partner is hungry. A solution will soon be found, perhaps involving the local pizzeria. A couple of hours later, you will be snuggling on the couch and laughing about it all . . . or better. With hindsight, it was no big deal.

But if your self-worth is low, you are (both) likely to have a very different evening. Even if your partner is not angry, you may experience a huge outbreak of self-criticism. Worse still, this may be followed by "self-justification" (for example, "Look at how busy I am, I can't think of everything!") or playing the victim ("Why is it always me who has to do the shopping?"). There will surely be drama—whether it's tragedy or farce is anybody's guess. Accusations may fly across the kitchen, followed by crockery if things get out of hand. There may be hours of sullen resentment ahead.

Why? Because the burden of self-reproach has inflated the original problem out of all proportion. When I'm acting out of low self-worth, I can beat myself up for hours for a silly mistake. Or attack the other person, in order to smoke-screen my dissatisfaction with myself. Or I may become anxious about my memory, worried about what else may be slipping out of control. I react to the other person's angry words, instead of just seeing the hunger or tiredness or anxiety behind them. I feel slighted or humiliated or resentful about the way I've been spoken to. In a hundred different ways, I re-experience my inner suspicion of being "less than" or "not enough."

On the surface, this drama is sparked by the remarks of the other person. But surely the fuel (and hence the bigger explosion) is caused by my own self-reproach? There is an important distinction between the trigger and the cause of a problem. The other person's remarks are certainly the trigger for the explosion, but the cause lies within, in the self-reproach that is often a by-product of low self-worth. Self-reproach is like a system of penalty points: it adds to the score we chalk up against ourselves. And these penalty points serve to amplify every explosion.

We saw the same penalty points earlier in the way that Pete was reproaching himself for his economic misfortunes. Notice how self-reproach leaves us vulnerable to the Four Plagues of anxiety, frustration, envy, and shame. These plagues not only sap our energy: they invariably damage our relationships with the people around us, as Pete experienced with his wife.

Life will always deliver its share of disappointments and frustrations. Whatever the reason, other people will sometimes do or say things that do not live up to our hopes, and certainly not to our expectations. These are precisely the moments in which we need to be kind to the self and not apply penalty points against ourselves in the form of self-reproach, blame, or negative rumination.

As we saw earlier, when distinguishing between guilt and shame, it is healthy to take stock of our actions and make appropriate corrections to our behavior. The problem for self-worth comes when we descend into criticizing ourselves. We can always reflect about whether "I should have said or done that." But when we find ourselves thinking "I should not be . . . ," then the trouble starts.

Practice: Dealing with Self-Critical Voices

You will need pen and paper for this exercise.

Note that the purpose here is to take stock of the self-critical voices, not to review any actions for which you feel guilty. A healthy stock-taking of our behavior does not pose any problem for self-worth.

1. Draw three columns with headings as follows: "The Voice," "The Owner," and "The Alternative." There will usually be several voices, not just one. So we need to address them one by one.

2. In the voice column, identify your prevalent self-critical statements. These could be "I am stupid," "I am not reliable/consistent," "Nobody could love someone like me," "My career is a mess," and so on.

3. In the owner column, see if you can identify a personality that goes with each voice. It may be a critical parent, a sibling, a friend, a teacher, or a former boss. It may also be a group, for example, "the neighbors." Sometimes, there is no specific owner, in which case you would leave this column blank.

4. In the alternative column, write a positive opposite. This has to be a true statement, not a "fake it 'til you make it" affirmation. So, if in the first column you wrote "I am unfocused

on my business," you might write an alternative statement such as "I am building connections" or "This is a time for exploring."

5. Continue until you have taken stock of all your self-critical voices.

6. When finished, review what you have written. Are there any patterns? Is there a particular parent or teacher still living (rent-free) in your head? Is there a theme? For example, do many of the criticisms center on being stupid/ugly/insignificant/hopeless?

7. If these voices are very troublesome and robbing you of energy, with whom can you discuss them? Like vampires, the best way to get rid of them is to show them the light of day.

Relationship Issues and Self-Worth

In any relationship, there are three realms or fields of play: My Stuff, Your Stuff, and Our Stuff.

My Stuff might include sorting out my career, dealing with my anxiety, or my tendency to eat too much. Your Stuff might include managing your anger, your issues from childhood, or your need to prove yourself. Our Stuff might encompass how we communicate, our plans for the future, and how we bring up our children (if we choose to have them). Many issues in relationships stem from confusing these three realms. Self-worth plays a big part in this confusion. Let's look at an example.

Sue and Geoff are a young married couple, with two children aged six and four years old. They met in their final year at university, where Geoff was doing a degree in management and Sue, an accomplished pianist, was studying art. Sue was attracted by

Geoff's air of assurance, his confident ambition that he would be financially self-sufficient by the age of forty. For his part, Geoff admired Sue's artistic grace and beauty, her unique style, and her capacity to hold a room spellbound when she played.

They dated for three years and then married. Geoff was promoted several years in succession and then decided to start his own design agency. Sue worked as a teacher for a few years but found urban classrooms a far cry from the artistic joys of her college years. So when the kids came along, Sue suggested she stay home to look after them, and Geoff agreed.

It's now nine years since their college days and Geoff is working night and day. His business is growing rapidly, and Geoff believes that he will achieve his dream of being financially independent within the next five years. This is important to Geoff, both for the benefit it will bring to his family and his own recognized need to prove himself to his estranged parents.

But Sue is unhappy. She's heard Geoff's story about financial independence for years, but the reality is that Geoff is never home, and that happy state of financial independence is always way off in the future. Now that the kids are in school, she's often alone and feels a bit lost. As well as teaching, Sue has tried administrative work, but neither career worked out. She has taken to overeating, which she blames on suburban boredom.

There are ever more arguments and each partner blames the other. Sue reproaches Geoff for not being a responsible parent and for missing valuable time with his kids. Geoff reproaches Sue for not sorting out her career, for overeating, and for becoming financially dependent on him. Their suburban dream home is increasingly the scene of raised voices.

It's a story that will be familiar to many a reader, and the challenges of juggling work and family life for young parents are never easy. As well as the sheer workload, there are the sleepless nights and temper-tantrums to deal with. (And the kids can be unpredictable, too!)

But let's look at all of this from the perspective of self-worth. We can get fresh perspective on what is going on, particularly if we can distinguish the three realms identified in the diagram opposite.

If Sue has low self-worth coupled with a fear of responsibility, she may try to bundle My Stuff into Our Stuff, thereby making the relationship responsible for her career, her eating habits, or even her boredom. If Geoff has low self-worth, he may be addicted to proving himself but still believe that the relationship is responsible for his need to over-work, because Sue is not working. A series of relationship issues therefore ensue, wherein Sue resents Geoff for his overworking and irritation, and Geoff resents Sue for not sorting out her career and for overeating.

In this dynamic of low self-worth, Our Stuff is often made up of blaming. A sink full of dirty dishes becomes ammunition (hopefully just metaphorically) in a war of blaming the other for what he or she is or is not doing. But there may also be silent resentment, sad resignation, or anxiety about the future. Yet surely the core issue is not the dishes, not even how we are communicating about the dishes. The root problem is the emptiness of their undiscovered self-worth.

Confusing Realms

The sad fact is that many a relationship might well look after itself, if only each partner had sufficient self-worth to take care of their My Stuff realm. For example, with a bit more self-worth, Sue might take responsibility for her career and the emotional factors that cause her to overeat. If Geoff only realized the difference between self-worth and self-esteem, he might see that his need to prove himself was his own and not a consequence of whether or not Sue worked. If even one partner in this couple raised their self-worth, the relationship might turn around.

In this more self-worthy dynamic, the Our Stuff discussions will be very different. There will be less blaming and much greater probability of either party taking responsibility for that sink full of dirty dishes, whether this is Geoff owning his need to prove himself at work or Sue owning her depressing days as her own issue to resolve. When one partner owns an issue as theirs, a loving companion usually wants to support them as best they can.

I'm not suggesting that all partners are supportive or that all issues in relationships are self-worth issues. Nor does this chapter pretend that self-worth alone offers a panacea for all relationship difficulties. Not all relationship problems can be resolved simply by positioning them in the three realms above. This example simply illustrates how self-worth can be both cause and remedy for some relationship issues by disentangling them from the total relationship spaghetti.

Many of our issues with other people are manifestations of our issues with ourselves. To take one example, the struggle to prove something to ourselves can cause us to be judgmental of others, can make us unavailable (even indifferent) to them, or can make us angry or reactive or irritated. Perpetual anxiety may cause a person to be over-controlling, jealous, paranoid, or unable to laugh and have fun. When low self-worth takes the form of dependence on others, this may lead to manipulation, evasion of responsibility, or casting people as saviors and subsequently as persecutors. As the Four Plagues of anxiety, frustration, envy, and shame set in—usually because of our attempts to prove things to ourselves—relationship problems soon get worse.

In all cases, the power lies with the individual to see how low self-worth is fueling their feelings and behaviors. When this awareness is followed by acceptance (including acceptance of responsibility), the process of growth and change is often already underway.

If you are reading this and experiencing relationship issues, may I invite you to explore how your own self-worth may be compounding the problem(s), whether magnifying the pain or driving the agenda? For example, does low self-worth trigger irritation, anxiety, or guilt and shame that then has ripple effects on the relationship?

If irritation is the primary issue, what expectations of yours are not being fulfilled? Where do these expectations come from? Why are they important to you? Must your self-esteem depend on satisfaction of these conditions? And if so, can you at least find a sense of self-worth, accepting (at least for now) that your relationship is imperfect?

If anxiety is an issue, how is this influencing your behavior and your feelings toward your partner? Are you harboring suspicion, jealously, or fear of tomorrow? Do you control, nag, or refuse to join in and have fun? What are you afraid of? Can you trust your power to deal with whatever tomorrow brings? And if not (at least not yet), can you find self-worth even in the person that you are today?

If feelings of guilt or shame dominate, in what ways do you feel unworthy? Would it help to acknowledge these feelings as yours and perhaps seek help to address them? Many of the deeper issues of shame come from childhood trauma, and you might need professional help to overcome them. Or they may be related to some sort of addiction, including alcohol, prescription medication, food, pornography, shopping, or work. Or perhaps shame is the aftereffect of infidelity. Remember that a sense of self-worth is unconditional and can therefore be kept alive even in the throes of addiction or guilt. Self-esteem may require us to live up to certain values, but self-worth does not. Self-worth can be accessed even on those days when we are not doing what we "should." So even when addictions or shame rule the day, can you tap into the strength of real self-worth, rather than trying to regain that self-esteem that seems to be evading you just now?

Ted's Story

One of the real-life examples of how self-worth can transform relationships comes from a man that we will call Ted. I first met Ted in the run-up to Christmas, during a particularly vulnerable point in his life. He initially came for coaching on some business issues, but it soon became apparent that, as well as these work-related issues, Ted had a rather complicated family situation. He was divorced, with two daughters from his marriage, now young adults, who lived with their mother in the UK. Ted lived in Europe and was in a three-year-old "new" relationship. He and his new partner had recently moved in together.

Ted felt that this new arrangement was creating complications in his life. His two daughters (influenced perhaps by their mother) point-blank refused to have anything to do with his new partner. Fortunately, she was quite understanding about this, but Ted still felt torn when it came to Christmas and other family celebrations.

His feelings of being conflicted were compounded by his guilt over the circumstances in which his marriage had ended. Ted had had an affair, which his wife discovered when he left his laptop unattended and email accessible. Years later, Ted was still carrying a substantial burden of guilt from this affair, and his ex-wife was still carrying an equal amount of resentment.

Ted had spent the previous Christmas in the UK, seeing his daughters as much as he could. He had returned to Europe for the New Year, feeling a huge sense of failure as a father and as a husband. He felt he no longer "belonged" with his own kids, nor even in his country of origin. He worried about what the future held and the effect all of this was having on his new relationship. He seemed to be in a no-win situation.

Distinguishing "Self" from "State"

Ted's story illustrates a classic trap of self-esteem: confusing your *self* with your *state*. In this scenario, the relationship with one's self depends on factors such as being happily married, having a soul mate, or having children. As many psychologists have observed, there is a distinction between personality and behavior. When we link our well-being with our relationship status or family circumstances, trouble invariably follows. We are back in esteem mode. While this may make us happy (even ecstatic) for a while, there will be real angst when the relationship encounters cloudy days or there are family complications, just as Ted was experiencing.

Self-worth makes you okay even when life is hard. Whatever decision you make in or about your relationship, it will be a better decision when it's firmly rooted in self-worth. When people let go of proving themselves, they often experience a fresh clarity and serenity. Accepting responsibility without the poison of self-reproach, they find they have new energy and decisiveness. The anxious let go of the burden of the future and those suffering from guilt and shame let go of the burden of the past. Self-worth creates a new sense of lightness.

This is exactly what happened with Ted. Separating his being from the complexity of his family proved very helpful in finding new perspective. Above all, he began to see how he was constantly awarding himself penalty points by incessantly reproaching himself about the circumstance that led to his divorce.

Ted began to distinguish reproaching his actions from reproaching himself. The plague of shame was particularly significant for Ted. While the actions that led up to his divorce had certainly been problematic for his self-esteem, Ted found it very helpful to imagine that someday (hopefully soon) he could again enjoy an intact relationship with himself, without the constant burden of self-reproach robbing him of emotional energy.

One Year Later

A year after that difficult Christmas, Ted was once again making his way back to Europe. Outwardly, not much had changed. Ted's daughters were still adamant that they wanted nothing to do with his new partner. His ex-wife still resented him. His partner was none too chuffed that he had once again headed off to the UK for Christmas but again acknowledged that she "knew what [she] was getting into" when she met him.

But for Ted, the big sea-change between one Christmas and the next was the relationship he had with himself. In his own words:

I have a new excitement about the year ahead. To be honest, at times I never thought I would be able to look at myself in the mirror again. The awful sense of alienation from my kids has nearly disappeared. I now realize the extent to which I was trying to prove myself as a dad, fueled by this dreadful sense of self-reproach about the divorce. Today, while I still wish I had acted differently, I know I can still be a friend to myself.

In a matter of months, self-acceptance had done more for Ted than years of guilt and self-reproach. Furthermore, it seemed to have mysteriously improved things with his daughters, too. When Ted stopped trying to prove himself as a father and just became interested in them as the young adults they were, they responded to his unspoken change of intent. A lot of Ted's alienation had flowed from a hollowness within, rather than any real sense of rejection by his daughters. Therefore, the slightest indifference or inattention on their part would echo down the empty chambers of his own heart.

Practice: Relationship Terrains

Choose a problem that bothers you, preferably something specific. For example, the way that your partner spends money or the way that they leave clothes lying around the house or the way that they speak about you to others.

This practice can be done alone or with your partner. If you are doing the practice together, then you may first need to recap the My Stuff, Your Stuff, and Our Stuff circles on page 83 and pay special attention to the first step below.

1. Set your intention to seek fresh understanding of the problem, rather than to solve the problem. If you achieve the former, you are well on your way to the latter. Without understanding, there will certainly be no long-term solution.

2. Using a pen and paper, draw three large circles for My Stuff, Your Stuff, and Our Stuff. If doing this with a partner, use a single page on which you both work, perhaps with pens of different colors. In this case, name your circles as X's Stuff, Y's Stuff, and Our Stuff, where X and Y are your first names.

3. Start filling in the components of the problem, beginning with My Stuff. Taking the example of the living room being messy, you might write "need for order" in the My Stuff circle.

    • Wherever possible, use descriptive rather than judgmental words. For example, "clothes all over the living room" is descriptive, "disorganized" is a judgment.

    • For an item to be in the Our Stuff circle, both partners need to agree on it. If one partner cannot agree, it has to go back into the circle of the person who wants it included. (If working solo, try to imagine if your partner would agree.)

    • If you are doing this exercise together, you cannot write things in the other person's circle. Later in the exercise, you can make gentle suggestions, but I suggest you avoid doing so, even by way of compliments. The power of this exercise lies in each person taking responsibility for their own circle.

    • If you are doing the exercise solo, you can write things in the Your Stuff circle. Please resist judgments. Think instead of the other's needs. For example, instead of "disrespectful," you might write "need to be seen and heard."

4. When you have filled in all three circles, review the total picture. What patterns do you see? For example, is everyone trying to prove something or trying to be understood?

5. Shift your attention to your own circle. You have no control over other people. The only person you can ultimately change is yourself. What are the needs that are operating here? The

need for order? Security? Appreciation? Validation? How can you get this need met from within, so that you are less dependent on another person meeting your needs?

6. What have you learned? If working with a partner, take a few minutes to appreciate each other.

Singles and Self-Worth

We have been considering self-worth in the context of couple relationships. However, we must remember that since the 1950s, the number of people who identify as single has grown steadily across the Western world. More than half of American adults are now single. In the UK, the overall population of singles increased by five percentage points between the 2001 and 2011 census. That's a huge shift.

The reasons for this are many and various and are well beyond the scope of this book. Millennials in particular are increasingly delaying not just marriage but traditional relationships in lieu of meaningful work, education, or alternative lifestyles. Behind the statistics, there are also many nuances. There are single people who are actively looking, singles in a succession of "living apart together" relationships, and other singles who are part of polyamorous relationships. There are happy singles by choice and involuntary singles by lack of opportunity. There are widowed or bereaved singles who once had the love of their life and see that as irreplaceable. For some people, being single is a state of conscious choice. For others, it's a product of circumstance. For quite a few, it's often a "transition state" toward a hoped-for future relationship.

At one time or another, most single people grapple with issues of self-worth. Their solo state confronts them with a starkness that rarely appears in cozy relationships. When you are dining alone or out for a solo walk on a Sunday afternoon, you get to confront issues of self-worth with no distractions in the surrounding silence. When another Christmas or birthday comes around, your friendship with yourself becomes "singularly" significant, in more ways than one.

This experience may vary wildly from one year to another. For some newly single people, for example, the surrounding silence can be a blessed relief. Particularly if they have emerged from a fractious relationship, complete with frequent quarrels or hostile silence, the initial months of singledom can be a peaceful paradise. As time passes, however, this happy honeymoon period often wears off. Being alone for an extended period of time can be tough. Loneliness can set in. Perhaps there are renewed attempts to rekindle that old flame or desperate attempts to light some new fires.

Beyond these distractions, there is the sound of silence, punctuated only by the ticking of the clock, the crackle of the fireplace, or the entry of the cat through the flap. Now is the time when you get to sit down face-to-face with the full reality of self-worth, unencumbered by family obligations or distractions. The Four Plagues of anxiety, frustration, envy, and shame may well pay a visit. So it's hardly surprising that many single people simply fly into the arms of the next encounter.

In any case, issues of self-worth usually crop up. Indeed, it is often during moments of sadness or loneliness that we get a true glimpse of what our real self-worth is. These moments can, therefore, be precious opportunities: it's often in those hours that real life-enhancing self-awareness takes place. It's precisely in these solitary moments that many people experience the difference between self-worth and self-esteem, distinguishing their self from their state. Not just intellectually but at belly level.

While self-esteem is a notoriously fickle friend—happy to dance with us in the sunshine—true self-worth is a loyal companion even on wintry days. When there is no lover around, the quality of your friendship with yourself is particularly vital. Unlike self-esteem, self-worth does not make demanding expectations, just that you be on your own side. For example, you might ask yourself:

- Can I be a true friend to myself, even if nobody else wants me today?
- Am I on my own side, or am I criticizing or judging myself?
- Do I take responsibility for my life or am I blaming society, another or my own gender, the city in which I live, or my upbringing?
- Can I look at myself with affection and love?
- Can I be grateful for the relationships I've had, rather than resentful at what life has not given me?
- Even if experiencing loss, loneliness, rejection, or depression, can I still choose to love myself?
- Do I accept myself as I am, or am I making self-acceptance contingent on changing aspects of me, my life, or my appearance?
- Do I choose to think constructively about myself, or am I stuck in a poisonous, bitter, or melancholic narrative?

Shift #3: From Self-Reproach to Self-Acceptance

The big shift in this chapter is from self-reproach to self-acceptance. This usually allows us to see relationship issues with fresh clarity. Whether self-reproach stems from frustration with a disappointing relationship, resignation about never finding the perfect mate, dismay at not being able to have children, guilt about the end of a previous relationship, or something else, self-worth does not ask you to give up your sadness or disappointment or even annoyance. But self-worth does ask you to end self-reproach for how you feel about yourself and to replace this with self-acceptance. It's impossible to experience self-worth while not practicing self-acceptance.

There are many misunderstandings about self-acceptance. Some people equate self-acceptance with being passive—resigned to whatever life throws at them. Naturally, most people rebel at being such a victim of circumstance. Self-acceptance does not (necessarily) mean acceptance of circumstances. But it does mean acceptance (and kindness) toward yourself. For example, when you see a photo (or a person) that evokes longing or sadness and you remember happier times, this is an opportunity to be extra kind to yourself, as opposed to judging yourself harshly for that relationship's end.

Self-acceptance makes people active, not passive, because they are no longer burning up energy by resisting their emotions or other facts about their lives. To take a simple example, if you feel you are not very attractive, you can waste many futile hours in wishing otherwise or in feeling resentful about how attractive people naturally get more attention, or you can love yourself as you are and get on with living life. As we saw in the first terrain, much of what torments us is often just flickering images, in particular the unfavorable assessments about life (and ourselves) that we make. As we watch that self-critical movie in our minds, we reproach ourselves over and over. Self-acceptance is about quitting this shabby movie theater and stepping outside into the sun.

If your partner is not showing sufficient interest in you, it's easy for this unfortunate fact to become a perennial complaint or the focus of hours of silent resentment or self-pity. With self-acceptance, you stop reproaching yourself for how you feel about this and you accept the sadness. You may (or may not) find it possible to accept this unfortunate fact about them. Either way, with self-acceptance, you find the strength to do something about it.

Shinzen Young's formula *suffering equals pain multiplied by resistance* ($S = P \times R$) applies perfectly in these types of situations. We magnify any pain by the degree to which we fight it. When we stop reproaching and start accepting, suffering diminishes. A big part of the Self-Worth Safari adventure is that of reconnecting with your intrinsic reality, rather than living in the mental movie theater of self-assessment and self-reproach. The terrain of romantic love can be painful enough without adding any additional penalty points. If you have lost a partner (or someone you hoped would be a partner), even if love has eluded you entirely, that's enough to deal with. You don't need the additional burden of negative judgment about yourself. The pain of loss heals with time, but self-reproach is like a cancer that eats away at happiness and energy.

Self-acceptance is a deep understanding of who you really are, with honest acknowledgment of (so-called) strengths and weaknesses as well as your needs. It means accepting your reality, even when it's not "enough."

Resignation?

A second common misunderstanding is that acceptance leads to resignation, perhaps even tolerating unacceptable circumstances or behavior. At the extreme, this could lead some people to tolerate abusive relationships. Or become resigned to a perpetual single state, instead of facing the challenge of doing something about it. Most of these people would claim to be practicing acceptance, when what they are actually practicing is more likely resignation or extreme toleration of circumstances, usually driven by a combination of fear and low self-worth.

So how do you know whether you are practicing self-acceptance or resignation? You can apply two relatively easy "tests." First of all, resignation is usually accompanied by feelings of loss and sadness and longing. The absence of the other person (or circumstance) throbs with pain or regret or bitterness. Acceptance is more peaceful. There may still be pain, but you feel differently about it. There is a sense of lightness, perhaps even joy, in true acceptance.

The second test is one of energy. If your energy plummets, then it's probably resignation. True acceptance does not usually result in an energy slump: it's a calm acceptance of the way things are, often accompanied by a sense of release. We are ready to quit that shabby cinema and get on with life.

A man recently told me he was at last "totally over" his recent breakup. Nevertheless, he managed to come back to the subject of his ex-girlfriend three times in the next thirty minutes. While he may well have become resigned to the way things were, he was clearly still nowhere near real acceptance.

Shift #3 is specifically about your *self*-acceptance, not about acceptance of your relationship with others. To be fair to my friend, while it may take him many months yet to accept the end of his relationship, he was a lot more accepting of himself and his preoccupation with her.

Self-acceptance is considered by many psychologists as essential for any change to occur. Making a decision to change seems to always require a moment of acceptance of some aspect of ourselves, our needs, or our boundaries.

Self-acceptance does not require us to tolerate circumstances. On the contrary, when we accept ourselves and our needs, we are more able to make requests of others. Instead of denying our reality, we can calmly state what is okay for us and what is not. We can skip a lot of justification, both to ourselves and to others. We stop self-reproach, that inner cancer that eats away at our emotional energy. Aware of a new sense of delight in our own being, we find the strength to make decisions and to carry them out. Self-acceptance is active, not passive.

Confusing Love and Happiness

Most people have an image of their ideal partner in their head. Whether single or in a relationship, we all have some long-standing ideas about what that person should be like. We have expectations about what they would do or what they would say. We also have expectations about what is not okay for us—usually the reasons why previous relationships ended.

Our happiness is therefore often mortgaged to our dreams of ideal love. Whether we explain this as the influence of advertising, childhood stories, Hollywood, iconic songs, or hormones, we invest a lot in these dreams. It's easy to see our ideal partners as the perfect solution to woes such as loneliness, lack of acceptance, economic insecurity, or the need for approval. Perhaps they hold the key to our sexual fantasies. Or they are that missing "other half" that will enable us to achieve our dreams. Right?

Wrong, according to the Spanish philosopher and therapist Joan Garriga. As he writes in his book *El buen amor en la pareja* [The right kind of love in relationships]: "Your partner can bring you happiness, but they can't make you happy. This is an important distinction." In Garriga's explanation, love and happiness are separate domains. Your happiness is your responsibility, not your partner's. Needless to say, this flies in the face of just about every lyric we've ever heard in a love song!

But if we look at this from the viewpoint of self-worth, doesn't Garriga have a point? Our relationship with ourselves is our responsibility, just as our self-worth is. Both belong in the realm of My Stuff, not Our Stuff. If I am single, great, I'm happy. If I am in a relationship, great, I am also happy. The happiness may be different, but it is not necessarily more or less. And even if I'm not happy (whether single or in a relationship), the amazing fact is that I can have self-worth anyway. This is nobody's responsibility but mine.

Romantic love is something of a lottery, and many people find that, in today's society, it's an increasingly haphazard one. If your number comes up, this is probably a happy blend of genetics, location, and serendipity. It's got nothing to do with merit, character, or your real worth as a person. So why would you anchor your happiness to such a flimsy reed?

Kids, Parents, and Siblings

All of our familial relationships touch us deeply. Being around our parents (or our memories of them) often brings up huge issues of self-worth. This is hardly surprising. Our initial sense of self is usually formed by reference to them.

A book like this one can hardly add to all the volumes written about the development of the child, the significance of sibling relationships, or good practices in child-rearing. Not to mention the millions of hours of therapy spent grappling with these issues we've developed from the first seven years of life.

I will simply make one observation here. If you are struggling with your kids, your siblings, or your parents, it helps to separate out the part of the problem that relates to your relationship with yourself. You may also find it useful to explore the ways in which this problem relates to contingent self-esteem or to unconditional self-worth. Making this distinction often throws some fresh light on whatever you are grappling with.

Let's say you are worried about your son because he has not done well on his exams. It's the most natural thing in the world to try to motivate him by appealing to his self-esteem. Even if you resist such crude tactics as extrinsic rewards or threats, you may be tempted to motivate him by appealing to his reputation with himself. "Look at how proud you will be, if you succeed!" Esteem mode, again.

If your son's self-worth is rather low to begin with, the worry of exam performance is now a contingency, and hence another potential failure. A self-worth approach might look something like: "I love you, exactly as you are, exams or no. You will always be special to me whether you pass or fail them. Now, what do you really want to do?"

Perhaps even more importantly, however, why are your son's exam grades so important to *you*? Esteem mode again?

According to all my friends who are educators, we are currently seeing an explosive increase in self-esteem and self-worth issues among kids and teenagers. Teen suicide is a growing public health crisis across the Western world. The Centers for Disease Control and Prevention reported recently that the suicide rate for teenage girls in the United States have hit a forty-year high. According to the CDC report, the suicide rates doubled among girls and rose by more than 30 per cent among teen boys and young men between 2007 and 2015. The World Health Organization reports that suicide is now the number one killer of teenage girls worldwide—more so than accidents, illnesses, and complications from pregnancy. In the United States, suicide is the second leading cause of death among teenagers (behind automobile accidents). These are shocking statistics.

Growing awareness of this crisis is one of the reasons for forming the Self-Worth Academy, as a resource center where people of all ages can access unconditional self-worth. (More about this at the end of this book.) My hope is that parents, teachers, and anyone involved with the young will find ways to share with them the shifts of self-worth so that our youth are no longer hostage to the tyranny of self-esteem, which is literally killing so many of them. Self-worth parenting could transform the lives of many people.

Self-worth makes us more courageous lovers, family members, and parents. We do not react so easily to the barbs of others (who are also dealing with self-esteem issues). We can love with less anxiety than when we are trying to prove things to ourselves. Most of all, we can love ourselves with a new sense of loyalty.

Grief and Self-Worth

Kindness and self-acceptance are particularly important when you are grieving the loss of a special person because of death, separation, or even redundancy. We might also mourn the loss of a pet. In all cases, we find ourselves reaching out to someone who is no longer there, and in their absence, we throb with pain.

Each experience of loss is unique. No matter how well schooled we might think we are by previous experience with bereavement, each new loss brings sharp thorns of pain and emptiness. So when someone says, "I know how you feel," you intuitively know that they don't. In this way, grief is a very solitary experience.

We can add to the pain of grief by reproaching ourselves for how we feel. We can blame ourselves for the end of a relationship or for not spending more time with the deceased when we had the chance. We can tell ourselves that we should be "over it by now." We may view ourselves as weak or useless, either because of their absence or the way we are coping.

Recovery from loss is a big subject, well beyond the scope of this book. If this is a special area of concern for you, I recommend the book *The Grief Recovery Handbook*, from which I've personally derived great benefit. Self-acceptance is a crucial starting point in the recovery process: acknowledging the feelings of what you wish had been different, better, or more. Self-worth is a crucial prerequisite for getting support and one of the fruits of the journey. Many people report that they have emerged stronger at the end of a grieving process. It can be another gateway—albeit painful—to a deeper relationship with themselves.

Love After Love
The time will come
when, with elation,
you will greet yourself arriving
at your own door, in your own mirror,
and each will smile at the other's welcome,

and say, sit here. Eat.
You will love again the stranger who was your self.
Give wine. Give bread. Give back your heart
to itself, to the stranger who has loved you

all your life, whom you ignored
for another, who knows you by heart.
Take down the love letters from the bookshelf,

the photographs, the desperate notes,
peel your own image from the mirror.
Sit. Feast on your life.

DEREK WALCOTT

Exercises for the Terrain of Relationships and Family

In your journal, record your answers to the questions that follow and play with making assertions of self-worth based on insights you derive from the exercises.

1. What are the ways in which you might be avoiding self-acceptance? Write down at least five (for example, being in

denial, striving to change things, focusing on something else such as work, compensation habits, blaming or judging, and so on).

2. How is self-acceptance different from self-pity? What is an example of this distinction in your life?

3. How might you link your self-esteem to your relationship status? Consider how you feel on birthdays, anniversaries, on holidays, or when you see people posting engagements on Facebook. What goes through your mind?

4. How might you outwardly reproach or blame your partner for things that, deep down, you are reproaching yourself for? Write down an example, without beating yourself up!

5. If you are single, how do you feel about that? About yourself?

6. When you next see a beautiful happy couple or person—who exemplifies everything that you long for in life—use that trigger as a reminder to send love to yourself. At first, this may feel a bit forced, even fake. But over time, it works. Note that this does not mean denying any sadness you might have; it means accepting your sadness and loving yourself nonetheless.

7. If you are grieving the loss of a special person, how is that impacting your sense of self-worth? How do you need to be kind to yourself? Could you use some support? Where can you find this?

8. Write a gratitude list, focusing on self-worth (in other words, you), not your relationship status/achievements.

9. If you were coming from a place of freedom, playfulness, and joy, what actions would you dare to take? In this terrain of relationships, what movie theater of the mind do you want to quit? What does stepping out into the sunshine mean to you?

10. Who can you talk to about these experiences?

Self-worth is a game changer in affairs of the heart, if we can just avoid those alluring sirens of self-esteem thinking. To download the resource Subtle Saboteurs in Relationships (as well as resources specifically for single people), go to the Resources page of SelfWorthAcademy.com.

(5)

Third Terrain:
Career and Work

"What we must decide is *how* we are
valuable, rather than how valuable we are."

EDGAR Z. FRIEDENBERG

OST PEOPLE SPEND more waking hours at work than in any other activity. If they are fortunate enough to have a job, that is. For many, the absence of a fulfilling job is their single biggest issue of self-esteem. Those who are not in work often have to battle an endless erosion of self-value that frequently accompanies a long period of unemployment. Meanwhile, people who do have employment seem to be working harder than ever to prove themselves.

Furthermore, at the present time, many people find themselves in some sort of transition. Whether between careers, countries, or sectors, more and more people need to reinvent themselves, often several times in a working life. At such times, self-worth is often called into question. Even retirement is being redefined, driven by longer life expectancy, concern over pension values, and a generation of baby boomers who have reimagined every stage of their working lives, so why not retirement, as well?

In my business- and career-coaching work, I see the effects of self-worth every day. Whether it's the new manager trying to prove themself, the negotiator who gives way too easily, the over-eager worker who always says yes, or the professional over-servicing a client, the issue of self-worth is never far away. When I add together all the effort that goes into pleasing others—plus the sometimes even greater effort that goes into proving ourselves—I wonder how anyone finds time to do real work at all!

Effects of Low Self-Worth

It must be acknowledged that self-esteem motivators often produce good results. The desire to make a difference, to have an impact, and to prove ourselves lies at the heart of many worthy endeavors. When we approach these objectives from an intact, healthy conviction of self-worth, our capacity to act is enhanced.

But what happens when self-worth is low? If you've ever had a boss or a colleague who was trying to compensate for a poor sense of self-worth, then you probably already know just how needy they can be. Sitting next to them all day is a penance; having them as a boss is a nightmare.

Among the many effects of low self-worth, we might list the need for constant praise or validation, perfectionism, micromanagement, inability to delegate, failure to take initiative, not asking for what is needed, frequent absences due to illness or depression, over-sensitivity, inability to take feedback, constant need to talk, inability to speak up, difficulty saying no (or yes), indecision, inability to negotiate, trouble dealing with stress, and inability to cope with change. And that's just the beginning.

Let's take an example. At work, have you ever encountered an unexpected explosive reaction from someone that seemed way out of proportion to the cause? A client once described how a new supplier had "exploded" over a small piece of negative feedback that she had given them. She offered to show me the email exchange and I can vouch for the fact that it would pass any test of nonviolent communication. The observations she had made to the supplier were reasonable and balanced, coupled with many appreciative comments about the work the supplier had done. When I read the explosive reply, it seemed obvious to me that the supplier had a significant self-worth issue. While some people with low self-worth become very quiet and withdrawn, others explode over trifles.

Resilience

Whether you are employed, independent, or looking for work, there is one thing you can be sure of in today's uncertain economy: setbacks. The marketplace is a tough place to be. Some people experience this in the form of rejection and disappointment. For example, salespeople get a daily dose of rejection that would cripple many others. For others, a setback takes the form of the latest reorganization or a new boss whose style is at odds with their way of working. Independent professionals may have to deal with the sudden loss of a contract, the arrival of a tax bill, or a late-paying customer. Uncertainty is everywhere; there is no hiding. Even the traditional public sector—often regarded as the safest haven in the turbulent seas of employment—is no longer immune.

Today's workplace is riddled with setbacks and harsh realities, except for perhaps a fortunate few who live in a cozy bubble. When I read books on personal development, I sometimes wonder if the authors live in a different universe than the majority of us who earn our livings in the rough-and-tumble of the real marketplace. When I come across exhortations like "take a nap in the afternoon" or "go for a walk in nature when stressed," I often get the impression that such authors are writing from the coziness of retirement or slow-paced lifestyle businesses, far removed from the hurried lot of common humanity.

I am writing this on a flight across the United States after two intensive days spent with a sales team, working from early morning to late evening to sharpen their sales and negotiation skills. I have huge respect for these people who start each month with a zero and live with the constant tyranny of quotas. I've been impressed by how they treat each new prospect with courtesy and respect, even though they know that many of these complicated technical proposals will end in rejection.

It takes tremendous resilience to survive and thrive in this market. If your self-worth is limited, your ability to bounce back from setbacks is weakened. For this reason alone, every investment we make in self-worth repays us handsomely in terms of energy and resilience.

I see evidence of this every week in my coaching work. The nature of the work that I do with clients invariably takes them out of their comfort zones. Along the way, therefore, there are more setbacks and rejections to deal with. This is one reason why we work on raising personal energy: otherwise, the fuel to drive the development will simply not be there. Developing one's career or business is rarely just a matter of clever strategy and tactics. As human beings, our energy levels are an equally vital dimension of successful working.

Esteem Mode at Work

How does energy erode? Let's take one example where energy is being consumed not by the demands of a difficult boss or a client but by an Inner Tyrant.

Edward is a consultant in his early thirties. A firm believer in self-esteem and his "optimized self," he invests in himself. Outwardly confident, he's a good communicator and presenter. Edward is ambitious, so he seeks regular feedback, both from clients and colleagues, in his constant quest for improvement and achievement.

Unknown to Edward, however, some of his clients and colleagues are starting to resent these feedback conversations. They are busy people (equally preoccupied with proving themselves), so they don't have the time to give Edward all the attention he seeks. Indeed, Edward is developing a bit of a reputation for being narcissistic and self-focused.

Sensing something is amiss in his relationships with colleagues, Edward redoubles his efforts. He takes courses in rapport-building, presence, and even mindfulness. He becomes even more aware of body language, breathing, and performance. Every meeting is now a battleground of self-improvement technique, in pursuit of that holy grail of self-esteem.

The struggle is a tiring one. Edward feels that his energy is being slowly eroded and, with it, his self-esteem. The more he pushes for self-esteem at work, the more it seems to be slipping away.

Modes

Edward is stuck in esteem mode, or what might also be called "desire to impress" mode. In the terrain of work, a mode is a tramline in which we get stuck. It's an underlying way of thinking that can shape many hours of our working week. Most of the time, we are not conscious of the mode in which we are operating, yet these modes can consume a lot of our energy.

What if Edward could appreciate his own self-worth, without the imperative of self-esteem, the need for positive feedback, and all the attendant directives of growth and development?

How might this realization transpose his search? How might his relationships with his peers improve?

On occasion, nearly everyone gets stuck in recurring patterns of thinking, so it's hardly surprising that a lot of my coaching work is supporting people to break the pattern. Let's consider the most prevalent of these modes.

It's easy to get stuck in a mode. Nearly everyone experiences this from time to time. It's usually easy enough to see that mode in hindsight but devilishly difficult to spot when we are stuck in it. My coaching work often focuses on getting people to ask, "Which mode am I in?" If you can identify it, you can usually change it.

Sometimes, it takes time to spot the mode, and this was the case with Edward. He was so accustomed to chasing approval that he did not (at first) see that he sought validation and by doing so undermined the very relationships he was trying to build. The exercise that helped him to see it was a reverse role-play, in which I played the part of someone like Edward and he played the role of the person being approached for feedback. In the role-play, I kept asking questions like:

- "How do you feel I performed in that meeting?"
- "Are you happy with my presentation?"
- "What does your boss think of me?"
- "What sorts of things could I do better?"

Suddenly, the blinders came off. As one self-preoccupied question followed another, Edward was a bit taken aback by the degree of self-focus, as well as by how quickly he became irritated by the questions. That's another problem with modes: we often don't see the effect they're having on the people around us.

Personally, I have been stuck in many of the following modes, with task mode still being a regular pitfall. In this mode, my subconscious thought is "I can feel good about me if I get through

Mode	Link to Self-Esteem
Engineering mode	Self-esteem = technical brilliance (designing the perfect solution whether or not anyone wants it)
Perfectionism mode	Self-esteem = no defects, no mistakes, being right
Strategizing-for-the-future mode	Self-esteem = what I will do some day, and who I will therefore be
People-pleasing mode	Self-esteem = being liked, respected, validated by others (my boss, the clients, my colleagues, my peers)
Worry mode	Self-esteem = fixing (I am the world's problem-solver; I'm prepared; I'm constantly rehearsing the next problem or disaster, anticipating issues in the future)
Anger mode	Self-esteem = identification with cause (asserting myself via the cause, so as not to be ignored; smoke-screening frustration with self; railing against the world and protesting about management, environment, gender, security, politics, and so on)
Victim mode	Self-esteem = low (caught between persecutors and saviors; seeking identity in destiny or tragedy; "look what's happened to me now...")
Time sheet mode	Self-esteem = billing the maximum hours
Qualifications mode	Self-esteem = degrees, diplomas, certificates
School mode	Self-esteem = learning the lesson (and life is reduced to a series of lessons)
Task mode	Self-esteem = getting through the to-do list

my key tasks for the day." I can hear that voice in my head even now, as I type this paragraph. This morning, I'm very much in task mode.

Siren Voices

· · · · · · · · · · · · · · · · · ·

We now know that, in one way or another, all these voices are in the self-esteem choir. When they sing in harmony and the song is beautiful and seductive, these voices are the sirens that can lead us away from an unconditional relationship with ourselves.

Perhaps I will get through my task list for today, and I will probably feel good about that. When I'm getting ready for bed and I think back over the day, I will no doubt feel better if I've managed to do the things I planned to do at 7 a.m. There is no problem with that. Indeed, I will hopefully tackle tomorrow's workload with renewed energy and confidence. I will be happy listening to the seductive voices of self-esteem.

But what if one of my afternoon tasks proves a lot more diffi-cult than I imagined? Today, I have a complex piece of research to design for a corporate client, which may well put me behind on my to-do list. I will then feel less satisfied about my perfor-mance. Self-esteem will almost certainly be impacted, even if I theorize that it shouldn't.

But even if I fail to do my tasks, and/or eat a packet of bis-cuits, and/or have an argument with a close friend, and/or fall prey to any of the modes in the table above, I can still access a core friendship with myself, which means I can get a good night's sleep and tackle tomorrow with a clean slate. That's the difference that self-worth makes: its roots go deeper than performance-based self-esteem.

Which mode(s) do you think you might get stuck in? Perhaps take a moment to review the table on page 113, before reading further.

Workaholics

. . . .

Twenty years ago, it was exceptional to meet people who worked literally all the time. Now it's quite commonplace to meet managers and professionals like Edward who work around the clock, particularly if they have global roles. For those based in Europe, they are often communicating with US colleagues late into the night, before waking early to deal with issues coming from the Asian offices. In between, they manage with little or no sleep.

The statistics are dramatic. Here are just a few.

- The average American worker receives thirteen vacation days every year, but 34 per cent of workers don't take a single day of that vacation in any given twelve-month period.

- Even when people do take vacation days, 30 per cent say they worry constantly about work while they are trying to relax.

- Between 1970 and 2006, the average number of hours in a working year for the average American worker increased by a total of 200 hours.

- Of those who admit to workaholic tendencies, 86 per cent state that they feel like they must rush through their day in order to get work done effectively.

- More than half of all workaholics end their work day feeling like they weren't able to accomplish as much as they could have.

Some of the consequences of workaholism are as follows.

- The divorce rate in relationships where at least one person is classified as a workaholic is 55 per cent.

- A study in the Netherlands showed that 33 per cent of workaholics have regular migraines because of the stresses of their job.

- People who work eleven hours per day or more have a 67 per cent greater chance of suffering from coronary heart disease when compared with those who work a typical eight-hour day.

- Anyone working twelve or more hours per day is 37 per cent more vulnerable to suffering an injury that is job-related, even in an office environment.

Even those without global responsibilities seem to be permanently stuck in task mode. They answer work messages from their phone, even during dinner at home. Upon awakening, their first thought is to check for messages. Their weekends are spent catching up.

It's not just the quantity of work that's problematic, it's the intensity. One of my clients once labeled this as "hurry sickness": the constant rushing to meet impossible deadlines, to meet expectations, to catch up with endless emails and messages, and to generally get the job done. Another client once spoke to me about the permanent state of guilt in which working parents live, not being "enough" at home because of work priorities and not being "enough" at work because of home priorities.

Apart from the demands of the job and the home, I see an even greater imperative coming from within: the need to be "enough" in the first place. This is particularly acute when young professionals have been rapidly promoted. They often harbor a deep unspoken suspicion that they are not worthy of the role they have landed. So there is an everyday imperative to prove oneself.

This behavior rapidly becomes a habit, one that is clearly well established with Edward. His preoccupation with his own impact is almost certainly a result of a deep-seated belief that he is not worthy. If he felt worthy, he would not be as addicted to feedback as he has been.

Shift #4: From Self-Evaluation to Usefulness

This takes us to an important shift in the Self-Worth Safari, one that is often neglected in the annals of narcissistic self-esteem. It's a bit paradoxical, odd, even contradictory—at least in theory. But it's very powerful in practice.

For nearly two decades, I have been coaching hundreds of people like Edward to shift their focus from self-evaluation (or self-preoccupation) to how their services can be *useful*. For example:

- changing questions such as "What did you think of my presentation?" to "Which aspect of the presentation was most useful to you?";

- moving away from ratings of each other (or ourselves) toward an open-ended exploration of value and the difference that we make in the world of each other;

- supporting independent professionals to set aside their preoccupation with credibility, strategy, or messaging and instead to focus their communication on being of service to others;

- encouraging salespeople to go into a meeting with an attitude of usefulness, rather than trying to "land the deal";

- describing a company's value proposition in terms of the impact on customers rather than self-preoccupied claims about ourselves or our methodology.

Why this emphasis on usefulness? Let me illustrate with an example from my own experience. For years, I hated giving presentations. Mention of the words "public speaking" brought me into that same grip of cold sweat as seeing that iconic *Lunch atop* a *Skyscraper* photograph, depicting eleven workmen having lunch sitting on a high beam in New York. I only had to visualize an audience (even a small one) in order to experience a host of anxious physical sensations, from rapid heartbeat and breathing to dizziness and a panicky contraction of core muscles.

I recognized that I could not escape presentations. The first one I gave was to a small lunch-time gathering in Northampton, UK. I did not sleep the night before, and I arrived an hour before anyone else turned up. A friend came along for moral support. I had endlessly prepared my "speech" on index cards, which shook as I gripped them. Yet, somehow, I got through and amazingly that presentation got me one of my first clients. I was delighted. But then I realized I would have to do it again!

I read books and attended seminars and teleclasses (early webinars) on public-speaking. But, if anything, my problems got worse. I became conscious of even more mistakes in my delivery, such as saying "em" a lot and speaking too quickly. The more I rehearsed, the worse I seemed to get. Those index cards continued to shake.

Around this time, I also started to deliver a series of workshops on business-building for new entrepreneurs. One Saturday morning, I was driving home and realized that the workshop had been less nerve-wracking than previous ones. I had almost enjoyed it! This was strange because, if anything, the topic and the attendees had been a bit more difficult than usual. Asking myself what was different, I could only see one factor: that through necessity I had become so engrossed in the content, and the conversation, that I forgot about my own performance.

I decided to experiment, to do less preparation and more "go with the flow." Along the way, I unintentionally gave myself permission to forget about my own performance and just focus on what attendees might find useful. I changed the feedback sheets, dropping the usual evaluation-of-the-session questions and instead asking more open questions about relevance and usefulness.

When we focus on usefulness, we shut out a lot of background noise. We can clearly hear the issues of the person in front of us or turn our attention 100 per cent to the content we are delivering and the context in which it is being received. We are not distracted by the voices of self-preoccupation.

It's a strange paradox, but *the more we focus on usefulness to others, the more room self-worth has to grow*. Precisely when we are not thinking about it, self-worth is expressed in our ability to focus on the issues and people around us.

If you are just starting out in your career, you may find this approach particularly liberating. It's normal to be concerned with positive evaluation. You have just left an education system that is preoccupied with scores. When a young professional discovers they can drop all the self-centered concerns to participate from a perspective of usefulness, they no longer have to worry about asking a silly question or appearing to know the answer. You are free to explore.

I've seen a vivid example of this shift during a workshop in Brussels with an NGO. A talented young man had a "eureka moment" when he realized that his natural sense of curiosity allowed him to have any conversation with anybody—without the need for permission or explanation—as long as he kept his focus on being useful. I still receive occasional emails from him, expressing how this has transformed his working days.

From such a standpoint of usefulness, self-worth is free to grow. Uninhibited by the claims of self-esteem, conversations flow where they are needed. By dropping the constant need for self-evaluation or to prove our credentials, professionals develop courage in their business interactions.

The often-surprising result is that self-esteem grows, too, precisely because we are no longer chasing it. I'm particularly thinking of a young woman, who, like me, was terrified of presentations. As someone who for years suffered the same torment, often for days and nights beforehand, I felt a great affinity with her suffering. She also described how excessive preparation often made the problem worse, by deepening her preoccupation with performance. Those siren voices, again.

In our work together, we focused on how to turn presentations into dialogues and how to embed questions about usefulness. Today, she is a confident public speaker with only a fraction of her former anxiety. She regularly presents to senior management with a degree of assurance she never imagined even a few years ago.

Another way to think of this is with the metaphor of "building a bridge from the other side." Instead of beginning with us/our expertise/our talents, we begin with the other: their opportunities, their risks, their complications, their issues. Then we build a bridge back to how we can be useful. In this way, the value of our work can be more easily understood.

Worthiness

As long as a person's sense of worthiness is basically intact—however obscured by a self-esteem upbringing or by education—Shift #4 can usually be done in a matter of days or weeks. However, if that intrinsic sense of worthiness is missing, or if a person has spent decades hooked on the drug of self-esteem, it may be much more difficult to make the leap.

One of the principal reasons for creating the Self-Worth Safari was to address this fundamental problem. I personally know scores of talented people whose careers have not even started yet because of this intrinsic sense of unworthiness. They pursue one qualification after another or they experience burnout after burnout or they get stuck in one of the modes on page 113; all the time what's missing is a basic sense of worthiness. Deep down, they worry, "Who am I to be doing this?" They often suffer from imposter syndrome, which we explore in depth in chapter 15.

A pivotal moment comes when they realize that the only answer to that question, for anybody, is an assertion of the right to be here. This realization often happens in a split second. It can be preceded by years of searching or futile struggle, and then one day they wake up to the epiphany that there is no need to prove anything at all. That can be a thrilling day, indeed.

How do you establish worthiness? Ultimately, this cannot be done by thinking; that will inevitably lead us down a self-esteem path that places more conditions on our worth. Worthiness can only be affirmed with action or decision. I know hundreds of people who are going from one workshop to another, in search of worthiness from a new thought, a new teacher, or a new experience (or quite often a new relationship). What is needed is an assertion: a split-second decision, action, or commitment to oneself. It is too easy to avoid that commitment via the distraction of the next book or workshop or another form of sophisticated procrastination.

Some seek worthiness with a new sense of purpose, particularly when it comes to their work life. There is no doubt that a strong sense of purpose is energizing and a great boost to self-esteem. But we should not confuse purpose with worthiness. I know a man who, today, has a great sense of purpose. But it took him several years to find that. Along the way, he had to assert a sense of loyalty to himself, even on those cloudy days when his sense of purpose was unclear. That's when self-worth really counts.

Practice: Pre-Meeting Anxiety

If you have a call or a meeting coming up about which you feel a degree of anxiety, then this practice is for you. It's useful for

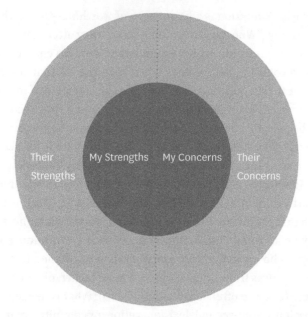

interviews, first meetings, appraisals, presentations—any occasion that makes you nervous and concerned about your worth.

1. On a large sheet of paper, draw two circles, one inside the other. Then draw a line down the middle, splitting both circles in half.

2. The inside circle is about you. In that circle, on the left-hand side of the center line, outline your positive strengths or talents (for example, creativity, structure, and so on), and on the right-hand side, note the things that you are concerned about (lack of results, inexperience, getting fired, and so on).

3. The outside circle is about them, the person or people you are presenting to. In that circle, on the left-hand side, outline what you perceive to be their strengths (for example, established clients, great technology, and so on). On the right-hand side of the center line, note their issues and risks

(need to demonstrate results to boss, reputation if things go wrong, revenue dropping, and so on).

4. You may struggle to write things in the outside circle. If so, congratulations—you have found the real problem! Your challenge is to discover these issues, whether by calling someone, using Google, or referring to notes or an annual report. What are their strengths and issues? Your meeting with them will be a lot stronger if you can get into their shoes.

5. Once you have discovered their issues, focus on how specifically you can reduce their risks or increase their effectiveness. Putting aside any lack of experience or other limiting factors (which are all about you), how can you contribute to *their* world?

6. Ask yourself: what are the likely complications they are facing? How can you make their life easier?

7. Prepare some opening questions for the meeting. For example, "Before we start, may I ask..." can be used in almost every situation. By listening to the answer, you move your attention from self-evaluation to usefulness.

Self-worth is not about bringing the spotlight back to you. It's about taking charge of the spotlight and shining it where you can have most impact.

Your Future Career

When people find themselves at a career crossroads, this shift from self-evaluation to usefulness is particularly valuable. At times like this, a vicious circle of thinking often forms that looks something this.

I experience a vague (or intense) sense of dissatisfaction with the state of my current career (or lack of career). I look around me at what others are doing, and my dissatisfaction becomes even more intense. I see others who seem to be much more successful than I am or who seem to have more meaningful careers. So I reach out to get some help. Perhaps I employ a career coach or mentor. They encourage me to examine my talents and strengths. I start reflecting on my passion and purpose. I do various talent assessments and personality profiles. So far, so good.

However, because my self-esteem is problematic, partly due to my dissatisfaction with my career, I struggle with those questions of passion and purpose and long-term career goals. It's hard for me to answer the question, "What do I want?" I come up with something so vague and nebulous that it's hard to translate it into any solid reality.

Eventually I get around to reformatting my CV or website. I broadcast this at every opportunity. I apply for every job that comes up. I get no response and my self-esteem drops even further. I feel more dissatisfied and frustrated. The vicious circle is now complete.

When we embark on career planning from the perspective of self-worth, we open up a very different approach that is much more successful. First of all, we acknowledge the dissatisfaction and the impact this has on self-esteem. We accept that our self-esteem could be better. At the same time, we remind ourselves that self-worth is not based on performance. We apply Shift #1, dropping the self-assessments and asserting our right to be who we are. Then we kick Shift #2 into gear, practicing some simple daily actions as an expression of self-worth, even if self-esteem is not ideal. With Shift #3, we switch from self-reproach to self-acceptance.

On this basis, we are now ready to do something different. Instead of navel gazing, we start exploring how our skills and talents can be useful. This is not a question about ourselves: it's a question about the marketplace or the world in which we find ourselves. As such, we are free to explore this to our heart's content. We can talk to anybody we like—or even don't like—because our focus is usefulness.

In my coaching work, I see the transformative effect of this shift every day. It's much easier for people to set up meetings, lunches, or cups of coffee, when they're not focused on selling themselves. Exploratory conversations are much more effective because they are not about "me, me, me." When CVs eventually get emailed, they are much stronger and more targeted.

Business Development

The same approach is equally powerful in business development. As some readers may know, I have spent the past two decades coaching professionals and salespeople of all kinds to shift from self-promotion to open-ended exploration of usefulness, and to design business-development strategies accordingly. Not only does this value-centered approach open up more opportunities, those opportunities are more lucrative when firmly rooted in serviceability and trust. Furthermore, the cost of sale is less, because a usefulness-based approach is conducive to strategic partnerships and referrals—far more so than a promotional approach.

Let's take a typical example. Sara is an independent consultant, now in her forties. For over a decade, Sara suffered from a recurring "feast to famine" cycle. Some years, she was so busy that she hardly had time to see her kids. Other years, the pipeline was empty and worry about her financial future plagued Sara. This cycle was repeated, so that Sara had not so much ten years of experience, but two years of experience five times over.

Every so often, Sara would engage in a flurry of "business development." Sometimes this took the form of networking. She also tried social media, email campaigns, newsletters, blogging, and getting on the speaker circuit. Each of these initiatives ran out of steam, sooner or later. Partly because of poor results, but most of all because Sara felt uncomfortable about doing them.

Business development is a tough game if self-esteem is low. Unfortunately, self-esteem is usually low when the pipeline is empty, which is precisely when we most need it.

When I work with people like Sara, we usually have a very honest conversation about self-esteem at the beginning of our work together. More than strategy or tactics, our relationship with ourselves is at the very root of our effectiveness in business development. We have to believe in ourselves on those days that others don't—and this is particularly important for independent professionals.

So how does someone like Sara switch from self-evaluation to usefulness? Practically speaking, this means having different conversations. In a first meeting with a client, for example, Sara might want to share some insights from the marketplace rather than simply presenting herself and her experience. She will focus more on exploring the specific *context* of the client's problem, then presenting her own *content* and solutions. Her marketing meetings will be primarily research-based. Her website will be less about her and more about real-life client issues.

When Sara has an opportunity, she will have a detailed understanding of what is most useful to the client. As a result, her pricing will be better. She will have a clearer picture of what they can afford, and her negotiation tactics will be stronger. When they try to discount her fees, she will have sufficient self-worth to resist and insights to caution the client against under-investing. All this will be possible because of her focus on usefulness rather than on self-evaluation.

When doing reviews with her existing clients, the same change of emphasis will be operative. Sara won't encourage them to evaluate her because she now knows this is just another form of self-preoccupation. Instead, there will be assessments of what was useful and what could be of even better service. These conversations will build trust with Sara's clients and as a result she will be likely to win more business.

This shift is so powerful that you'd imagine everybody would be doing it. Nothing could be further from the truth. In reality, so many companies and individuals are utterly obsessed by the need to prove themselves. You can see this on their websites, their proposals, their constant quest for ratings about what you think of them. It's not just individuals that have an insatiable hunger for self-worth; entire organizations do, too. Self-preoccupation is rampant.

If you are in sales or in business development, this is perhaps good news for you. By dropping self-preoccupation and self-evaluation, the potential to stand out is enormous. When value is understood as usefulness, not self-justifying adjectives, a very different conversation happens between a provider and customer. The need to discount is removed. The potential to grow revenue by stopping discounting has added millions to the bottom line of some of our larger technology and consulting clients. Self-worth has tangible value.

That Difficult Boss

If you've ever struggled with that awful boss (or client), you have firsthand experience of one of the worst nightmares of working life. Not only does a difficult boss render each day one spent in hell, but they are also destructive to self-esteem. This is particularly true in early working life, when we don't always have better reference points to perceive what is really going on.

Perhaps you are working for a bully who enjoys their power over you. Or you are dealing with sexual harassment, working for that lecherous guy who you don't ever want to be caught working late with. Or you have to endure constant criticism and nitpicking. Or public embarrassment and mockery. Perhaps you're with that outwardly friendly type who subtly creates insecurity and is manipulative and controlling. Or the boss whose tendency is to react, rather than respond. The list goes on.

One of our Safari participants had a blend of this situation. She works as a contractor in a big financial-services organization. Around the time she started her Safari, she was working with a new boss who was instantly critical and dismissive of everything that she did. Every day became a battleground, and she was constantly defending herself. She feared for her job and hence for her family's income.

When you're stuck with a difficult boss, you have two problems. The first is the *situation*: the awkward meetings, the anger, getting through the day. The second is the effect on *self*: the erosion of confidence and joy, the fear of the future, sometimes even not knowing who you are anymore.

Our Safari friend found it helpful to separate these two problems. It was obvious that there was not much she could do about the first problem. Though not completely powerless, it was clear that she was not going to change her boss's way of working. No matter how unjust or intolerable he was, there was a limit to what she could do to influence the situation.

However, she decided that she was *not* going to allow him to influence her sense of self. Armed with this decision, she made a point of looking him straight in the eye, calmly giving explanations when necessary (as they most frequently were), and not allowing fears to undermine her self-belief. In this context, she found Shift #3—from self-reproach to self-acceptance—very helpful. She could accept her fear without slipping into negative descriptions of herself.

This allowed her to make Shift #4, from self-evaluation to usefulness. How could she be useful and helpful in the revised setup, rather than preoccupied with herself? She soon discovered she was not alone: others were also being bullied by this arrogant boss. She became even more determined and looked him straight in the eye every time they had a difficult encounter.

This is when self-worth is all-important. Dealing with difficult people is one of those situations where we get to deepen our belief in ourselves. Paradoxically, the day that you don't feel you are dealing well is the day when you get to be a loyal friend to yourself, precisely and perhaps especially when you feel you could have performed better.

Our Safari friend practiced this to the letter because she had to! There was nothing else to do. Each day, she met conflict squarely. When things did not improve, she eventually initiated a formal complaint. Self-worth is not just a thinking process; it often leads to action. As she herself puts it, "I knew that 'in action' means taking an action and I simply had to do something. It was a defining moment for me and one that I will never forget."

In this real-life story, we see a truth illustrated yet again: that an *external* problem (in this case, a difficult boss) can strengthen our *internal* relationship with ourselves and be a catalyst for self-worth to grow. Much as I discovered through loss and bereavement, she discovered through dealing with adversity. This "defining moment" is when self-worth gets deepened.

How does the story end? Her complaint was not only upheld, but her contract has since been extended twice in the same company. She now works for another boss, and there remains an uneasy awkwardness with the difficult guy. But each time she meets him, she still looks him straight in the eye.

Job Search

Being without a job, or doing a job far below one's expectations, can be a lonely and demoralizing experience. On top of all the practical difficulties, such as financial worries, many people have to endure regular setbacks, loss of peers, and the erosion of self-esteem that being unemployed often brings.

In this setting, the benefits of focusing on self-worth, as opposed to self-esteem, are very real. First of all, you can accept and befriend the feelings of low self-esteem rather than fighting them. When setbacks occur, you can be kind to yourself and not add self-reproach on top of the burden of rejection.

It takes real self-worth to do this. I have seen how the combined effect of rejection, loneliness, and uncertainty can test even the bravest of souls. It's so easy to become discouraged, depressed, or even bitter. Even more perniciously, a strident hardness can set in.

Let's take Martin, for example. Martin is a senior technology manager in his mid-forties who has been unemployed for two years. He has applied for a succession of global roles and usually makes it to a second or third interview. On two occasions, he has been offered a job, only for the prospective employer to cancel the deal at the last moment.

What is the problem? At first encounter, Martin is insightful, knowledgeable, and friendly. He has a string of impressive achievements behind him and the outward confidence you would expect in a senior leader. However, the longer you spend with Martin, the more you encounter a certain narcissism. He talks incessantly about the impact that he wants to make, often inserting his views and war stories in the middle of discussions wherein these have little relevance. He has yet to appreciate that all his undoubted talents have to fit into the glove of usefulness.

If Martin could learn to fully accept his self-worth and drop the need to prove himself, he could free himself from many imperatives. Above all, he would be more attractive to potential employers. I wonder if the last-minute job cancellations are due to the employer's unease about hiring a potentially difficult and self-preoccupied senior manager?

The last time we met, I could not help but notice how Martin's tone had darkened. He refuses to acknowledge any issue with self-worth: the only problem he sees is that people don't value him enough. He's slipped into anger mode. A vicious circle is forming as repeated rejection leads to a thickening shell of denial and resentment. It will probably take a hard knock to break open that shell.

If Martin could only find the roots of self-worth, he might be released from his incessant railing against the state of the world. He could rediscover the talent and the curiosity of his younger self. He could focus more on being interested, rather than trying to be interesting (Shift #7). With his connections, I have no doubt that softening into self-worth would open doors to new opportunity. Self-preoccupation is a veritable blight on the lives of many unemployed professionals.

The Question of Purpose and Meaning

The world of work has evolved enormously since the end of the Second World War, particularly in terms of what people find meaningful. The postwar generation found fulfillment by having a job and feeding their family. If you had a job, a car, a house, and security, you were successful.

As more and more people enjoyed higher levels of education, as organizations became more complex and intertwined, success came to involve being some sort of manager, leader, or expert. It was no longer enough to have a job. You now needed goals and achievements, too.

In the yuppie 1980s, investments were added to the list. People chattered about how their house value or shares were growing by the week. Financial planners stepped in, and suddenly everyone could be a millionaire. It was no longer enough to have an income; what mattered now for many people was their net worth.

Of course, many people also became teachers, nurses, social workers, or worked for nonprofit organizations. They chose careers that had meaning for them and aligned with their values, instead of goal-driven careers with self-focused purpose.

There are subtle differences between *purpose* and *meaning*, though there is little consistency in how these terms are used and are sometimes used interchangeably. I distinguish the terms as follows.

Purpose is a clear-cut vision or goal, usually a future state toward which a person wants to head. Examples of this future state may be a business they want to build, a career they wish to establish, a house they wish to own, or a status they wish to achieve. Their purpose may be linked to a vision of society or something they want to achieve for themselves.

Meaning is the wider context that makes a purpose significant and is usually closely linked to a person's values. Examples include a belief in quality, in harmonious relationships, or in creating prosperity in the wider world.

If we look at the current world of work, we can easily distinguish environments in which one element is clearer than another. For example, in a large corporate organization, there will be no shortage of stated purpose. Most goal-oriented management thrives on precisely that. But how many of these goals have meaning?

On the other hand, walk into an incubation hub of social entrepreneurs and you are in a hothouse of meaning. Everyone

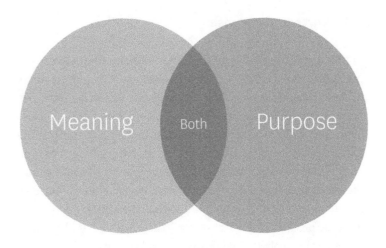

wants to change the world, yet they often change their plans more often than their socks. There is often a tsunami of meaning but not always a consistency of purpose.

Since the millennium, we have seen increasing numbers of people who want both: meaning and purpose. This is not an easy blend to achieve. For many people today, their self-esteem is therefore caught between a rock and a hard place. Many feel that they face either a lucrative but meaningless corporate racket or a low-income existence as a charity worker, social entrepreneur, or poorly paid service professional.

Some turn to self-employment, as a way to hopefully experience both dimensions (purpose and meaning). Yet a huge number of independents also struggle, often taking fewer holidays and working longer hours than they did in their traditional jobs. On top of that, they have to cope with a tyrannical boss 24/7—themselves. And if that boss is in full pursuit of self-esteem, requiring that every day is rich in both meaning and successful purpose, you can just imagine the stress that results. Welcome to twenty-first-century living.

Self-Worth and Purpose

In this stressful world—where jobs are expected to deliver both purpose and meaning—self-worth becomes an easy casualty. A classic example of this is the socially conscious entrepreneur, who, for example, starts an eco-business. They pour heart and soul into their "baby," rich as it is in both meaning and purpose. Every waking moment is spent thinking about the marketing, the communication, the partnership-building, and the ever-present problem of cash flow. Because they believe so deeply in their work—even more so than the aspiring corporate director or the ambitious lawyer—they may feel guilty about enjoying themselves. Taking any time off can seem like a luxury, even on weekends. Their entire identity is bound up with the eco-business.

This can be dangerous not only for general well-being but for self-worth. When serious setbacks occur, it's personal. Their very identity is threatened. Beyond a dream of passion and purpose, who are they?

If you listen carefully to that chorus of passion and purpose, it will not take you long to hear a second melody of self-validation underneath. When you hear someone say, "I want to make a difference," the subject of the sentence is very clear; the difference to be made is often rather vague and abstract. The quest for meaningfulness is equally, and often primarily, a quest for self-esteem. We want to carve our initials on the tree of life by doing something meaningful.

I've noticed that the distinction between self-esteem and self-worth is particularly useful to social entrepreneurs and independent professionals. When they protect the roots of self-worth, they can pursue passion and purpose to their heart's content: knowing that whatever happens, they can maintain a core friendship with themselves. In this way, they recover swiftly from setbacks and they are free to live their dreams.

We seem to be living in the Age of Purpose. Many books start with purpose and meaning. *Find your life path or life goal. Write down your mission statement. What is your passion?* These questions can be onerous to people when self-worth is low. So it's easy to grasp at abstract notions such as, "I want to make a difference."

My humble suggestion is to start where you are, with the people you know and who believe in you. Whatever state your career is in, find your worth in yourself as you are today, with no conditions, not in some rose-tinted dreamy future. You are not what you do, any more than you are your relationship status or your shape. Your self-esteem will fluctuate, but your self-worth does not have to.

ARTIST AT WORK
I trace
with trembling fingertip

the naked calligraphy
of your body

my hands
creating you

out of this darkness

so that dawn
finds you

drawn with such
exquisite passion

that it tells
the sun

to look:
'Look!'

And the sun
reaching in the window

can not help but touch
to see if you are real.

'Hands off!'
I warn.
'She's mine!'

And the sun
sulks

as I cover you up
my masterpiece

and finally exhausted I
... fall asleep.

DÓNALL DEMPSEY

Exercises for the Terrain of Work

The following exercises offer opportunities to reflect, by writing down answers to these questions in your journal, and to work with others who may support you in your self-worth journey. You may also find yourself offering the same kind of support in return.

1. How does self-worth affect you at work? Where has it held you back? When has self-worth helped you?

2. In which modes do you tend to get stuck? Review the table on page 113 to consider the possibilities.

3. Choose something you would like to change about your work. If you were absolutely convinced of your value and were not

seeking to prove anything to anyone, including yourself, what difference might this make to how you tackle this challenge?

4. Why do you want to make this change (in Q3)? Are you trying to prove something to yourself? If so, what?

5. If you were free of this imperative, how might that influence your objective?

6. If you work in sales or business development, how could you adapt your approach to be more useful? Think about your website, client-review meetings, and proposals, as well as first meetings with prospects. Who might be partners in that quest?

7. Is there a difficult boss or client in your life? How do they represent an opportunity to believe in yourself, to deepen the roots of self-worth?

8. What drives you: purpose, meaning, both? Something else?

9. What would you do if you were not afraid? If you were to be more courageous in your choice of career direction, what would you choose?

10. Ask someone to introduce you to an imaginary ideal customer or employer. How would they describe you? Notice your gut reactions to their description.

11. Who can support you as you work your way through these questions?

12. Can you incorporate ten-minute breaks into your day, when you can just be with you?

Check out the Self-Worth Academy website for upcoming events, coaching services, and resources to support you in bringing self-worth to the terrain of your career. You can also download the following resource (and others) from the Resources page of SelfWorthAcademy.com: From Self-Evaluation to Use-fulness: 20 Questions to Boost Your Career. These are questions to ask yourself, and others, when you want to add value to what you do.

(6)

Fourth Terrain: Money and Status

"Too many people spend money they
haven't earned, to buy things they don't want,
to impress people that they don't like."

WILL ROGERS

APART FROM A fortunate few, most people have to think about money. For many of us, financial issues get in the way of a good night's sleep. Financial necessity often takes priority over thinking about the self, at all. For the fortunate few, the nearest they get to a financial problem is when the sun is shining brightly and it's hard to read the screen on the cash dispenser. But even they often have sleepless nights, haunted by questions of achievement or status.

The majority of people engage in some sort of exchange, usually of time for money. Whether they are working for others or for themselves, they think about the hours they spend at work and the rewards that this brings (or doesn't).

In *Your Money or Your Life*, authors Vicki Robin and Joe Dominguez take the reader through a valuable exercise to calculate their real hourly wage. I've noticed that most people who do this exercise and establish the amount of life energy they trade for their salary find the result to be a bit of a shock.

The core concept of the exercise is simple. There are usually many hidden costs to your employment: getting to and from work; the clothes you buy to wear at work; at-work meals; the amount spent to relax and wind down after the stress of a work day; dealing with job-related illness; and all other expenses associated with maintaining your working life. For example, you might replace the washing machine or buy a new phone because you don't have time to get the old one fixed. All these costs need to be deducted from your net income after tax. Viewed that way, most people earn less than they think.

Additionally, most people spend many more hours working than they know. As well as those hours at work, there are those spent in preparing for work, traveling to and from work, winding down after work, shopping to make you feel better since your job feels hard, the cost of other go-to reliefs plus all the other hours linked with maintaining your job. Not to mention the hours spent checking emails last thing at night, first thing in the morning, and on the weekend.

If you subtract from your net income the total amount you spend maintaining your work life and divide the reduced net earnings by your total hours of work, including doing activities like those mentioned above, you will have your real hourly wage: exactly the amount of money that you exchange for an hour of your time. If you want to make this number even more precise, read *Your Money or Your Life* and work out the details.

When you make your own calculation, be aware that most of us forget to include things. For example, what about the hours spent lying awake at night, worrying about a work problem? Or the new iPhone that you bought because you couldn't be without a phone and wait for the old one to be repaired? The examples and the checklists in Robin and Dominguez's book are useful.

One way or another, you now have a rough idea of your real hourly wage. How do you feel about that?

Energy

I've seen many a high-earner surprised to discover that, in real terms, they were not so far removed from the minimum wage. One man—quite astute in finance—exclaimed, "I cannot believe that I exchange so much of this finite irreplaceable asset [his life] for so little of a transient asset [his real hourly wage]. You would never tolerate this exchange rate in business!"

Even for people who are reasonably satisfied with the exchange rate, there is still the question of *why* they do it. For those who love their work, the answer is easy. But for many people, work is a means to an end. That end may be to succeed, to be their best, to have an impact, to pay the bills, or to leave a legacy. Whatever the reason, there is a huge energy exchange, day after day. The pursuit of an income accounts for the single greatest exchange that most people engage in. Just paying the rent or mortgage alone requires days of work each month.

Meeting Needs

The conscious (or unconscious) driver behind earning money is to meet needs. At a basic level, this is about paying for housing, buying food, and perhaps providing for the family. For most people today, however, this is also about meeting the needs of a lifestyle that includes holidays, entertainment, travel, self-development, leisure, and personal appearance. As you may notice, some of these are the very prerequisites of self-esteem that we discussed in previous chapters.

Even beyond these considerations, there are other drivers, often linked to proving ourselves. When we tell ourselves that we need a new car, this is not just about getting from A to B. As often as not, are we not making a statement of identity with our clothes, our cars, our technology, and our vacations? As Maslow outlined in his famous hierarchy, there are many levels of needs.

Being Vigilant about Needs

As already discussed, there are huge industries with vested interest in creating needs for you every day. Our entire economy can be viewed as a needs-creation machine: not just the obvious consumer needs but also our needs to look good, to achieve, to have the right lifestyle, to be a success.

The majority of people spend their lives trying to fill these needs. You can see this on a busy shopping street any weekend. But it's equally manifest in the numbers of people flocking to higher education, to fitness centers, and to personal-development courses. These needs may be on different levels—as Maslow charted in his hierarchy—but they are still *needs* directing how the majority of people spend their time and money.

Satisfied needs tend to create more needs. We have no sooner achieved our dream of buying a house then we decide that we need a better garden. Now that we have a bachelor's degree, we need a master's. The holiday creates a need for another holiday, plus perhaps a better job to pay for the better holiday.

It's wise to interrogate our needs from time to time. I used to think I needed a Mercedes, a flat in London, and a high net income. I've since discovered that I can live happily on a fraction of what I used to think I needed. Nobody thinks less of me, at least nobody whose views I worry about. Most people don't even notice. They are probably too preoccupied with their own need-fulfillment.

Here are some questions to help you interrogate if a need is real:

- How many hours per week will it take to pay for this and maintain it (at my real hourly wage, as defined above)?
- Who specifically cares whether I have this or not?
- What story am I telling myself to support this spend?
- By embracing this car, holiday, travel, and so on, what am I saying no to? (Creativity? Relaxation? Development?)
- How can I simplify my life? What benefit would that bring?

Reducing my needs has freed me to do many things I could never have otherwise, including writing this book. By interrogating and eliminating some needs, I learned a new sense of loyalty to myself, shifting away from my perceived needs. I discovered that self-esteem can more often be enhanced by eliminating a need than by getting the need met.

But not always. I've occasionally made the mistake of going too far by trying to eliminate a real need. For example, I need a certain amount of travel and variety in my life. From time to time, I've tried to do without this and instead opted for more stability and routine. After a few months, however, my energy drops and inspiration suffers. I've learned that it's important to get this need met. Some needs are real, not just the product of consumerism.

Needs and Wants

It's helpful to distinguish "needs" from "wants." For me, a certain amount of travel and variety is a need, not just a want. For example, I need occasional changes between city and country life; I may want a scuba-diving holiday in the Philippines. I need occasional conversations with true friends; I may want an exotic car. I need meaningful work; I may want some clients to pay me more.

It's not always easy to distinguish, because wants have a habit of presenting themselves as needs. So I might say, "I need to go diving" or "I need a cream cake," when these are really wants. Language doesn't help!

Needs are core essentials, without which I cannot perform at my best. Just as I can overstate my needs (by confusing them with wants), I can also understate them. Reviewing my needs and wants is therefore important. Why? If I expend too much energy in pursuing needs that are merely wants, then my happiness can suffer. But if I go into denial about needs, then my happiness suffers, too. And so can self-worth.

So how do you distinguish if that new car (or proposed holiday, or that desired lover) is a want or a need? It's a need if:

A. it's related to basic shelter, security, food, or physical well-being;
B. it's essential for emotional well-being—this is often where needs like belonging or affection become important; or
C. it's vital for us to perform at our best (order, variety, inspiration, and so on).

Everything else is a want. It may well be a want that you choose to satisfy, but it's still a want. You can find a full checklist of needs and wants in the Resources section of SelfWorthAcademy.com.

When people have low self-worth, they find it hard to explicitly state their needs and wants. Often, they find it hard to even identify them. They will either dismiss the whole exercise as "more self-preoccupation" (as I've often done) or they will become so consumed by a long list of needs (many of which are actually wants) that they define as essential for their self-esteem.

We all have needs. We would hardly be human if we didn't. A healthy sense of self-worth allows us to freely identify our needs and express them. The very act of doing so is liberating. It's an acknowledgment of our self-worth, a recognition of our value as a person.

Proving Ourselves

I have coached many people who firmly believed that it is essential to pay for private education for their children. If they had not done so, they would have reproached themselves for the rest of their days. They would have felt themselves less than ideal parents.

Others might read this with horror or even mild amusement. The question is: what are your imperatives? Do you believe that your children need piano and several language lessons? Or that you need swimming, yoga, or travel? Why are your imperatives important to you?

Much of the time, we are trying to prove something to ourselves. Our lifestyle—actual or desired—is a product of our expectations. So is the way in which we raise our kids. As noted already, entire industries educate us every day about new possibilities for "reaching our full potential." For good reason: every need of ours—from cars to personal development—is a business opportunity for someone. Every day, we are being constantly encouraged to prove things to ourselves. The smiling faces on the TV adverts (or at the fitness center or yoga studio) demonstrate what you, too, can have, if you would only "invest with us," of course.

The extent of this is very deep—much more so that most people realize. Many Safari voyagers have been quick to say, "I'm not proving myself to anyone," only to discover that the next dilemma they encountered was symptomatic of the very need to do so. Even if we're not proving anything to anyone else, how often do we get caught up in demonstrating things to ourselves?

The entire economy thrives on cultivating anxiety and envy, two of the Four Plagues. It's often anxiety and envy that drive people into shopping malls, onto websites, and even into courses on personal development. It takes real vigilance to notice when we are proving things to ourselves.

Shift #5: From "Should" to "Could"

The Self-Worth Safari is all about tapping into our intrinsic self-worth, as we move away from proving anything to ourselves. We have so far seen four shifts illustrated in three terrains:

- In the terrain of physical self-worth, accepting ourselves as we are. Ceasing self-assessments, moving toward self-assertion instead (Shift #1). Taking actions because we are worth it, as an expression of self-worth, not as a condition of self-esteem (Shift #2).

- In the terrain of relationships, decoupling self-worth from relationship status, and moving from self-reproach to self-acceptance (Shift #3). Taking action derived from freedom, playfulness, and joy.

- In the terrain of career and work, shifting from self-evaluation to usefulness (Shift #4). Acting from a desire to contribute rather than to please or impress.

In the terrain of money, the invitation is to shift from what we "should" do to what we "could" do. It's not our lifestyle or educational aspirations that are harmful; it's our constant need to prove things to ourselves that does the damage. We can embark on any course of action with more freedom and courage if we

feel empowered by a sense of creativity and joy, not pressed by concepts of necessity and imperative.

We *could* put the kids in private school, or we *could* use a good local comprehensive school. We *could* do that next course or get that next qualification, or we *could* focus on using the qualifications and skills we already have. We *could* take that diving trip to the Philippines, or we *could* enjoy a holiday closer to home.

Simply by declaring that we have it, we create a sense of free choice for ourselves. If we declare the opposite, then we will prove ourselves right and continue to live by necessity. If we choose to believe that we need a long and arduous course of self-development in order to change, then we will also make that a reality, and change will be long and difficult. And probably expensive. If we choose to believe that we need an MBA, then we will have to invest both the time and the money to acquire it.

When we come to these decisions from the vantage of choice, then we gain new perspective about our needs, seeing more options and possibilities. Being less "needy" and "should-driven," we make better decisions. Why? Because we are less blinded by trying to prove things to ourselves. We gain a degree of freedom from those plagues of anxiety, frustration, envy, and shame.

Social Status

While some cultures evaluate success in financial terms, others place more priority on social status. Depending on your country and upbringing, this may be connected to your education, manner of speaking, cultural taste, style of dress, and so on. Even a postal or zip code can speak volumes about status, as can a discreet label on a cuff link.

As with "the house on the hill," social status proclaims, *Look at me, I am a Success.* Much of the time, other people don't even notice—after all they are preoccupied by their own need to prove themselves. When we try on that expensive suit, with the right logo, the person to whom we are usually broadcasting our status is the person in the mirror.

Those brought up to value social status may find that it is so ingrained that it's hard to see. In a matter of seconds, they draw conclusions about people based on their accent or clothing or leisure pursuits. When you mention sport, they ask you which gym (or club) you use and your answer says far more about you than you may have intended. In Belgium, "de" in a surname, which often indicates nobility, carries a wealth of meaning that is totally invisible to the outsider. In the UK, Kate Fox's humorous book *Watching the English* contains fascinating examples of the shifting sands of class in modern-day England.

For some, it's very hard to separate self-esteem from social status. In their eyes, stepping out of the social game constitutes giving up, which already feels like failure. Social approval is all-important. Individual expectations are often intricately bound up with generations of familial and cultural expectations.

In this context, being able to separate intrinsic self-worth from contingent self-esteem is especially valuable. Asking someone to renounce their entire cultural heritage (such as their values around education) is a big ask, often bigger than asking them to give up their spending habits.

Shift #6: From "Proving Oneself" to "Valuing Oneself"

It is helpful to remember that it is possible to strive for status with self-worth intact. Self-worth is not about abandoning our drive for excellence; it is about not being a slave to excellence.

When a person seeks to assert themself with real conviction, it helps to have a solid core of self-worth to begin with.

Many people live their lives following the logic of Have, Do, Be. For example, when I *have* sufficient money/qualifications/ achievement, then I will *do* the things I want to do, and finally I will *be* the person I want to be. Self-worth is about consciously inverting this process. Starting by being the person I want to *be* (valuing myself), I now *do* the things that fit with my values (self-esteem) and end up (at least sometimes) *having* the things I want or need. The usual narrative is something like this:

- Have: "When I have a better job (or qualification)..."
- Do: "then I will be able to work fewer hours (or take care of myself, or take holidays)..."
- Be: "and then I will be happier with myself."

Inverting that usual narrative looks something like this:

- Be: "No matter what happens, I am going to be loyal to myself..."
- Do: "so I choose to make the best possible use of each hour of the day, without slipping into self-reproach or negative self-assessments..."
- Have: "in order to open up fresh possibilities of a better job (or a different situation in life)."

Releasing ourselves from what we "have" often seems most difficult when we "have not." It's relatively easy to dismiss the importance of money (or education or good looks or a valuable network) when we have these things. But privilege is always invisible. It's a lot harder to set aside the absence of these things, which often takes real courage. But this is precisely when it's most valuable to drop the attachment to have/have not. The day that a person can do so, without self-reproach, self-worth can really start to grow.

From personal experience, I find Be, Do, Have to be a very powerful way of thinking. The quality of my "doing" is better. My capacity to act is enhanced, when I let go of what I have or have not. I can live with the imperfections of circumstances—even the imperfections of myself. As you can imagine, there are still days when I get attached to doing (for example, getting through my tasks) or having (a new car, a publication credit, or a certain business success). In these moments, it takes conscious effort to refocus my attention on such questions as, *Who am I being in the present moment?* Every time I make the shift away from having or doing to being, I experience a lift in energy, usually within minutes. I can stop the tiresome scenario playing in my head and deal with present-moment reality. The doing somehow gets lighter and the having (or not having) less significant.

In our consumer society, notice how much of human experience has drifted into having. The most obvious is how we speak of a relationship: "having someone special" in our lives, in much the same way as we would have a pet, a new pair of shoes, or a vacation. The commoditization of human experience is everywhere. The liturgy of a consumer society is that "we deserve to have," and if we question this, we may well be told that we need to work on our self-esteem. Notice how the twin melodies of consumerism and self-esteem form a perfect counterpoint: we establish self-esteem by buying the world's goods and having "perfect" experiences and relationships.

Once you step out of that circular narrative, the sense of liberation is thrilling. Intrinsic self-worth never depends on having—not money, not status, not even a relationship. Nor does it depend on doing: you can have self-worth unconditionally, even when you lose the deal.

So who do you want to be today? Adventurous? Curious? Useful? Happy? Loving? You are totally free to define your answer and to change it tomorrow. Or to change it even in an hour from now.

See Me!

....

Everywhere you look, people's hunger for attention is palpable. At work, you see people striving for their voices to be heard at meetings and in decision-making. At home, it may take real effort to get a partner's full attention. One of the saddest sights I've seen recently was an excited child running out from school trying in vain to get her dad's attention, while he was engrossed by something on his phone. The image of that little girl tugging on her dad's sleeve burned itself into my brain as an icon of our attention-deficit society.

We can blame all this on demanding jobs, social media, rising levels of self-preoccupation, virtual working, globalization, education, parental neglect, technology, and a host of other causes. No doubt many factors blended together to produce our attention-deficit society.

Whatever the causes, few people are getting the attention that they would like. While some feel invisible at work, for others the issue is loneliness in their personal lives. Still others are trapped with partners or in families who exhibit indifference or lack of interest. For many young people, the pain is lack of identity. As we saw in the terrain of the body, even attractive people can feel invisible. There are so many ways to be ignored.

While this invisibility is painful for many, it's particularly acute if self-worth is low. When others are not listening (or don't call back or forget your birthday or ignore your contribution), it's all too easy to see this as proof that you don't matter. A vicious circle quickly forms. Each little act of neglect becomes yet another manifestation of low self-worth. We almost expect to be neglected. So we may strive even harder or become resigned to indifference.

I call this the "attention-deficit spiral of hunger." Let's look at a couple of examples. Marianna believes she is living in a fake world dominated by image, and she feels a loss of connection with the people around her. At the same time, she's confused about her professional identity and her self-worth is low. Socially, she often perceives that she is valued for her looks but not her intelligence.

Her inner insecurity is mirrored by external events, particularly at work. When she goes to a meeting, low self-worth leads her to anticipate being ignored and neglected; she doesn't feel "heard." Her boss interrupts her, or her colleague Paul is clearly not listening to her, and each small act of neglect reflects back her low self-worth. The attention-deficit spiral kicks in, undermining her sense of self-esteem.

Paul is an introvert and works as a financial analyst in the same company as Marianna. For Paul, meetings are a nuisance so he's frequently thinking about something else. Despite possessing above-average intelligence and considerable confidence in his intellect, Paul also has low self-worth. Being short and stocky and quiet, he feels invisible to attractive women like Marianna and he's not had a date in over a year. He sits silently resentful in the same meeting. Each time he looks up and sees the distant look on Marianna's face, his own lack of self-worth is reflected in her indifference.

In a hungry attention-deficit world, it's all too easy for people to interpret each minor act of neglect as validation of low self-worth. Every day could contain literally a hundred acts of indifference: the newsagent who doesn't make eye contact, the barista who doesn't return our "Good morning," the colleague who walks past with a preoccupied frown, the email not answered, the friend who didn't call, the date who didn't seem enthusiastic. The city becomes a rude and hostile place. Everyone is broadcasting; nobody is listening. So many people yearn to be seen and heard.

Keys on the Inside

Both Paul and Marianna have to run the daily gauntlet of their attention-deficit city, just like everyone else. Neither of them can do much about the self-preoccupation of other people. But each of them has the power to stop their *own* attention-deficit spiral, simply by separating *external* neglect from *intrinsic* friendship with themselves.

It's not the indifference of others that hurts; it's the way that this pierces us within. If Paul could be a real friend to his short and stocky self, he could perhaps be curious about what really lies behind Marianna's distant frown. The indifference written on other people's faces usually has nothing to do with us. Even when low self-worth might tell us otherwise.

If Marianna believed in herself just a little bit more, she might be able to counter Paul's inattention or her boss's interruptions with a touch of lightness and humor. She would almost certainly perform better at meetings. And even if she didn't, she could still be a friend to herself.

The key to dealing with the attention-deficit economy does not lie in changing society. We can break the negative spiral with a loyal, unconditional friendship with ourselves. Viewed in this way, each act of indifference has little to do with us. But we can use it as an opportunity to affirm a deep commitment within.

Compassion

Huge numbers of people desire to be seen. So if you're being ignored—whether at work or socially—the good news is that you are not alone. It's not personal. It's part of the universal condition of twenty-first-century living.

The next time that you feel hurt by someone's indifference or rejection, you can safely assume that they are experiencing this, too, in some other area of their lives. If either Paul or Marianna had sufficient self-worth to find compassion for their colleagues, perhaps the two could work together with a greater sense of connection.

The desire for connection is everywhere. The more we crowd into cities and become hyper-connected by technology, the lonelier we get. The problem is deeper than loss of companionship or confusion about career direction. As we see with Marianna and Paul, it stems right from a core vulnerability.

You are almost certainly surrounded by people who struggle with self-worth. Outwardly, they may appear confident and even the life of the party. But appearances can be deceptive. Even those whom you might envy—because of their money or status or looks—can still be struggling with self-worth and isolation. A lot of loneliness hides behind those high walls and haughty airs.

Perhaps we can also be compassionate toward those people who appear desperate to prove themselves with their pursuit of money or fashion or status. The universal plea behind all the attention-seeking words and selfies is "See me!" This desire to be seen drives entire sectors of the economy as well as a lot of human behavior. When my colleague Claudia Vettore runs sessions on compassion and mindful communication, she often sees very emotional reactions to the question "When was the last time that you felt seen, listened to, felt?" This question reveals a deep vulnerability in the most unexpected people.

If you are searching for good business or career ideas, here's a great place to start. How can you help others be more visible? Perhaps you can start by giving them your attention. You already have self-worth, so nothing can be taken away from you.

Living the Dream

Does self-worth imply that we have to renounce money, achievement, and social status? Certainly not. The pursuit of our dreams motivates many worthy actions. Living life on the basis of self-worth, we will naturally want to take care of ourselves and our real needs. As already noted, self-esteem helps us to feel good, even while we are still striving to achieve these estimable things.

The point is that we don't want to be *ruled* by them. That's the problem with living on the basis of self-esteem: it's a bit like living in a totalitarian state, where the actions of the dictator may often be benign, but basic freedoms are still missing.

For example, on the day that you feel you are making progress with your career, when you get good feedback from the boss or the client, when you feel you are learning or are appreciated by your colleagues, then self-esteem will be good. You will want to do even better tomorrow. There is no problem with self-esteem on those sunny days.

Even in adversity, self-esteem can be helpful. Perhaps you are bored or frustrated with your job. Or you are not appreciated by the organization in which you work. Such frustration is often the catalyst for change. Again, there is no problem with self-esteem on those days, even when the wind is blowing against you. You can still be motivated by the dream.

But when we begin to make negative judgments about ourselves, when we make our friendship with ourselves conditional on how our financial situation or career is developing, perhaps by linking our self-worth to our net worth, that's when the trouble starts. In such moments, we are being ruled by our dreams and not simply motivated by them. That's when we need to be able to access something deeper than self-esteem.

When we are firmly in touch with our self-worth, then our self-esteem is nourished even on adverse, wintry days. So when the boss is critical, we can still look him in the eye and not sink into depression or victimization. When we reflect back on a week in which we did not achieve very much, we can bounce back and make next week more productive. In a very real way, self-worth empowers us to live our dreams.

Ozymandias
I met a traveler from an antique land
Who said: "Two vast and trunkless legs of stone
Stand in the desert . . . Near them, on the sand,
Half sunk, a shattered visage lies, whose frown,
And wrinkled lip, and sneer of cold command,
Tell that its sculptor well those passions read
Which yet survive, stamped on these lifeless things,
The hand that mocked them, and the heart that fed:
And on the pedestal these words appear:
'My name is Ozymandias, king of kings:
Look on my works, ye Mighty, and despair!'
Nothing beside remains. Round the decay
Of that colossal wreck, boundless and bare
The lone and level sands stretch far away."

PERCY BYSSHE SHELLEY

Exercises for the Terrain of Money and Status

Many of the following exercises involve reflection, and I invite you to record your insights in your journal. Some items below ask for you to shift your money and status habits of thought.

1. What are your imperatives? List at least five, ranging from lifestyle choices to achievements or personal-development aspirations, such as education.

2. Why are your imperatives important to you? What expectation of yourself is driving them?

3. In what areas of your life are you practicing Have, Do, Be? Consider not just material "haves" such as money but also

education, relationship status, time, energy, and lifestyle. Why are you waiting for these conditions to be satisfied?

4. Choose an item of spending that you can change. Please don't make this another "should": on the contrary, try to choose something than you "could" do relatively easily, perhaps to shop in a different store or to drop a subscription that you are not using anyway.

5. Review your needs. What are they? Which are needs and which are wants? Which core needs are met, and which are not?

6. Where might you have more freedom in your life, if you were less concerned with proving things to yourself?

7. Do you sometimes sink into a state of powerlessness about money? If so, how can you be compassionate toward yourself at these times?

8. Write your money story, in 100–200 words. Is it a story of survival or of being a victim of circumstance? Is it a story written in the past or in the future tense? What does this tell you?

9. Apart from money or possessions, what else constitutes "status" for you? Educational qualifications? Style? Accent? Achievement? How might these judgments—often applied to others—be subtly ruling your own self-worth?

To download a copy of a Needs/Wants and a Be, Do, Have checklist, as well as the Energy Inventory, please go to the Resources page of SelfWorthAcademy.com.

(7)

Fifth Terrain: Friendship

"Let us be grateful to people who make
us happy; they are the charming gardeners
who make our souls blossom."

MARCEL PROUST

IT ALWAYS AMAZES me that, for all the books about intimate relationships, there are so few written about friendship. Next time you enter a bookshop, try to find even one. Contrast this with all that's been written about finding love or an epic sex life. Strange, isn't it?

Given current rates of divorce and relationship breakup, it's increasingly likely that any permanent sense of belonging will be derived more from friends (and family, hopefully) than from a person's intimate relationships. Partners come and go. It's estimated that most people will have three to five major relationships in the course of their lives. Friendships often outlast love relationships.

With real friends, we can be fully ourselves. We feel safe and supported. We can speak freely without fear of judgment. In the words of Charles Lamb, "Tis the privilege of friendship to talk nonsense, and to have her nonsense respected." We can listen, too, because that's how we respect our friends.

I'm not talking here about Facebook friends, that diverse and wide-ranging collection of people we have met along the way. I'm referring here to the two to ten people who really "know" us for who we are. Our friends are those who really "see us," if we allow them. Here we run into a classic problem for people with low self-worth: they find it very hard to let people see them for who they really are, which in turn perpetuates a cycle of isolation. Let's take Elsa, for example.

Elsa will soon be thirty. When she was twenty-one, she had a huge party in her home city of Stockholm to celebrate her birthday. Elsa was still in college and had a host of friends of both sexes, with whom she's since been able to keep in touch via Facebook. She looks back on those days as the happiest of her life.

Since leaving college, life has been tough for Elsa. She first moved to Paris and then to London, in an attempt to establish her career. She does not feel that her career moves have been particularly successful. To make matters worse, Elsa thinks that her friends have generally done better than she has; their Facebook posts parade a procession of engagements, promotions, and exotic holidays that have somehow eluded her. On top of all that, after having invested six years in an emotionally exhausting relationship, she's recently been dumped by her long-term boyfriend.

She approaches her thirtieth birthday party with a deep sense of apprehension. She's not made any close friends in London and she's also lost touch with her friends back home. She has more than 1,500 friends on Facebook, yet she's never felt so lonely. Running through all of this is a deep sense of failure and low self-worth.

Like many singles in cities, Elsa signed up for the usual array of evening classes, health clubs, yoga and dance classes, as well as the ubiquitous internet dating. However, when socializing,

Elsa comes across as aloof and somewhat snobbish, so she's not made deep friends. People perceive that she is judging them, which she probably is.

Loss of Connection

Elsa's story is typical of many experiences in today's urban life: hundreds of virtual friends, lots of chat and messages, yet nobody with whom to spend a Sunday afternoon. We all know a lot of people, but how many of these are real friends? Of those who are, how many are available for friendship right now, this week? With how many do you feel a deep sense of connection?

It is possible to catalog a long list of social forces that erode friendship. This is a far from exhaustive collection:

- demanding jobs, busyness, people always in a hurry;

- individuals preoccupied with their own growth, doing courses, attending classes or activities;

- exhaustion and tiredness;

- mobility; constant changes of job/city/home; people moving away, losing touch;

- established cliques or social groups unavailable to newcomers or outsiders;

- people living virtually, spending more time on social media; less chance of a casual conversation (for example, on transit) when everyone is engrossed in their phones;

- loss of traditional meeting places (for example, pubs, churches, parish events);

- transience, more and more people drifting through social groups, meet-ups, spiritual movements, discovery experiences,

"Do you have someone
special in your life?"
"Yes, me."

and so on, but not staying long enough in any one group to form deep connections;

• growing numbers of people living across borders, being away for months at a time.

In short, it's harder than ever for friendships to take root. It's therefore not surprising that, in several studies, increasing social media use has been correlated with loneliness. It seems that the more connected we appear, the more disconnected we really are from each other.

As we see with Elsa, this disconnection has consequences for how we feel about ourselves. It's hard to maintain self-worth in isolation. Somehow, we need "the other" to help us to see ourselves. Our friendships with others—even with one or two people—are vital to maintaining a sense of friendship within. In the company of a close friend, we get to see ourselves.

Solitude

It is important, however, that we distinguish loneliness from solitude. There are many people whose lives may on the surface resemble Elsa's but who are not at all lonely. Some people enjoy solitude. They are happiest of all in their own company. For those people, being around others can be very fatiguing. These people are usually called introverts. They derive energy from being on their own.

Many of us are ambiverts. We need time on our own, but we also need the company of friends. I certainly fit this pattern. After enjoying companionship for several hours, it's as if I need to go away and "digest" the conversation quietly. If I don't do so, I can become tired and inattentive. I also enjoy many solitary activities, such as walking, swimming, and running.

At the same time, I also need friends and companionship. If I were in Elsa's shoes, the sense of disconnection she's experiencing would rob me of energy and confidence. Sooner or later, my relationship with myself would be impacted. Looking around at other happy people, I would wonder what was wrong with me.

When we feel a sense of connection and belonging, solitude can be very enjoyable. It can be a relief to go away for a quiet weekend or a solitary holiday. Equally, even while away on holiday, I look forward to coming home and telling others about it, as well as hearing what they have been up to.

As the poet John O'Donohue has described in *Anam Cara*: making friends with solitude can represent the awakening of a new creativity. Instead of running away from solitude, I have learned that it's better to move into it. In this way, new ideas and experiences often appear, as if whispered from the surrounding shadows. Throughout the ages, many artists, writers, and thinkers have discovered the gifts of solitude.

Loneliness

You can be lonely in a crowd. Loneliness often has very little to do with the number of people around you; it's a perceived sense of disconnection from others. If anything, there is probably more loneliness in cities, even if there is more solitude in the countryside.

Much has been written in recent years about the link between social media and loneliness. Several studies have attempted to correlate loneliness and Facebook use, but it's far from clear which is the chicken and which is the egg. Does Facebook use lead to loneliness, or is its use a result of isolation? It's hard to say. In any case, correlation is not the same as causation.

From a self-worth perspective, what is perhaps more disturbing is the unwritten expectation that we should *not* feel lonely, that loneliness is a problem to be fixed. It's hardly surprising that Elsa feels lonely: she's lost her boyfriend and she's far from her hometown and college friends. What is more damaging is that Elsa judges herself harshly for being lonely. Not only does this hurt more than the loneliness; it led Elsa to armor herself with a veneer that became a block to real friendship.

Loneliness can be tough, but it can also be an opportunity to establish self-worth. In order for that to happen, we have to embrace loneliness, rather than flee from it. This truth was captured hundreds of years ago by the fourteenth-century Persian poet Hafiz:

> *Don't surrender your loneliness so quickly.*
> *Let it cut more deep.*
>
> *Let it ferment and season you*
> *As few human or even divine ingredients can.*
>
> *Something missing in my heart tonight*
> *Has made my eyes so soft,*
> *My voice so tender...*

It is often in the lonely places that you get to plumb the depths of your relationship with yourself. When you stop running away from loneliness and face it—without judging yourself negatively for that experience—then the "seasoning," as Hafiz names it, can begin. You come home to yourself.

Judging Others

In parallel with the external forces noted above, a set of internal forces are just as destructive to a sense of connection. Let's start with one of the principal culprits.

If self-worth is low, we often slip into judgments about others. It's easier to blame a friend for being late than to admit to one's own inner sense of insignificance. It's easier for Elsa to judge her co-workers or the people at an evening class than to face the self-resentment lurking silently within. Low self-worth very quickly leads to judgment of others and just as readily to being swamped by their criticism.

People can compensate for low self-worth in other ways, too. Some develop a hardened shell—often accompanied by sarcasm, aloofness, or pretension. Others talk incessantly, like "Garrulous Gary," my (somewhat judgmental!) nickname for certain people I know. My colleague Monika Majvaldova once mentioned that she learned to listen compassionately to endless talkers, according them both her attention and respect rather than trying to interrupt or manage their flow or judge them (as I confess I would be more likely to do). Intrigued by her approach, I've taken to practicing this myself. What I've noticed is the "hole inside" that drives the garrulous to fill every pause with words. Interestingly enough, they usually reveal the hole, if I can listen long enough. (I'm still learning!)

Judging others, even filtering them out, can be a smoke screen for my own self-worth issues. I wonder how many people (and opportunities) I have missed over the years, because of the judgments I've made about others. In judgments—whether of myself or of other people—I'm learning to recognize the weeds in the garden of self-worth.

Shift #7: From "Being Interesting" to "Being Interested"

In the terrain of friendship, I find the following question to be a simple test of my own self-worth: when listening to a friend tell a story, am I listening out of interest or am I listening in order to reply? In other words, is my focus on being *interested* or trying to be *interesting*? If the latter, why? What am I trying to prove?

Sometimes I don't like the answer, and then I have to resist the urge to judge myself negatively for that. The truth is that most of us have a range of responses. Sometimes, we are genuinely interested and we accord our friends the full focus of our attention. Other times, we are looking for the gap where we can drop into "That reminds me of the time when . . ." or ask a question that makes us look clever, if only in our own eyes.

Often, being interested just takes remembering. As long as I remind myself, I can switch out of "interesting mode" and focus on the other person. It's a lot easier to be curious about someone else than to be worried about being entertaining, and generally my self-worth is reassured by the switch.

A conscious focus on being interested is rewarding at many levels. The quality of connection with others almost instantly improves. I often wonder if this is due to the simple fact that people are now so accustomed to poor levels of attention, they gravitate toward those people who accord them their full presence. You learn so much more. Listening carefully, you hear what's not being said; you hear the subtle ways in which people try to prove themselves, the recognition that they crave. The writer Mark Nepo puts it this way: "To listen is to lean in, softly, with a willingness to be changed by what we hear."

Most people find this shift quite easy to apply. Once we give ourselves permission, it's generally easy to be interested in others. During social occasions that might otherwise be a source of dread, being interested is a game changer. We don't need any special experience or qualifications. We just need to remember to adopt an attitude of curiosity.

Most Safari voyagers have found this distinction to be quite refreshing and novel. As one man puts it, "I honestly never thought about conversations that way before. From as far back as I can remember, I've tried to be interesting. Often this was unconscious: I was not aware I was doing it. Putting down the burden of being interesting has been a huge liberation. I enjoy social interaction so much more than I used to."

Beyond Technique

It's not surprising that the shift from being interesting to interested has often started out as a technique, a bit like driving a car. This is particularly true if self-worth is low to begin with. However, over time, being interested is so rewarding that it soon gets adopted as a way of life.

A few Safari voyagers have even reported that being interested can become so fascinating that they sometimes need to make the reverse shift. This is particularly true to highly empathetic listeners, who are genuinely curious about others and who can easily forget to claim their own space in a conversation. As self-worth develops, most people can find this balance easily and naturally. If you are genuinely interested in others, you will find no shortage of people who are eager to tell you their story.

The shift is powerful both in professional life as well as in personal life. Customers sense very quickly whether you are genuinely interested in them or just interested in landing the deal or getting paid. Colleagues, too, can quickly spot the difference between those who are interested versus those who are trying to draw attention to themselves.

Having coached hundreds of business people on this distinction, I receive emails, sometimes years later, with comments about how powerful this shift is—both in work and in social terrains. We don't need any special qualifications or permission to be interested. From a standpoint of simple curiosity, we are entitled to talk to anyone in the world, to ask them questions, to explore their views or ask for their advice. They may occasionally wonder why we are interested, and then we tell them, as simply as possible. Being interested is a passport to any conversation with anyone.

Boundaries

There are times and places when we need to protect ourselves, to set boundaries on our interest or on what we allow other people to do or say in our presence. Most of us would object to physical violence. But do we tolerate shouting, sarcasm, or mockery? What about constant interruptions? Or the friend who only gets in contact when they need something? Or those who cancel at the last minute, oblivious to any trouble that you may have gone to?

When people have high self-worth, it's easy enough to draw lines. And to allow for a certain flexibility, too. After all, people who have too rigid boundaries about humor or interruptions can be very tiresome.

But for people with low self-worth, every social encounter—even with friends—can be daunting. The smallest bit of teasing can be blown into a traumatic drama of disrespect. Or they allow others to mock them without drawing a line and expressing that they are not okay with that, instead silently fuming with resentment. Then, when finally drawing a boundary, they do so explosively. Every nuance of conversation is fraught with danger.

It's important that we look after ourselves, and this sometimes means setting limits with certain situations or people. It takes self-worth to do so and though we may sometimes reproach ourselves for not handling a situation better, it's important that we respect ourselves first and foremost. If we nurture the roots of self-worth, we can deal with specific situations as they arise.

For example, most of my friends know I place a high value on reliability. This means I have little tolerance for last-minute cancellations or no-shows. Nor have I any plans to develop such tolerance for people whose only loyalties are to their own whims and changing mood. On the contrary, as one year follows another, my "Flaky Filter" is applied more and more. All around me, I see the damage caused by flakiness: the spaces reserved, the frantic rescheduling, that special dish organized, the travel arrangements made, the other invites turned down, and the disappointment caused to everyone else when others don't show up. You get the picture.

Earlier in life, I kept silent and just shrugged my shoulders, swallowing my own annoyance when people canceled at the last minute or just didn't bother to show up. But as my own self-worth has grown, I now voice a boundary when this behavior is not okay with me. Indeed, I go further, systematically removing such people from my life and work in order to limit the corrosive effects of unreliability. In choosing to do so, my intent is to make conscious space for the reliable people and to protect my energy from being wasted by the flaky.

Sure, I could learn to be more tolerant and even spend hours in therapy examining my own frustration. But I choose otherwise: my self-worth is better served by putting a clear boundary in place, much as I would want to protect my garden from marauding wild goats, rather than learn to accept them!

In practical terms, the issue is often the difficulty of deciding *where* the boundary should be. For example, is that gentle teasing okay or not? Is it me who's being too sensitive or too rigid? Should I be okay with that level of flirtatiousness? If I stop her repeated interruptions, will I just destroy the mood? By the time one has thought through the answer to all these questions, the moment has usually passed and it's too late to do anything, anyway!

By now you have hopefully developed a sufficient foundation in self-worth to know that you are okay already, whether you set that boundary or not. Our effectiveness at boundary setting may well be important to our self-esteem, but it doesn't have to be a condition for self-worth. However, setting a boundary can be an invaluable *expression* of self-worth (Shift #2). If boundaries are a particular problem for you, I suggest you think of them in this way. Otherwise you might create another trap for your reputation with yourself.

Boundaries can be set lightly and humorously, without drama or explosion. One of our Safari participants had us in tears of laughter as he described how he started to set boundaries with that "friend" who only ever called when he needed something. As he role-played the extravagant (and impromptu) ways in which the "friend" would invite himself over (only when in need), the whole group howled with laughter at the ingenuity and the realization of how often they experienced this, too. Another participant told us a similar story about the friend who was always complaining and the various ways in which she would try (in vain) to shift the conversation to a more positive tone. These are the occasions during which boundaries become important.

In this chapter, we are considering boundaries in the context of friendship. The ability to set boundaries is a fundamental skill in maintaining self-worth in general. For this reason, chapter 14 is entirely devoted to boundaries.

It's often wise to rehearse the type of boundary you want to set. For example, if every time your mother calls, she is critical, you might want to decide how you're going to deal with that, gently but firmly. Because you are worth it.

Friendship Saboteurs

How are you as a friend? When it comes to friendship, it's very easy to focus on what we want from the other person. It takes considerably more courage to take stock of ourselves. Here is a list of what I call "Friendship Saboteurs": the behaviors that can erode friendship. What would you add?

- Fixing other people or interfering in their lives, even with "good" motives
- Criticizing; as W.H. Auden says, "Whatever you do, good or bad, people will always have something negative to say."
- Gossiping
- Not being genuinely interested in others
- Being too busy; preoccupation with own plans, no time
- Being co-dependent; needing to be needed
- Interrupting, not listening, talking too much
- Being used, using others
- Blaming
- Not respecting another's space
- Playing the martyr or the victim
- Being flaky and not showing up
- Advising other people how they should live their lives

Notice how low self-worth increases each risk. When we don't feel good about ourselves, it's all too easy to slip (usually unconsciously) into the behaviors above. Sadly, the net result is that the friendship then gets eroded and sometimes, nobody quite knows why.

Let's take an example. Many years ago, I learned to stop "coaching" in conversations with friends. Full of enthusiasm for my newfound skills, I fondly imagined that people would be delighted when I supported them to see their challenges from fresh perspectives. Well, often they weren't. Even when I asked questions, rather than giving specific advice, I noticed how my intent (in this case, to "coach") often just produced annoyance. Friends want real friendship, not coaching. Any attempts to do so—however well intentioned—provoked irritation.

In recent years, I've also encountered a few people who feel they are being advised/coached even when this is *not* the case. Perhaps some have developed an allergy from an overdose of advice, for example, previously given by family or from friends. Others (perhaps with low self-worth) may feel that people are constantly "talking down" to them, even when they are not.

In any case, people want friends who are genuinely interested in them, not people who are trying to "improve" or "fix" them or even draw attention to their potential. Today, I consciously try to avoid falling into these pitfalls, though sometimes I fail to spot this in time. On such occasions, the challenge is not to slip into self-reproach.

In our Safari groups, we often hear a wide range of Friendship Saboteurs. Some people confess that they are compulsive problem-solvers. Others own up to being hopeless at keeping in touch, to not listening, or even to being the complainer. One man talked about saying yes to everything and then struggling to meet his commitments.

Taking stock honestly is all part of self-worth in action. We don't have to beat ourselves up for any of these behaviors. We can recognize them and put them right, simply because we're worth it.

Practice: Being a Friend to Yourself

This practice is particularly powerful in times of loneliness, loss, or rejection. Perhaps you had hopes for friendship or romance and it's become obvious that the other person cannot (or will not) reciprocate your feelings. As well as feelings of sadness and hurt, you may also be experiencing resentment toward them, for example, for setting certain expectations and then disappointing you.

1. Find a place where you will be undisturbed for at least thirty minutes (one hour is better).

2. Close your eyes, take a few breaths, and get in touch with how you feel. Angry? Sad? Hopeless? Gutted? Lonely? Depressed?

3. Place your left hand on your heart and acknowledge your right to feel this way. If tears come, let them flow. Or you may find yourself swearing, shouting, or muttering through clenched teeth. Or you may just experience a dull ache of dejection. Whatever the feeling, let it move through you, all the while keeping your left hand on your heart as an assertion of self-worth. Typically, this takes ten to fifteen minutes, but it may be longer.

4. When the storm has passed, a feeling of calm usually follows, though this can be a melancholy calm. Notice when you get there. Bring both hands to your heart at this point, and you may switch to a lying down position, if you are feeling tired or low in energy.

5. Affirm your unconditional friendship with yourself and repeat your mantra. This affirmation may feel woefully inadequate just now, but like a seed in the middle of winter, it contains all that is needed for the summer ahead. Wrap yourself around this seed of unconditional self-worth and nurture it. You may drop off to sleep, as you come home to yourself and begin to rest within.

6. Notice the need of yours that is operating, perhaps for affection, appreciation, or shared experience. But resist the urge to fall into that story or any form of self-reproach or self-resentment. You can provide unlimited affection and appreciation to yourself, though it often appears otherwise.

7. As energy returns, you may wish to continue with the morning routine as described in chapter 3. Or put on some music.

"Grow a green tree
in your heart and perhaps
a singing bird will come."

CHINESE PROVERB

If time or circumstances do not allow this, stand for about a minute with your left hand on your heart and remind yourself that you can be a loyal friend to yourself... no matter what.

True Friends

This is a good week. I will get unhurried, face-to-face time with three friends. I'm not always this lucky. Travel and schedules often mean that my friends and I are in different countries and time zones.

With these friends, there is no role-play. I can show up just as I am. There is no need to impress or win their favor; none of us will be editing what we say. There will be laughter, some of it no doubt at my expense, and it will all be fun. They already know about the projects I'm working on and they will be interested to hear more about them. I will be equally interested in the developments in their lives. As I always do, I will come away grateful for their presence in my life.

Other weeks, I will not be so surrounded. I may be in hotel rooms on the other side of the world, trying to find something edible from the room service menu. Or noticing a happy group at a neighboring table while I dine in the company of my book.

From a self-worth perspective, it's all the same. Perhaps I will be happy with my book. Perhaps I will be sad to be so far from home. Perhaps I won't be thinking about myself at all. I simply don't know. But what I do know is that having drilled down to the groundwater supply of self-worth, there need never be another drought of self-reproach. No matter how friendship with others may fluctuate, I know I can be a loyal friend to myself in all circumstances.

What does it mean to be a true friend to myself? Being loyal to myself means respecting myself at all times, no matter what is going on around me. Even when I don't live up to my expectations of myself—*especially* in those moments—it means being "on my own side." It means taking care of my core needs, not putting myself down. It means treating myself at least as well as my friends do.

The Arrow and the Song

I shot an arrow into the air,
It fell to earth, I knew not where;
For, so swiftly it flew, the sight
Could not follow it in its flight.

I breathed a song into the air,
It fell to earth, I knew not where;
For who has sight so keen and strong,
That it can follow the flight of song?

Long, long afterward, in an oak
I found the arrow, still unbroke;
And the song, from beginning to end,
I found again in the heart of a friend.

HENRY WADSWORTH LONGFELLOW

Exercises for the Terrain of Friendship

While a few of the following exercises are reflective, many ask you to develop self-worth in practice.

1. How do you feel about social occasions such as birthday parties, after-work events, or family dinners? How does this link to your self-worth?

2. What judgments do you most frequently make about others (for example, they're loud, uncultured, boring, inauthentic, weird, and so on)? How might these judgments be directly or indirectly linked to your own feelings of self-worth?

3. Reviewing the list of Friendship Saboteurs earlier in this chapter, which ones do you recognize? Any others? For a further checklist, together with more about the behaviors that often unwittingly sabotage friendship, see the Resources page of SelfWorthAcademy.com.

4. List your closest friends. How do they support your self-worth? How do you support theirs?

5. Choose a forthcoming social occasion (or family event) and consciously go there with an attitude of "being interested" (versus trying to be interesting or being tuned out). What difference does that make to your experience of the event?

6. When you keep in touch with others, do you do so when you have something *interesting* to tell them or when you are genuinely *interested* in how they are?

7. Do you enjoy your solitude? Or are you lonely? No wrong answers. Is there any self-reproach (or self-blaming) that you could usefully drop?

8. Who can you talk to about any issues of loneliness? Ideally, choose someone who is not affected, so you may wish to avoid having this discussion with siblings or family, at least for now. The objective is to explore your feelings, not that you feel better by obligating anyone else.

9. What boundaries might you need to set? See more on boundaries in chapter 14.

10. From the basis of self-worth, you know you are already okay. On that basis, what actions around friendship, if any, do you want to take?

(8)

Sixth Terrain: Environment and Leisure

> "We are a culture of people who've bought
> into the idea that if we stay busy enough,
> the truth of our lives won't catch up with us."
>
> BRENÉ BROWN

FOR MANY YEARS, I could read a quotation like this and, intellectually at least, think that I understood it. I could nod my head at the wisdom of valuing myself. But if you looked around me, at the place I lived or the way I spent my "spare" time, you would get a very different picture.

One of the people who helped me to see this was Thomas Leonard, the founder of Coach U, the International Coach Federation, CoachVille, and the International Association of Coaches. I met him once in London (where we had an interesting conversation about both being survivors of Catholic boarding-school education) and had the pleasure of participating in many of his teleclasses, until his untimely death in 2003.

Thomas had a deep appreciation of the entrepreneurial spirit, and he was also a firm believer in the importance of physical environment, both as an essential ingredient of productivity and an even more essential ingredient of one's relationship with oneself. Among his most memorable lines for me was "space management is more important than time management," by which he meant that it was vital to pay attention to the environment in which we work. His "Clean Sweep" program included such items as ensuring that you had adequate space, light, and air; that papers were neatly filed away; and that your infrastructure (such as computers or appliances) were all in good working order.

At the time, all of this was new to me. My living and working spaces were often random and rather chaotic. Decorating or renovating was always low down on a busy agenda. My relationship with my physical environment could best be summed up in the phrase "It will do."

Environment

If you walk into someone's home, you learn a lot about them in a matter of seconds. The state of a home or office reveals a lot more about us than anything we might say. Our environments reveal our values, ranging from beauty, inspiration, ostentation, family, serenity, joy or gloom, hurry, learning, harmony, and a thousand more.

Deeply embedded in these values lies our relationship with ourselves. I remember visiting the apartment of a man I had always assumed to be self-assured. The sad dilapidation of his home told a very different story. With an incredible lack of care written all over the scuffed paintwork, a dirty kitchen, and a weird juxtaposition of colors, it had "don't care" written all over his own relationship with himself.

My mind went back to my own early years, to the lack of care I showed to my own living and working spaces. Today, I see clearly how this was an outward reflection of a lack of care toward myself. Why? Because I did not believe deep down that I was worth it. There were always more important things to do, other things that took priority.

To this day, my expectations are not lavish. I choose to prioritize free time over extravagant space. I prefer to live light and mobile, instead of bogged down by a host of possessions. But I pay attention to where I do my various activities such as coaching, writing, or planning. Let's take a practical example.

Seeing the Horizon

I'm writing this chapter in Ortigia, in Sicily, in early summer. I'm here to work with Claudia Vettore to prepare a pilot program for the Self-Worth Safari. My day began by running around the island, along a coastline of clear-blue Mediterranean water, stretching away into the horizon.

When planning or preparing for the future, my experience is that it's important to be able to see the horizon. One of the reasons that clients liked to do strategy days at a home office I had in Brussels is the nearly 360-degree perspective from the top floor of an Art Deco building, which gives a view across the eastern side of the city and northward toward the Atomium. People tell me that they can think more clearly about the future when they feel they are "sitting above it," rather than trying to conjure it up while bunkered down in some anonymous meeting room or surrounded by the chaos of their daily workspace.

What you look out at makes a difference to your day. One of the less-considered awful effects of poverty is the lack of open space that often accompanies it. When working in Guatemala with Education for the Children (EFTC), I was struck by this poverty of space available for kids to play in, in the slum neighborhoods where they grow up. When the school doors open in the morning and they burst into the playground, this is perhaps the only space in which many of them can freely and safely roam.

We each have our own needs for space. Some people need routine and familiarity. Variety of landscape is quite important for me. For my own planning, I have used rooftop cafés, viewing platforms, mountain tops, art galleries, anywhere where I can see the horizon. It makes a material difference to the quality of my thinking.

Clean Sweep

After studying Thomas Leonard's material and doing his Clean Sweep program (see CoachU.com), I was particularly influenced by the Physical Environment section. By keeping my car clean, my papers filed away, and making sure I had a good view from my workplace, I found I was also changing my relationship with myself. Almost overnight, I became more productive and decisive. When I walked into my home office, I actually wanted to work, no longer feeling dragged down by piles of neglected admin or anxiety-inducing chaos. I recovered more quickly from setbacks and disappointments, of which there were plenty during those early years of building my business.

At the time, I saw the impact purely in terms of productivity and physical environment. Today, I understand that this was the visible tip of the iceberg. Below the waterline, there is no doubt that it affected my entire relationship with myself. Looking back, I can see that a degree of self-worth was growing from an enhanced sense of taking care of myself.

To illustrate, let's take the example of being rejected by a prospective client or suffering a financial setback. In earlier years, I would come home dejected, see the uncut grass on the lawn, the pile of unopened mail inside the front door, and the dilap-idated state of my home office. Depending on circumstances, I would easily give way to anxiety, resentment, self-reproach, or depression. That rejection or disappointment would echo down the hollow chambers of the emptiness within, finding a response in the chaos of my physical environment. From both within and without, I would question my own worth. The latest setback would be yet more evidence of this void.

Once I started to pay attention to my environment, however, my space became a welcoming shelter. Rejection or setbacks still hurt. Indeed, I probably experienced far more disappointments in those early months than in the relatively sheltered existence of my previous career. However, I would drive home in a clean car of which I was proud. (Back then!) My home office reminded me of my vision, which was written large on one of the huge whiteboards that dominated the walls. There was no unopened mail. There was a clean sweep of admin every Saturday morning. I would recover in minutes or hours instead of in days or weeks.

Why? Because I was unconsciously developing a belief in myself, in my own value as a person. When setbacks occurred, I saw them just as setbacks, not as evidence of a lack of value within. The void was starting to close.

Shift #2 in Our Environment

Back in the first terrain of this book, in the context of our bodies, we discussed repositioning our relationship with our physical well-being from being a condition of self-esteem to being an expression of self-worth. We now apply exactly the same shift in thinking to our physical environment. Indeed, the relationship with our home and office environments is likely to be an external mirror of our new relationship with our physical body.

So when we wash the car or tidy a messy room, we don't do so as a condition of self-esteem. We do it "because I am worth it" (or whatever your mantra is). It's an expression of who we are, not an application of Have, Do, Be thinking.

Some prosaic chores may suddenly start to acquire fresh meaning. When I cleared off my table before leaving for Sicily a few days ago, for example, I was not just doing so because I "should" or I "had to." I did it because I feel I deserve an ordered space when I return home.

This shift of intention, from condition to expression, is important. If we embark on a frenzy of renovation in order to feel better about ourselves, we are back on the drug of self-esteem. Not only does this approach run the risk of failure, it reinforces a "performance mentality" that deepens a conditional relationship with the self. This is the exact opposite of unconditional self-worth. With this understanding, it might even be better to leave the desk messy, or the car unwashed, rather than risk your friendship with yourself. Try lying in the sunshine instead.

Many people report that shifting their approach to their environment, to make it an expression of their worth, helps them recapture a sense of wonder. This sudden sense of amazement is beautifully described in Louis MacNeice's poem "Snow":

The room was suddenly rich and the great bay-window was
Spawning snow and pink roses against it

The sudden shock of awareness described in this poem is a wonderful experience of connecting to our surroundings and also to ourselves. When you gaze in amazement at the striking image of roses against a background of falling snow, or in appreciation of the cozy contours of your own fireplace, you live an aesthetic experience of your core self, that is deeper than any self-assessment or self-appraisal.

In these moments, you are brought back to the wonder of your own being: the extraordinary mystery of being here. Your core self comes alive. Beauty is a gateway to a new level of self-awareness.

Practice: The Micro Clearance

Over the years, I have coached many people on energy levels, and the Micro Clearance is one of the little gems that time after time brings tangible benefits in terms of effectiveness. It's a perfect expression of self-worth in action.

Professionals usually know they need the Micro Clearance when things get too much. When they look at the piles of unattended papers and emails, when the whiteboard is full of tasks, when the yellow sticky notes are falling off the wall, when every glance around their space falls on yet another thing to do. Most of all, when the energy to sort it all out just isn't there.

The Micro Clearance is best practiced in ten- to fifteen-minute intervals. The keys to success are a) doing it little-and-often and b) not getting attached to the results. Anything you do is an expression of self-worth. Prepare to be surprised at the effectiveness of this innocuous little practice if it's done in this spirit.

1. Choose a tiny area that you wish to clear, such as the corner of a desk, a subset of emails, or a drawer. Make this as small as possible. Please do not choose an entire room, closet, or email folder. Make your chosen target as small as you like.

2. Start clearing. Dump, delete, or do, but act rapidly, in seconds. If the email is over a month old, delete it. If you can reply in two sentences, by all means do so, but your priority is clearing. Get rid of it.

3. If you need to keep a file or an email (for reference or audit purposes), move it into a single box (or folder) labeled by year. Do not attempt to create subfolders or anything sophisticated. Just get rid of that object, paper, or email as quickly as possible.

4. Moving things into a garage, cupboard, or other location is okay, as long as it's out of sight. Please don't move things onto shelves or into the hallway, the utility room, or anywhere else you will see daily and where the sight will drain your energy. You can always clear the garage later, when you have the energy. When you do so, use the same technique, one corner at a time.

5. You may be tempted to carry on, surfing the energy wave of your early clearances. If so, choose an equally small target area next. The primary purpose here is to build your energy, not to reorganize your life.

6. Pay particular attention to junk in corners of the room or of the desk. Blocked corners somehow seem to be particularly corrosive to energy. It's best to start in corners and work around from there.

7. Savor the sight of that cleared space. Because you are worth it.

Sources of Pleasure

When life is fun and inspiring, even a clean, uncluttered table can be a source of pleasure. Or a nice coffee or your favorite music or an energizing dance rhythm or watching a comedy clip on YouTube.

Our society tends to glorify big, expensive pleasures. Via social media, we are bombarded with other people's "peak experiences" every day: exotic restaurants, new cars, adventure holidays, or check-ins to international airports on the other side of the globe. Sure, many of us enjoy these things. But the sources of pleasure and enjoyment associated with real self-worth are more likely to depend on *frequency* rather than *intensity*.

To clarify, I'm not suggesting that pleasure is a necessary foundation for self-worth. That would slide us back into conditional thinking, making self-worth conditional on enjoying life. But the ability to enjoy pleasure on a regular basis is a natural *consequence* of self-worth. For example, who is going to be most secure in his happiness: the guy who lives for his annual ski vacation but trudges through the rest of the year or the guy who enjoys sport with his friends at home a couple of times each week?

An unconditional sense of self-worth is not immune to the ecosystem in which we live. Although the roots of a hardy plant can grow in most types of soil in many kinds of weather, some conditions are still better for it than others. Regular enjoyment is a bit like rain and sunshine. It's an ecosystem in which self-worth thrives.

I'm grateful to people like Thomas Leonard for teaching me that frequent breaks were more conducive to happiness than big annual holidays. Particularly for entrepreneurs or people who work as independents, Thomas always advocated quarterly holidays over annual ones. He argued that we needed to have perspective restored frequently, given the intensity of our relationship with our businesses. Having practiced this for many years—and also failed to do so at times—I can testify that it makes a big difference, both to productivity and to self-worth.

It's almost impossible to enjoy something without feeling that we deserve it. Sometimes this does not come easily. Like many people, I was brought up with a "work hard" ethic. In many organizations, I still see a macho culture around me, where people almost compete with each other to talk about how little they sleep. A workaholic culture has been lauded in many schools, offices, and farms for many a decade. Our role models were often hard workers. And who has not learned to congratulate themselves for having worked hard? Few people reading this book will be unfamiliar with this type of conditional self-esteem.

Pleasure calls for something else entirely. When something is a source of pleasure, we do it for its *own sake*. We may set goals (as in sports), but if an activity is a true source of pleasure, we can still enjoy it even when we don't achieve our targets. Indeed, if this is not the case, the activity is probably no longer a source of pleasure.

With this understanding, work can also be a source of pleasure. For anyone who experiences even the occasional bliss of being lost in a creative moment or the mental exhilaration of solving a problem or the delight of real collaboration, then the joy of work will require no explanation. Even getting through mundane tasks can bring its own pleasure. Anything done attentively or mindfully, for the inherent fulfillment the task brings, can be a source of joy.

Pleasure puts us in touch with ourselves, with our self-worth. If we have difficulty experiencing pleasure (perhaps due of a nagging sense of guilt that we should really be doing something else), then we probably struggle with self-worth, too. The constant call to something else (work, family, studies, fitness, and so on) is often a smoke screen: a "worthy" distraction from a hidden inability to enjoy our own company.

Therefore, the practice of pleasure can be a valuable exercise in self-worth. Find yourself at least ten (ideally twenty) sources of pleasure that can nourish you regularly, several times per day. These can range from your favorite coffee to a walk outside to a brief message exchange with a friend. More and more people are finding that moments of mindfulness become a refreshing oasis in the middle of the working day. Whatever you choose, you will soon find more.

Joy in the Moment

The ability to enjoy simple pleasures is probably one of the most accurate indicators of self-worth. People who don't value themselves invariably struggle to enjoy life. Or else they require a lot of external stimulation, such as alcohol, drugs, attention, or shopping. On the other hand, when you feel good about yourself, even watching the rain on the window can be pleasurable. The sunlight through the trees becomes your art gallery. Even the most mundane task in a daily routine can be a joy.

"Because I'm worth it."

If we allow it, our days can be filled with hundreds of plea-surable moments. But what gets in the way of enjoying them? The usual answer is our stresses and preoccupations. If I don't notice the sunlight or don't taste the coffee, it's usually because my attention is elsewhere. Perhaps I'm worried about a presen-tation or how to respond to an email.

We're often preoccupied by what we don't have and blind to what is there. We don't have the perfect shape, and we fail to enjoy the robust health we do have. We think about the absence of that perfect partner and take for granted our many friends. We may be frustrated that our career is not at another level and we're blind to the kindness of supportive colleagues. It's so easy to think about what is not there and completely miss what is.

When we focus on pleasure in the moment, our attention is brought back to reality. This is its beauty and power. We are not thinking about tomorrow or yesterday. We can release ourselves to the enjoyment of what is, today. This includes our experience of ourselves in that moment—in other words, our self-worth.

Practice: Joy in the Moment

This practice is particularly valuable when life is stressful, when there is an avalanche of things to do, or your brain is hijacked by worry. It's also effective in times of sadness or loss.

While this practice works with any pleasurable activity over any duration, it's designed to be done in ten minutes. Obviously, some sources of pleasure—such as swimming, cooking, and (hopefully) sex—will take longer. You may need to adapt the instructions below depending on what you are going to do.

Ideas for brief joy-in-the-moment activities include listening to music, walking, dancing, watching a comedy clip, consuming your favorite coffee or ice cream, petting a dog or a cat, taking a shower, doing some stretches or meditation, reading (not work-related), calling a friend, brushing your teeth, watching kids at play, or just lying down.

1. Deal with the Pleasure Saboteurs: those voices in your head that may deny you the pleasure of the next ten minutes. Examples: "I'm too busy for this," "I'm not entitled," "Adults don't do this in daytime," "This is not the moment," and so on. Whatever these voices are, they need to be shown the door. Even if you are in the middle of the most complex negotiation of your life, you are entitled to a ten-minute break. Do something physical and decisive to brush off the voices (take thirty seconds for this). Perhaps walk outside or turn off your phone. Boundaries are important for pleasure.

2. Assert your right to these ten minutes and set your intention to express your self-worth in whatever activity you are going to do. (Shift #1 and #2 together.) A good quality coffee is pleasurable. When sipped with self-worth, it's even more powerful. For thirty seconds, as you begin, repeat your mantra.

3. For the following ten minutes, try to suspend all mental activity as much as you can. According to Ovid, "A field that is rested gives a beautiful crop." Your mind probably works very hard. Why not give it the gift of rest for just ten minutes? Instead of thinking, can you turn your whole attention to the joy of your activity. As David Whyte notes, "The antidote to exhaustion is not rest . . . but wholeheartedness."

4. When distractions happen, no judgment. Just repeat your mantra and resume the activity.

5. If you wish to prolong the pleasure, please do so.

6. As you conclude, notice how you feel, particularly your energy level and mental sharpness. Remember this for next time. When can you do this again?

Some Safari participants have found it helpful to give their Joy in the Moment activity a name, such as the "Power of Now Walk," the "From John to John Gift of Coffee" or the "Pinou Time" with their pet cat.

Everything is waiting for you
*Your great mistake is to act the drama
as if you were alone. As if life
were a progressive and cunning crime
with no witness to the tiny hidden
transgressions. To feel abandoned is to deny
the intimacy of your surroundings. Surely,
even you, at times, have felt the grand array;
the swelling presence, and the chorus, crowding
out your solo voice. You must note
the way the soap dish enables you,
or the window latch grants you freedom.
Alertness is the hidden discipline of familiarity.
The stairs are your mentor of things
to come, the doors have always been there
to frighten you and invite you,
and the tiny speaker in the phone
is your dream-ladder to divinity.*

*Put down the weight of your aloneness and ease into
the conversation. The kettle is singing
even as it pours you a drink, the cooking pots
have left their arrogant aloofness and
seen the good in you at last. All the birds
and creatures of the world are unutterably
themselves. Everything is waiting for you.*

DAVID WHYTE

"It's the simple things in life that are the most extraordinary."

PAULO COELHO

Exercises for the Terrain of Environment and Leisure

1. How do you feel about going to the gym? Or running or yoga, whatever your "must get to..." activity is. Is it a true source of pleasure for you?

2. Write your own list of ten to twenty pleasures, ideally those in which you can indulge regularly.

3. Make a self-worth playlist of music that makes your heart sing and that reinforces an unconditional relationship with yourself.

4. What gets in the way of enjoying your job? Could you have more pleasure at work, even if your present work is not ideal?

5. What minor changes could you make to your daily environment that would bring you joy and remind you of who you are?

6. What would be a useful mantra to support you making these changes as an expression of self-worth?

7. Where do you experience beauty in your life?

8. When you walk through your door upon coming home, what is the first thought that goes through your head? What does that tell you about your self-worth?

At the beginning of the book, you may have downloaded the Self-Worth Stocktake. It might be interesting to do it again now. See the Resources page on SelfWorthAcademy.com.

"A man who stands on
a hill with his mouth
wide open waits a long time
for a roast duck to fly in."

**PROVERB OF
DUBIOUS ORIGIN**

Part II
Self-Worth in Action

· · · · · · · · · · · ·

(9)

Common Setbacks

"Those who were seen dancing were thought to
be insane by those who could not hear the music."

FRIEDRICH NIETZSCHE

IN THIS SECOND part of the book, we take a look at the
"thrills and spills" on the Self-Worth adventure: we deal with
self-worth in day-to-day action. We also take a look at some
of the domains into which we might further apply self-worth,
such as leadership and negotiation.

By now, you have probably experienced at least a taste of that
belly-level feeling of self-worth, described by Irene in the open-
ing chapter. Even when self-worth is clear and well established,
there are occasions when our core relationship with ourselves
will still be called into question. Though we may now have a clear
mental distinction between self-worth and self-esteem, we can
still become very unhappy with ourselves when certain events
occur or certain states develop in our minds.

Self-worth does not provide immunity to fear or setbacks.
If you are rejected by a potential employer or lover, if you have
to disappoint another person, if you fail to live up to your own

expectations of yourself (perhaps especially then), you will experience a body blow to your relationship with yourself. In that moment, whether you call this self-worth or self-esteem will matter little: your sense of self will often suffer.

In this chapter, we look at some of the most common setbacks to self-worth.

Making Mistakes

A few months ago, we had 248 people registered for a webinar, for which we were using software new to us. We rehearsed not just once but twice. We thought of everything... or so we imagined... except for a little configuration detail that only allowed a maximum of a hundred people onto the call. I didn't realize any of this until I finished the webinar to be greeted by more than seventy emails from disappointed and frustrated people who had allocated an hour in their agenda but then could not log on. To add to the frustration, the attendees that were on the call failed to get the end-of-webinar landing page that had been expressly designed for that purpose. Net result: a significant loss of time and money, plus a lot of frustration for key followers. *Grrr!*

For several hours, I went into a vortex of self-reproach. Why didn't I remember to check? Why did we bother with this clever end-of-webinar landing page idea? Why don't we have a better server? And many more questions that I'm sure you can guess! In short, I was doing what I do all too well: self-reproach, coupled with reproach of others, the webinar platform, technology, my neighbor's dog, and anyone else with the misfortune to cross my path that particular afternoon.

The result? My self-esteem plummeted. Not only immediately, because of my frustration, but even more so later that day when I realized I was being grumpy and irritable with everyone around me. Let's face it: it's a webinar, not a life-support machine. I should be able to shrug this off. And I wasn't. So then I was even more annoyed with myself. You get the picture.

I wish I could tell you this was all over in a couple of hours. Well, it wasn't. Real life is not Hollywood. It took a night's sleep for me to wake up to reality and to reconnect to unconditional self-worth. In this renewed space, even my self-reproach can be shrugged off. Just as self-worth does not depend on getting it right, it does not depend on my being grumpy either. I can make amends and move on. Self-worth does not require that I live up to my own expectations.

The vast majority of people were understanding and forgiving. That was never the problem. The big issue was the critic in my head, the plague of shame. Reconnecting with self-worth silenced that critic.

The phrase "beating ourselves up" is a pretty accurate description of what happens when we make mistakes. Particularly for those of us driven by a desire to "get it right," mistakes tend to assume a magnitude that other people find odd, even peculiar. We can lash ourselves with recrimination, both for the mistake and for the resulting feelings about it. We can even reproach ourselves for the self-reproach in an ever-deepening spiral of negative judgment.

I saw this same phenomenon of self-reproach repeated the day that a friend left an umbrella in a restaurant at lunchtime. His first reaction was to be furious with himself. His exact words were "I cannot believe that I'm so stupid. I'm always doing this, leaving things behind." He wasn't mourning the loss of the umbrella. It had neither financial nor sentimental value. He was angry with himself for what he perceived as his "stupidity." Again, that plague of shame.

This is where a sense of self-worth can come to a speedy rescue. Self-worth makes no demand that we think well of ourselves all the time. We can literally laugh at our own self-reproach. We can befriend ourselves precisely in that moment that the self most needs a friend. As Kipling put it, in his famous poem "If," we can "meet with Triumph and Disaster / And treat those two impostors just the same."

From the vantage point of intrinsic self-worth, both triumph and disaster are indeed equal imposters. Neither is a necessary precondition for a sound relationship with ourselves, though both of them would like to play that part. With self-worth intact, we can enjoy our successes and learn from our mistakes, without swearing allegiance to either and making them king and ruler of our universe.

Negative Feedback and Rejection

I once heard a radio interview with Boris Becker talking about how he had become the world's top professional tennis player. When asked if there were other kids as talented as he was, he responded that there were many. So why did he succeed? He replied that he was able to deal with feedback, to take on board the sometimes harsh comments from his coaches and trainers. He went on to use a phrase that has stayed with me years after the interview: "Feedback is the breakfast of champions."

However, feedback is not a breakfast that is easily digestible. This is particularly true if self-worth is low. In my early life, I found it very difficult to deal with criticism, especially if it was given in public (as it often is in classrooms, for example). I was easily embarrassed. Criticism, even when kindly delivered, could discourage me for hours or even days.

Looking back, it would be easy to judge the manner in which some of that feedback was given. However, I now recognize that this was only part of the problem. No matter how well a critique is delivered, it will land differently for someone whose self-worth is weak than for someone with self-worth intact.

Let's take an example. In a group setting, two young professionals receive critical feedback about their presentations. One of them has a weak sense of self-worth. He will probably feel vulnerable, exposed, embarrassed. He will worry about what others are thinking. He will probably not even absorb the positive comments, dismissing them as there just to sugarcoat the more substantial negative judgments. He may even conclude that presentations are not for him and that he should avoid them in the future, insofar as he can. This synopsis roughly describes my own reactions throughout my twenties.

His colleague, though outwardly perhaps less confident, is more relaxed and playful. She treats work presentations much as she treats sports or flirting, as an activity to be engaged in but not as a reflection of who she is. When critiqued, she may well feel that some of the comments are subjective or unfair, but these arrows don't get through to her very intact sense of self. Like her friend above, perhaps she does not relish this ordeal either, but her self-worth is not on the line. Being more detached, she can do presentations if she has to and can endure criticism. In the end, she treats people's opinion of her as just that. Opinion. It's not a reality.

I once heard a saying that "other people's opinions of us are none of our business." It's very easy to dish out this advice to someone else; it's a bit harder to apply when it's one's own turn. If your feet are firmly planted in the ground of self-worth, you can see the truth of this and let go of negative (or unfair) comments. But on days when the defenses of self-worth are thin, it's easy for negative feedback to "get through" and self-esteem suffers.

Yet again, this is where a self-worth approach to negative feedback is quite different from a self-esteem approach. If I have to deal with critique with self-esteem, I have to somehow counter the negative with "positive self-talk" or affirmations like "I am smart/creative/talented" and so on. A self-worth approach is different: I accept the pain; I notice my tendency toward self-reproach; I resolve to be kind to myself, even though my reputation with myself may be suffering in that moment.

From my own experiences, I find this approach, which is very much the approach of self-compassion, brings two advantages over my earlier self-esteem thinking. First of all, it consumes a lot less energy. Dredging up all those positive affirmations in the middle of a negative day takes a whole lot of work. Second, it's more real. The problem with a lot of positive self-talk is that it feels fake. Although we've all probably found the energy to "fake it 'til you make it" on occasion, there are many days in which faking just doesn't work.

It's always worth remembering that many people's judgments of you are frequently driven by their *own* self-worth issues—for example, their need to sound clever, to be right, to assert power, or their fear of being ignored. One of the questions that often helps me is "Why do they need to make that judgment?" (applying Shift #7, from "being interesting" to "being interested"). The answer is usually not far away: you can sometimes hear it in their tone of voice or see it written on their face. On some occasions, I will ask the question aloud, though I usually have to first check with myself what my motives are in doing so.

We will always be on the receiving end of harsh or unfair judgments. That's life. Much of the time, the people doing the judging won't have studied nonviolent communication, either. You can expect many judgments to be superficial, arbitrary, unkind, or plain unnecessary, and they are often delivered out of a person's need to assert their power and have little to do with you, anyway. Nevertheless, even when you feel you "should know better," you can occasionally expect a negative impact on your self-esteem,

"Never wrestle with a pig.
You will get dirty, and
besides, the pig likes it."

GEORGE BERNARD SHAW

either for the judgment or for the way you deal with it. That's a good day to be a friend to yourself. Self-worth provides a safe place to come home to.

Not Living Up to Your Values

Anyone reading a book like this probably knows their values and will be trying to live in accordance with them. Some readers may be driven by success, others more inspired by contribution. Nearly everyone values a sense of freedom and joy in life. They want to love and be loved. Some people value inspiration, others routine or stability. Some have strong values around beauty, not just superficial glamour but the deeper sense of beauty articulated by Keats: "Beauty is truth, truth beauty,— that is all / Ye know on earth, and all ye need to know."

No matter what our values are, there are times when we sense we are not living up to them. Perhaps we feel we are being less than honest by withholding key information from someone. Maybe we do a hurried job that does not do justice to our values around quality. Or we are not keeping a promise or feel awkward because we know deep down we are pursuing a selfish agenda.

Consciously or subconsciously, we sense a gap between what we would ideally aim for and what we are tolerating about ourselves. This values gap is not just about ethics. It may also apply to how we communicate, the physical environment in which we work, or even how we care for ourselves.

These gaps are usually awkward to confront, so we might avoid doing so by developing compensation behaviors, such as criticizing others or overeating or even creating an entire story that smoke-screens the gap. If, for example, we have behaved selfishly toward a member of the opposite sex, it is easier to build an entire story of what "men" or "women" are like than it is to face the value gap in our behavior. Or we blame that demanding boss, when we know at heart we are just doing the bare minimum at work.

Before we judge ourselves too harshly, we might first try to understand that when we do these kinds of things, we are probably being driven by self-esteem. As we've seen, self-esteem tends to demand that we think well of ourselves pretty much all the time, and tactics of denial help us maintain the notion that we're living up to our values.

But what happens when we do things like withhold vital information or eat too much or do a sloppy job or catch ourselves criticizing others to take the focus off our own contribution to a problem? What happens to our relationship with ourselves?

In short, it usually suffers and we feel bad. We may even drift into states of depression, dissatisfied with ourselves and how we are failing to live up to our own ideals. Self-esteem usually takes a nosedive. And if we turn to the bottle or the fridge or the pharmacist for comfort, self-esteem will probably plummet even further.

This is when we want to practice self-compassion, but here's the problem: it's hard to practice self-compassion if you don't believe you are *worth* it. When we are turning to the bottle, the fridge, or the pharmacist, that sense of worthiness is called into question.

Perhaps the ultimate test of self-worth is how we respond when we find we are not living up to our values. In these moments, our core relationship with ourselves is uncovered and laid bare in all our humanity and vulnerability, without the ornaments of self-esteem, achievement, pride, or good performance. Can we still be kind to ourselves in those moments?

My mind goes back to a recent encounter in which I wanted to make a good impression. I didn't exactly lie, but I was very economical with some of the truth and positively profligate with other elements of it. The net result was that false expectations were created, not solely by me but I certainly contributed to the situation. For a couple of days, my self-esteem took a hit and I knew I would have to set the record straight and that there would be repercussions. So I procrastinated and judged myself harshly for that, too.

In the end, the crucial conversation took place, and I had to be honest about my part in the misunderstanding. Though somewhat relieved at the other person's reaction, I still didn't feel good about my motives or my communication. I had to acknowledge that I had exaggerated certain things. I also had to acknowledge that my self-esteem had been dented.

However, on this occasion, my self-worth managed to stay intact throughout the process, as if it had become Teflon-coated; none of the issues stuck. Indeed, it was that intact sense of self-worth that allowed me to make amends, overcome procrastination, and acknowledge that the whole sorry episode left a sour taste in my mouth. I can only wish that I had accessed this resource earlier in my life, when struggling with my own self-reputation often gave rise to weeks and months of unnecessary angst and various forms of cover-up behavior.

Practice: Daily Self-Worth Habits

The following are simple ways you can introduce self-worth habits into every day that may inspire you to practice other ways of bringing your friendship with yourself to the forefront of all your activities. Strengthening this relationship will lend you more resilience when you experience setbacks.

1. With your first sip of coffee/orange juice/water of the day, affirm your friendship with yourself and say your mantra, aloud if possible. (The more you practice this throughout the day, the better your self-worth gets.)

2. In the morning, as you think about your day ahead, remember that there is nothing that you need to prove to yourself. You will no doubt have many things to do, perhaps even a

call or a meeting that you are worried about. You may have to prove something to someone else (a manager, a client), or you may have to satisfy a regulator or an authority. Affirm that you are okay with you, even before the tasks of the day begin. Self-worth is unconditional.

3. As you enter a building or conference room (or make a call or initiate a session), set your intention as "How can I be useful?" rather than "How can I prove myself?" (Shift #4.) You will conduct a better meeting.

4. When you're feeling disappointed, rejected, ignored, lonely, or any number of other so-called negative states, be an extra-special friend to yourself. It's normal that you might feel sad and for your energy to drop. Create a gesture (for example, placing a hand on your heart) to consciously send love to yourself and avoid slipping into self-reproach.

5. During a break, practice Shift #2, doing something as an expression of self-worth, not as a condition of self-esteem. Take a quick walk or have a healthy drink, play music, dance, or watch a comedy clip. Do something that gives you pleasure in the moment.

6. When you catch yourself doing a self-assessment (whether positive or negative), ask yourself, "Why do I need to make this assessment?" Adjectives are not realities, they're just stories we tell. Stop assessing and start asserting (Shift #1) by making a decision, letting the assessment go, moving on. You may need to assess your work or your actions, but you don't need to assess *you*.

7. When planning for the future, ask yourself if you are trying to prove yourself or if you are valuing yourself (Shift #6). On the basis of valuing yourself, you can be as ambitious as you please. From a self-worth perspective, there is nothing to prove.

8. When not knowing what to do about a problem, ask if it is something you need to accept or something you need to change. With self-worth, you get to choose the battles that you fight. Not everything needs to be "fixed" for you to feel good about yourself.

9. In conversation with yourself or others, watch out for words like "I should," "need to," "have to," "must," and replace them with words like "I could . . ." (Shift #5). From the perspective of self-worth, there are no imperatives.

10. When you're facing indecision, solve problems from a stance of self-worth by imagining more possibilities. Two options can feel like a tough dilemma, three options usually represent real choice. What other options are there?

11. Notice those conversations, tasks, or social situations that drain your energy. Is the problem in the situation or in the expectations you have about yourself in that situation? Try being *interested*, rather than *interesting* (Shift #7). What difference does this make?

   - If the energy drain continues, think about changing the situation. Are there people, places, or tasks that have become so energy-sucking that your self-worth is being corroded? Please remember to be accepting of yourself while grappling with this issue (Shift #3).

   - Self-worth does not require you to be self-sufficient. Who can you talk to about the issues that you face?

12. Enjoy your food and affirm your friendship with yourself as you savor it, no matter what you're eating. Ideally, we want to eat well as an expression of self-worth rather than as a condition of self-esteem (Shift #2). However, what's even more vital is that we don't make self-worth contingent on this, or else we just create more emptiness within.

13. As part of getting ready for bed, write a gratitude list. Find at least three things you liked about yourself today, even while you grappled with unsolved problems. Tomorrow is another day.

Loneliness and Bereavement

At some point in their lives, nearly every human being suffers the loss of another. The most obvious example of bereavement is the death of a loved one, but there are many less obvious causes of intense grief: separation, loss of a pet, friends moving away, relocation to a country of origin and finding it utterly changed, redundancy, or even a young adult leaving home.

When these events occur, our self-worth can suffer a setback. Our loved ones and close friends are inextricably entwined with our sense of self. When we lose them, a part of us seems to disappear with them. One of the sentences you will frequently hear from the bereaved is "I no longer know who I am without them." This is not just an empty saying, it often expresses a literal truth.

Bereavement is often followed by loneliness. The loss of a loved one leaves an aching hole in the heart, which it seems that nothing can fill. We doubt if we can ever again be ourselves, laugh, play, or feel connected as we did before.

With seven billion of us on the planet, hyper-connected more than ever before, one would be forgiven for fondly imagining that it was only a matter of time before loneliness was eradicated. Sadly, all indicators point the other way. In a 2017 study of loneliness in Britain, more than nine million people reported that they often or always felt lonely. As a result, the UK government appointed the first ever Minister for Loneliness.

It seems that the more connected we are, the lonelier we become. I grew up in a small village, where your neighbors not only knew you but also your entire family history, your peculiarities, complete with funny stories from decades past. In my current urban setting, today in Lisbon, only a few neighbors know me by name. Like me, you may have several hundred friends on Facebook, but how many would notice if you didn't post for a couple of weeks?

Each person's experience of bereavement or loneliness is different. This is one of the reasons why both are hard to talk about. Most people respond not so much by listening but by telling you what happened to them, in the belief that their experience will somehow be useful to you. Sometimes it is, but often it is not. Each experience of loneliness and bereavement is unique.

We may also be taken aback by fresh experiences of loss or loneliness. We imagine that it will be somewhat like last time, and we are surprised—even shocked—to find that this time it's different. We try to cope the way we did last time, and it does not work. We begin to think that there might be something wrong with us.

As I personally discovered during a loss-filled 2016, the effect of bereavement on self-esteem can be very corrosive. Logically, I could tell myself that what I was experiencing was normal, even healthy. I could do my best at self-compassion. But emotionally it felt as if a part of me had disappeared and could never be regained.

Looking back on that year now, I can see that I was like an old chair being stripped of all the coats of varnish that had ever been painted over its surface. For a long time, all I could see was a mess. The veneer that I had shown to the world—self-sufficiency, confidence, ability to take initiative, energy—was just being scrubbed away. I wondered what would be left of me when the scraping was complete.

I had spent a lifetime defining myself by my roles in relation to other people. I was a son, a brother, a husband, a father, a businessman, a provider, a friend... the list went on. As one loss followed another, it was as if each of these roles were being peeled back and scraped away. I had known myself only through these roles, so I'd seen the chair only with its various artwork and veneers. I had no idea what the woodwork looked like.

During times of loss and bereavement, what is most evident is what is being taken away. An experience of loneliness is an experience of what is *missing*. Perhaps this is why loneliness and loss are so corrosive to self-esteem. Together they act as paint stripper for the soul.

When we resist the urge to fill the emptiness with displacement activities and distractions, we eventually glimpse the fine old wood from which the chair is made. We begin to appreciate that the various veneers (however shiny) were just that, not the chair itself. Even while still living in the shadow of loss, our eyes adjust to the gloom and we begin to make out the shape of a new relationship with ourselves.

In my own case, I already had a vague intellectual grasp of self-worth. But it took an experience of successive losses to teach me emotionally about self-worth, to make it real. As I began to glimpse a new springtime, I was better able to cope with times of sadness and loneliness. A new adventure began in the depths of winter.

Insecurity

Over a ten-year period, Dr. Carlo Strenger of Tel Aviv University's department of psychology has researched social anxiety and depression, phenomena which he first recognized were surfacing with increasing frequency in his clinical practice. Noticing a surge of this fear in his patients, he began an interdisciplinary research project, and his book *The Fear of Insignificance: Searching for Meaning in the Twenty-First Century* sets out his findings.

His conclusion was that the fear of insignificance is due to "global access"—our contemporary ability to endlessly compare ourselves with the most "significant" people around the world. "The impact of the global infotainment network on the individual is to blame," writes Strenger. "A new species is born: Homo Globalis—global man—and we are defined by our intimate connection to the global infotainment network, which has turned ranking and rating people on scales of wealth and celebrity into an obsession."

In the past, being a lawyer or doctor was a very reputable profession, he explains. Today, even high achievers constantly fear that they are insignificant when they compare themselves with success stories promoted daily by social media, constantly afraid that their rating on a variety of scales may drop." This creates highly unstable self-esteem and an unstable society," he concludes.

Homo Globalis is facing a difficult predicament: we have the weight of the world's expectations on our shoulders. We need to be fit, successful, busty, ripped, happy, fashionable, glamorous, in love, in leadership, in business . . . the list goes on. Homo Globalis is expected to be confident, emotionally intelligent, cool, trendy, good-looking, and smart, expectations which are further reinforced as each generation of children reach the age of dating and work.

On top of this, Homo Globalis is expected to possess self-esteem at all times. No matter what happens, "you need to believe in your selfie." This is the great "amen" of twenty-first-century living, and if you are not a believer, "you may still have some work to do on yourself."

Some people, particularly those of my generation and older, may envy millennials' supposed sense of entitlement and globalized vista of possibility. But look just a little closer and you see that many are living under the greatest tyranny since the medieval church invented the binary choice of heaven and hell in order to keep the faithful in line. The Tyranny of Self-Esteem starts early and leaves you entirely on your own with that responsibility. "We give you the tools: it's up to you to use them" is now the ubiquitous refrain of school and the workplace. The subtext is unambiguous: you are entirely on your own with your toolkit.

A postwar vision of social cohesion has now been replaced with the Age of Individual Responsibility. When it comes to your career, your healthcare, your retirement, your relationships, and so on, the refrain is always the same: you are on your own in all these spheres.

The net results are the plagues of anxiety and insecurity, long established even before you enter the workforce or even glance at the daily news. Women in particular get a raw deal. As well as shouldering all the responsibilities traditionally shouldered by men, women also have to cope with a biological clock that rapidly counts to forty at largely the same pace as it did a hundred years ago, even though an increasing number of young women do not finish college now until their late twenties. This leaves a painfully short time for those women so interested to establish a career, repay student loans, find a partner, and have babies.

At every age, people of all genders are grappling with the Tyranny of Self-Esteem and its ubiquitous offspring: incessant insecurity. We see this insecurity manifesting itself everywhere—in the hunger for attention; the increasing consumption of medication; the rising rates of depression; the growth of a long list of stress-related conditions, including obesity, heart disease, Alzheimer's, diabetes, gastrointestinal problems, and asthma. We see the constant clamor to prove oneself, to parade achievements, holidays, acquisitions, peak experiences, and even spiritual enlightenment. At every turn of the road, yet more peak experiences are proffered, a whole new array of expectations to live up to.

There's a lot of money to be made from cultivating your insecurities. Gyms, yoga studios, personal branding experts, coaches, therapists, spiritual gurus, and image consultants may vary in their approaches . . . but nearly all take credit cards. Not many of them want you feeling too smug or secure in your skin.

In the meantime, what happens to the individual sitting alone in the city apartment (as more and more are), contemplating career uncertainty, endless possibility, and total responsibility?

At the very least, unconditional self-worth offers a refreshing oasis in the middle of this clamor. In this space, there is nothing to prove, neither about your body's shape nor even the shape of your emotions. The incessant demands of self-esteem can be quieted, at least for a time, to allow us to reconnect with ourselves.

During times of insecurity, it is possible for self-worth to get damaged. One group of people at risk are those who suffer a prolonged struggle, for example, a long period of both economic and relationship battles that weakens their fundamental faith in themselves. The young are also vulnerable, until they discover all the things they can say no to and still have a good life. Anyone can experience a loss of self-worth through the experience of insecurity. Our mobile society also leaves a lot of people unsure of where they belong, which can knock self-esteem around.

Self-worth provides a citadel to retreat to on those days when you perceive your defenses of self-esteem lie in tatters. We saw this with Pete at the beginning of the book. No matter what is going on around you, no matter what you are about to lose, you do not have to lose your relationship with yourself. You can be a friend to yourself in all circumstances.

Recovering from Setbacks

While walking along a beach near Lisbon, I once had an interesting conversation with a friend who described how she often feels "gutted" by disappointment, particularly rejection. Her use of the word "gutted" was not just a figure of speech: it was as if each rejection felt to her as a visceral disembowelment. She readily admitted that she would never judge another person in the way that she judged herself for each setback. The sense of "not being good enough" was palpable.

I readily understood the feeling: I've experienced it often enough. At least when working in sales, you get plenty of practice with rejection. In the words of John O'Donohue, you get to "school your mind in the art of disappointment." Affairs of the heart are another matter: it's easier to school the mind than to school the heart.

Whatever our aspirations or values, there will always be some things that don't go according to plan. Whether it's mistakes that we make, values that we don't feel we have lived up to, or experiences of rejection, loss, or bereavement, there will always be occurrences that threaten to derail our relationship with ourselves.

Disappointment has a subtle way of undermining self-worth. On the surface, we are disappointed at something or someone *external*: the person or event that did not unfold as we hoped. However, below the waterline, there often lurks a sense of disappointment with *ourselves*. Questions like "Why do I always fail at this?" or "What's wrong with me?" can easily hide in the muddy waters of disappointment.

At such times, it's all too easy to take the hurt personally, to feel that your very sense of self has been disemboweled by the hurt and loss. In many cases, there is a double hurt: the rejection plus the negative judgment of self, often with words like "useless," "a nobody," "hopeless," or "an idiot." All of this happens in seconds and often without our awareness.

As Randy Pausch put it, just after he was diagnosed with pancreatic cancer, "What matters is not the cards we are dealt, what matters is how we play our hand." In terms of self-worth, we are going even one step further: what matters is being a friend to ourselves, no matter how the game is going. So what do we do instead?

This is when the seven self-worth shifts become important. Spotting and stopping the negative self-assessment (Shift #1) will be a big help. Accepting the hurt and being especially compassionate toward yourself (Shift #3) will help you to discover how to be your own friend at times like this. Most important of all, perhaps, is the discovery that it is possible to separate your sense of self from the "slings and arrows of outrageous fortune."

Let's apply this to the arena of romance, though we could just as easily apply this to a business or career rejection. Perhaps you pin your hopes on the attention of a certain person, but they do not seem to reciprocate your feelings. You think about them day and night, but it soon becomes painfully obvious that they do not think about you in the same way, perhaps not even at all. That hurts, right?

If this happens a lot, it's easy to build an armor of hardened indifference. For example, judging the other person ("They are not the person I thought they were"), becoming resentful at the entire gender in question, or even becoming hostile to love relationships in general. Some may even withdraw from the "dating game" entirely.

Notice how all of these responses are driven by the need to think well of ourselves all the time. Self-worth offers a different approach. Far from denying the hurt or making the other person somehow inferior, we are invited to go deeply into the experience of loss but without making any assessment of ourselves, good or bad (Shift #1). We start taking care of ourselves because we are worth it, which might include dropping some expectations of ourselves that day (Shift #2). We are invited to accept things as they are, even when they're not good, without slipping into self-reproach (Shift #3).

We cannot do much to diminish the pain caused by another, but we can do a lot to stop the penalty points, as well as the consequential suffering caused by ourselves. We can use the experience of loss and hurt to learn to love ourselves. In this sense, no experience is ever wasted.

Nobody is immune to occasional visits from those Four Plagues of anxiety, frustration, envy, and shame. Self-worth gives us an infection-free safe zone into which we can retreat to rebuild our defenses. From the safe point, we can see that what often terrifies us is our reputation with ourselves. Self-worth frees us from that tyranny.

Ending the Stories

The Indian teacher Anthony de Melo once wrote, "What makes you happy or unhappy is not the world and the people around you, but the thinking in your head." Much of the suffering caused to the self is caused by a *story*, not by a *feeling*. For example, it's not (just) the disappointment you've had, it's the story you tell yourself about what that rejection means about you. It's not (just) the mistake I made, it's what I fear the mistake says about me. It's not (just) the loss I've suffered, it's the melancholic story I'm now telling myself about life.

My colleague An van de Steen has a maxim: "Feel the feeling, not the story." A sense of unconditional self-worth helps us to distinguish the *feeling* (sadness, confusion, frustration) from the *story* ("I always fail at this" or "The world is unfair/crazy"). It's not uncommon to meet people who have been living a story for years. This may be a story about society, the economy, men/women, opportunity, or even themselves. These stories are often riddled with assessments and resentment, which is why Shift #1 and #3 are particularly important. The story is invariably backed up with "facts," diligently collected and curated to support the story, of course.

The story can also be accompanied by quite a lot of emotion, particularly tales of rejection or injustice. However, this emotion is usually induced by the drama of the story, not a primary current-day feeling. The presence of strong emotions is not (by itself) evidence that the suffering stems from story or from feeling. We need to look at what we are responding to: a current reality or a story in our heads.

Many Safari participants talk about a new sense of lightness when they put down the weight of the story. Even if that story is factually correct, how well is it serving them today? Getting rid of an outdated story sometimes takes time (and even therapeutic support), but some can be done in a matter of minutes. The moment of recognizing a story we have been living as just being a story often opens us up to a new lightness and freedom. One day, we suddenly discover we simply don't need that old story anymore. We can blow it away, like a feather.

Invictus
Out of the night that covers me
Black as the pit from pole to pole
I thank whatever gods may be
For my unconquerable soul.

In the fell clutch of circumstance,
I have not winced nor cried aloud.
Under the bludgeonings of chance,
My head is bloody, but unbowed.

Beyond this place of wrath and tears,
Looms but the Horror of the shade.
And yet the menace of the years
Finds, and shall find, me unafraid.

It matters not how strait the gate
How charged with punishments the scroll
I am the master of my fate:
I am the captain of my soul.

W.E. HENLEY

(10)

Saying Yes and No

> "When you say 'Yes' to others, make sure
> you are not saying 'No' to yourself."
>
> PAULO COEHLO

MANY PEOPLE HAVE difficulty saying no. The reasons are many and varied: fear of offending others, desire to serve, people-pleasing, over-optimism about one's capacities, high expectations of self, desire to impress, fear of missing opportunities, and so on.

The ability to say yes and no is an important life skill that influences both career and personal happiness. People with low self-worth are often smitten by a double-edged sword. First of all, they struggle to make decisions. When they experience difficulty accessing what they really want, it's hard to decide what is the yes and what is the no. Let's say you have two job opportunities. If you are obsessed with proving yourself, it may be hard to decide which job to take. Perhaps you would really like one, but you feel you "should" choose the other.

Second, even when the preferred option is clear, people with low self-worth often struggle to express that choice to others.

They may fear causing offense, making a mistake, unknown consequences, or cutting themselves off from a future opportunity. So instead, they procrastinate. And in doing so, they think worse of themselves, which exacerbates a problematic relationship with self. Another vicious circle occurs: low self-worth diminishes the capacity to make decisions, which in turn reduces self-esteem.

Not only does this result in many missed opportunities, low self-worth also creates a lot of suffering. In addition to the agony of decision-making, how many people endure jobs (or relationships) for years due to their inability to say no? The fear of disappointing another person cripples their ability to say yes to themselves. The good news is that self-worth can help to restore that balance.

Thinking Differently

Over the years, I've heard this topic ("Saying No") discussed extensively at many kinds of workshops. In business settings, the focus is often on productivity, and the discussion frequently turns around priorities, to "what" we are saying yes and no. Various structures are put forward to resolve the typical dilemmas, such as Stephen Covey's four quadrants, to help distinguish what is important versus what is urgent. Many apps have been created to guide you to your next priority. (Ignore them and keep reading! Distraction is one of the ways in which we escape difficult decisions!)

The real issue for many people is one of conflicting commitments or priorities. Often, several commitments are important, several priorities are urgent. For example, there are the demands of customers but also the demands of your own business development. There are demands of the kids and the demands of the job. Competing commitments are crowding into that very finite space called "this afternoon."

If the conflict can be resolved by an app, then it was probably not much of a dilemma in the first place. The hard yes/no conflicts are those caused by competing commitments, which are often linked to our values. So we *feel* bad about the conflict.

In more personal dilemmas, this conflict is usually better understood. Here the talk (hopefully) takes a more compassionate turn. It's less about the "what" and more about the human who is struggling and the nature of their struggle. One of the most useful discussions I've heard recently was about reframing a no, treating it as a redirection toward something else. Another conversation focused on the context that created the conflict, guiding the person to their true commitments in the wider context of their values.

From a self-worth perspective, what matters most is that we befriend ourselves during times of reflection and decision-making. When feeling conflicted, it's especially important to be loyal to oneself. Let's explore this a bit further.

Effects on Self-Esteem

When facing a conflict, one of the hidden questions is often "Do I feel entitled to choose in the first place?" The sad reality is that often we don't. For example, we are caught between an important work deadline, the kids, and our own self-care. No matter how imaginative we are with solutions, no matter how we reframe our commitments, there will be casualties. And one of the main casualties can be our self-esteem, accompanied by that nagging feeling that whatever choice we make will be the wrong one.

Working parents will be particularly familiar with this dilemma. A client once described motherhood to me as "living in a permanent state of guilt." When she chose work as a priority, she felt guilty about neglecting her kids. When she opted for home life as a priority, she worried about neglecting her work. She was caught in a permanent lose-lose game, a classic double bind.

The same issue gets played out when a professional is trying to pursue multiple career paths. In their heart, they know they need to focus on one. But they keep getting distracted by clients, problems, issues, and responsibilities that often do not earn them much money. Yet they fear letting go, worrying they may miss a vital opportunity or perhaps reluctant to say goodbye to a disappointing investment.

What usually happens? Self-esteem suffers, which diminishes their energy to make that necessary decision. Feeling bad about themselves, they doubt their capacity for success. Self-belief suffers and so the whole vicious cycle diminishes their ability to make progress on the dilemma.

This is when the first three shifts of the Safari are important. The first shift reminds us to stop assessing ourselves (negatively) for having the conflict. We saw this vividly illustrated with Pete, in chapter 2. When Pete stopped losing energy to self-blame and started taking care of himself (Shift #2), his capacity to think and act was enhanced.

Shift #3 is particularly important. When practicing acceptance, we not only accept ourselves but work to remove self-reproach from the equation. We make ourselves okay with whatever avenue we take and even with possible future regret, as beautifully summed up in Robert Frost's Poem "The Road Not Taken," in which the poet accepts:

I shall be telling this with a sigh
Somewhere ages and ages hence

With self-worth, there is acceptance of choice and even of potential regret. But this does not stop us from choosing a road... and taking it. Self-worth enhances our capacity to choose and to act.

Practice: Dilemmas

List some of the areas in which you are struggling to say yes or no. These could be conflicting work projects or a career direction, difficult commitments to friends, unhealthy compromises with self-care, agonizing relationship decisions, or struggles with family members. Before reading further, opposite each issue, note the consequences for your self-esteem.

Next, reflect on the dilemmas you've listed. Just for today, allow yourself to be okay with each option, whether you make a choice or just accept the dilemma. Trust your capacity to deal with it.

1. How do you feel?
2. Does this standpoint (being okay with yourself, trusting your capacity) throw any fresh light on your options? If so, what?
3. What might you do if you had nothing to prove? (To anyone, not even to yourself.)

The Role of Self-Worth

As someone who has struggled with many dilemmas, may I extend my compassion to you as you deal with some now. Struggles with competing commitments represent some of the hardest times in life and I'm not going to roll out any clichés about growing through difficulties. Personally, I would nearly always have been happy to say "pass" to the growth, particularly when I was elbow-deep in the problem.

I also understand that self-esteem suffers, often before, during, and after a decision. When we let go of a dream or an obligation or even a nuisance, the relief is not always immediate. Self-esteem may take a hit. We wish we had been able to deal with the dilemma in a better way.

But the good news is that while self-esteem often suffers,

self-worth does not have to. Whether today you are going to face up to that dilemma or postpone dealing with it, you can still have self-worth. Please affirm your friendship with yourself while you think about each of your dilemmas.

I once recommended the exercise above to an acquaintance who was putting off addressing a long-term dilemma in his marriage. He had two young boys, whom he loved dearly, but he and his wife were clearly growing apart. Twice they had sought counseling but to no avail. He knew he had to make a decision and would shed tears at the thought of what this would mean for his boys.

He felt encouraged by the thought of being a friend to himself, even while he was living with his indecision. He sought counseling for himself, from the standpoint of "I am worth it" rather than "because I have a decision to make." For nearly a year, he continued to do the best he could in the marriage and as a father, even though he could not see a solution. His wife became more and more distant and it later emerged that she was having an affair with a colleague. In the end, he also met someone, which in turn triggered their separation and divorce. While the ending was not exactly amicable, it was certainly not the disaster he had dreaded for his kids.

Whether it's a work or a personal dilemma, you do not have to reproach yourself for the feeling of being conflicted. Even while you live with the indecision, you can find your self-worth and be a friend to yourself. This does not mean that you do not care, nor that you reject the aspiration to be more focused. You are just not ready today.

Many people who have wrestled with a truly agonizing dilemma can tell you how useless a lot of the clichéd questions and aphorisms are. There are often no simple answers. In both leadership and personal life, there can be painful consequences to real-life decisions: sometimes for others as well as ourselves.

We are not just agonizing over whether to spend the winter in Bali or in Europe, or whether to take a beach or mountain vacation. The really tough choices in life often involve hard consequences for loved ones, the death of a dream, or a clash in values. While coaching legends may feature single-question stories (such as "What would you do if you were not afraid?"), the harsh realities of real dilemmas are rarely resolved by a single question.

So it's important to befriend ourselves when we are struggling with choice, to avoid the pitfall of making self-esteem contingent on an unconflicted life. We do not have less self-worth when besieged by doubt. Indeed, this is when self-worth is a real source of strength: even when the choice is not yet well-defined.

Sure, life is easier when each yes and no is clear. Indeed, a no is often more defining that a yes. After all, if we cannot say no, what value does our yes have? All true. But there is someone with primordial value, before a no or a yes is ever uttered: you.

Conflicted
Gored by the horns of dilemma
I lie bleeding, staring immobile
at a ceiling of projected horror

Hopes dashed
Dreams shattered
Desolation on every side
Nowhere to hide

Adding up again the pros and cons
The now familiar credits and debits
Yielding the same relentless zero sum

Stretched on the rack of indecision
The sound of four a.m.
Notching another bone-splintering shudder
Onto that taut timeline of anxiety

Finally, as dawn sends its first rays
Through a crack in the weary curtains
I surrender and turning to one side
Sink into a restless sleep

To prepare for the consequences
Of ultimate loyalty, of allegiance
To the core of my being

(11)

The Desire to Contribute

> "Once we believe in ourselves, we can risk
> curiosity, wonder, spontaneous delight, or any
> experience that reveals the human spirit."
>
> E.E. CUMMINGS

IN THE CHAPTER on work, we saw how purpose and meaning are important drivers in today's marketplace. For many young people in particular, it's no longer enough to be successful; they want to know they are making a difference or contributing to something worthwhile. For people of all ages, a sense of purpose is usually important both for energy and self-esteem.

Lack of meaningfulness drives increasing numbers of people out of the working world, often preceded by lengthy absences due to stress and burnout. It's not solely the workload that causes stress; it's the lack of alignment between their personal values and the culture of the organization for which they work. As one person once put it to me, "I feel I have to lock my soul and spirit into my car as I armor myself to walk into that building." That's a hard way to start the day.

Twin Strands

When a person wants to "make a difference," there are usually two things going on in parallel. First and foremost, they want to make an impact: whether that is by creating an enterprise, caring for dogs, or contributing to world peace. Second, they are making a statement about themselves, carving their initials on the tree of life, saying "I was here." This second strand of self-validation is very often a condition of self-esteem.

If we are firmly rooted in self-worth, each of the two strands supports the other, like the double helix of DNA. The desire to make an impact drives us on to bigger or better things—to give up that boring job and find a better one, even when this pushes us out of our comfort zone and causes us to run some risks. In doing so, we discover hidden reserves of our own power, we enhance our capacity to act, and our self-esteem grows. In turn, we dream bigger dreams and our ability to contribute is enhanced.

It's a perfect dance partnership of impact and self-esteem, sometimes one leading, then the other. When setbacks occur, at times we draw strength and inspiration from the result we want to bring about; at other times we remember our own strengths and commitment to ourselves. It's a positive yin and yang, even in the face of difficulties or adversity. So far, so good.

The Need to Be Needed

However, if core self-worth is missing, a very different dynamic comes into play. The most familiar example of this—which many of us have probably encountered at some stage in our lives—is the "needy helper" (or manager), whose hunger for validation overshadows their every step. Driven by "the need to be needed," this person constantly looks for people or projects to rescue.

They cannot resist "fixing" people or situations and are often perceived as interfering without being asked to ever get involved.

Sadly for them, they frequently drive away the very people whose validation they crave. While their initial attempts to "help" may be welcomed (particularly in a crisis, where they often excel), people soon find their help to be suffocating. Whether with friends or co-workers, many of us have encountered such people, perhaps even recognized in them some of our own tendencies.

This latter realization can be a tough one. Nobody wants to be a needy helper or compulsive fixer. Not only is it exhausting, it's a generally futile habit that only drives people away. This loss of connection is particularly painful for the "fixer," as they usually possess sincere values of service and usefulness to others.

The core issue is often one of self-worth. When values of service are coupled with low self-worth, service is performed with a constant undercurrent of neediness, such as the need for approval or validation, the need to be liked or accepted, the need to be seen, or the need to be in control. Sensing this dependency, others flee or become resentful, often without being able to put their finger on precisely why they feel this way.

The Role of Contributing in Building Self-Worth

It would be easy to conclude that focusing on one's own self and well-being somehow entails a withdrawal from service roles, perhaps even from all aspirations to contribute. Sometimes, this is indeed necessary for a period of time, for example, following a burnout or bereavement. There are times when we need to focus wholeheartedly on our own needs and recovery.

But contributing is not the problem. The "need to be needed" is the deeper issue: the constant drive to seek validation in external causes or service to people. It's a need that can never be satisfied because no matter how much you do, it is never enough. You may build temporary self-esteem by doing estimable things, but the feel-good factor can be contingent and fleeting.

On the other hand, when you build real self-worth—by focusing on the shifts outlined in the previous chapters and by living these in your life—then a whole new landscape opens up for contributing. Now you are free to contribute as an uninhibited expression of your own values, not in a needy pursuit of validation or as a condition of self-esteem. You can give with joy and freedom, without being attached to rewards or glory or attention. You are, therefore, at much less risk of service fatigue or burnout.

Not only is this a different experience for the individual, but the service lands very differently with others, too. For one thing, they are free to accept our assistance or not. We no longer need to be needed. We find ways to empower people, to encourage them to be active partners in whatever we are doing, rather than passive recipients of help. There is less drama and more lightness and joy.

In this spirit, contributing adds to self-worth, but as an *expression*, rather than a *condition* for thinking well of ourselves (Shift #2). As with physical fitness, we engage in a service activity for the intrinsic pleasure it affords us, as opposed to desperately checking the scales of gratitude afterward for hoped-for recognition. People may thank us or not. We are not dependent on their gratitude. Gratitude will often be welcome, but it's not the main driver of the activity.

During the writing of this book, I encountered a memorable example of such free-spirited contributing in action. Over dinner, I was chatting with a retired Massachusetts-based attorney, who mentioned that he did some work with a US-based organization called Habitat, which renovates homes for needy people. I was curious. Between courses, I inquired a little more. Bit by bit, my new acquaintance revealed the tremendous pleasure he took in chucking his tools into his pickup truck in the early morning and driving to a preassigned destination to do physical construction work with other like-minded people. He contrasted this with the very different days in his earlier working life, doing trial work in courtrooms before juries. While he had enjoyed considerable success in his law career, it paled to insignificance in comparison with the obvious pleasure he derived from contributing to Habitat.

My dinner friend did not need to be needed. There were many other ways he could fill his time. He was contributing as a pure expression of self-worth. He was not fishing for compliments. The conversation would probably have never happened had I not probed a bit, indulging my own curiosity.

Many of the best contributors I've come across keep quiet about it. They are not needy, nor are they contributing in order to draw attention to themselves or their "personal brand." They are happy to contribute as an expression of their own values, rather than for a particular result. Whether they are contributing at work, to a charity, to the local community or school, they just get on with it. The activity of contributing is its own reward.

Looking Outward

People with real self-worth don't usually live narcissistic lives, constantly cocooned in a safe bubble of smug contentment. They are active people with the energy that comes from a deep sense of self-belief. Many of them possess values about contributing to others, because they know from experience that the exercise of compassion is a tangible expression of self-worth.

As the psychologist Tasha Eurich noted in her article "The Right Way to Be Introspective," there is no intrinsic link between

introspection and self-insight. While the latter is indeed cor-
related with happiness and stronger relationships, there is no
correlation between abundant self-reflection and satisfaction.
She describes her surprise at the result of her own research: she
expected the results would show that people who spent time and
energy examining themselves would have a clearer understand-
ing of how they tick and that this knowledge would have positive
effects throughout their lives.

"But to my astonishment, our data told the exact opposite
story. The people who scored high on self-reflection were more
stressed, depressed, and anxious; less satisfied with their jobs
and relationships; more self-absorbed; and they felt less in con-
trol of their lives. What's more, these negative consequences
seemed to increase the more they reflected."

My experience is that people with real self-worth are not
lost in self-contemplation. Those who are may be trapped in
an experience of past trauma or else hooked on the drug of self-
esteem. When people have self-worth, they are more likely to
turn outward. Their thoughts naturally evolve toward how they
can contribute to the world, how they can be useful.

The diagram on the next page attempts to summarize the key
shifts of self-worth—as we now understand them—in the con-
text of our relationship with others.

As we can see, both Contributors and Needy Helpers are ori-
ented toward others but with a different foundation of self-worth.
Narcissists are caught in the worst of all possible worlds: an end-
less spiral of self-reflection.

We can spend a lot of energy on self-reflection but emerge
with no more self-worth than when we started. It's the quality
of our thinking about ourselves that matters, not the quan-
tity. As we start accepting ourselves, rather than assessing; as
we become interested in the world around us, rather than try-
ing to be interesting—we let go of neediness and we focus on

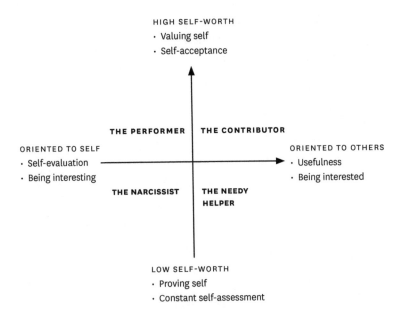

usefulness. This is how we build value in the marketplace as well as how we build friendship. Hopefully, your experience of these shifts has encouraged you to turn outward at least as much as inward, living in action a warmer friendship with yourself.

On Giving

Those who dare give nothing
Are left with less than nothing;
Dear heart, you give me everything,
Which leaves you more than everything
Though those who dare give nothing
Might judge it left you less than nothing.

Giving you everything,
I too, who once had nothing,
Am left with more than everything

As gifts for those with nothing
Who need, if not our everything,
At least a loving something.

ROBERT GRAVES

(12)

Self-Worth in Leadership

"Being confident and believing in your own self-worth is
necessary to achieving your potential."

SHERYL SANDBERG

I
F YOU HAVE ever worked for a leader who had low self-worth,
you will know from personal experience what a nightmare
this can be. In the workplace, the list of problematic behav-
iors produced by low self-worth is mind-boggling. Here are just
a few of them:

- inability to delegate, need to control everything;
- ego-boosting behaviors, such as talking nonstop or needing
  to be right all the time;
- inability to tolerate disagreement or real discussion;
- difficulty making decisions;
- unethical behavior, often driven by compulsions;
- breach of trust and confidentiality;
- attracting the wrong people, for example, sycophantic or
  manipulative persons with their own agendas;
- irrational outbursts, sometimes in anger;
- inability to retain good people, loss of valued team members
  who find better places to work.

We see such phenomena exhibited by many leaders, both in organizations and in society at large. We don't have to look far to see entire countries led by people who exhibit these traits. At times, it often looks like the world belongs to the dysfunctional.

Even as I write these paragraphs, I'm hearing from a young, talented woman with a highly sought-after combination of skills, who is leaving her job because of the behavior of a bullying, misogynistic CFO. This organization is about to lose a talented deal-maker. They will spend tens of thousands of dollars replacing her, as well as running the risk of losing key customers in the process. There is no guarantee that the first person to replace her will work. As she is well thought of within the organization, it is almost certain that others will follow her out the door. The cost of this CFO's behavior to the organization is a lot higher than his salary.

It is not the purpose of this book to discuss the pros and cons of various leadership styles. Many books already exist on the subject; leadership is probably the number one topic in management and business studies. For this reason alone, however, it's important to include at least one chapter about how self-worth shows up in leadership and to reflect on this frequently neglected dimension of leadership development.

Ideal or Real?

When it comes to leadership, it's often hard to distinguish the stuff of legend from the stuff of reality. Many of the so-called traits of great leaders are at best subjective, at worst idealizations founded on make-believe. Sometimes these models of leadership are based on a handful of companies, often companies that ceased to exist a mere decade after the legend was published. It's so easy to expound the traits that we would *like* to see, as opposed to those that show up in real life.

In the legends of leadership development, "great" leaders are invariably portrayed as purpose-driven souls, uniting people behind a common vision, inspiring loyalty and perseverance, deeply anchored in personal values, and nearly always possessing great charisma. However, if you have spent any amount of time around the captains of industry or politics, you will be painfully aware that the harsh reality is frequently rather different, as my young friend above can testify. Not surprisingly perhaps, no shortage of models propose some sort of evolutionary thesis—whether of society or of human consciousness—that somehow the future will be different from the past. In this way, the models could be right after all: the real world hasn't got there yet.

In this typical idealized future, ego and hierarchy will usually be abandoned, replaced instead with self-managing enlightened teams who will collaborate for the common good. Wisdom and wholesomeness will prevail and we will all live happily ever after.

Please resuscitate me when we get there. Meanwhile, back on Earth, we do our best to cope with the world as we find it. If we are fortunate, we occasionally come across role models of noble leadership that restore our faith in humanity and in the future, as opposed to those who cynically manipulate the masses with a blend of "bread and circuses," threats, or even plain brute force.

So what can we do? If you are a leader or HR professional wishing to influence things for the better, what fresh insights can we bring from the perspective of self-worth?

Followers

Lots of attention gets paid to the traits of leaders, but from the perspective of self-worth it may be even more important to look at the traits of followers. Let's examine for a moment how feelings of self-worth (or lack thereof) might influence people being led and hence set the stage for the people doing the leading.

Frank is in his fifties and feels that his known world is fast collapsing around him. He's been made redundant three times and worries about his future. His feelings of vulnerability are magnified by a sense of being "left out." He feels that today's society belongs to a young, educated, attractive, and mobile generation, all of whom appear to pay no attention to people like him. What type of leader will Frank vote for: a modern neoliberal or a "strongman" personality that promises a back-to-basics, conservative agenda?

It's not just Frank's age or his social status that dictates his voting pattern: it's his feelings of low self-worth. When self-worth is low and large numbers of people feel disempowered, the stage is set for the Strongman Agenda, or a "taking back control" promise. Sound familiar? We often focus on characteristics of political leaders, when it might be more effective to deepen our understanding of the followers, connecting with them rather than lecturing or mocking them.

Much the same plays out in many workplaces: leaders are subconsciously chosen on the basis of the people being led. Confident and attractive people are regularly promoted ahead of intelligent and caring people. Why? Partly because bosses tend to favor people in their own likeness and image, partly because of the icons of leadership that we are shown, but most of all because it somehow feels safer to choose such confident people in the first place. *It's often the insecurities of followers that define the traits of leaders.*

Think about it. Suppose you are choosing someone to take over your family business. Do you choose a deep thinker or the person who's willing to confront non-performance? Do you favor the confident extrovert who is the life and soul of the team over the introverted technocrat or the caring and sensitive people-pleaser? Which would you choose? Why? Don't we often feel that the team will somehow be safer in the hands of a confident person than in the hands of a competent one?

Why do so many competent people (let's call them Contributors) defer to those who exhibit confidence, who are physically imposing and often dominate meetings, even when they are not as smart, not as caring, and may be possessed with a self-serving agenda? Somehow, even when followers have misgivings, everyone frequently feels those people that we'll call the Winners are a safer choice, particularly if the Contributors are feeling insecure. You won't have to look far to see how a lack of self-worth leaves the space free for the Winners, and not for the Contributors.

Toward a Culture of Self-Worth

The world of bullying CFOs is not going away tomorrow. We all hope it will someday, and I believe the best way to bring that day forward is by focusing our attention on developing self-worth with followers and especially with the middle layers of management.

When young managers learn to "lean in," as Sheryl Sandberg describes it, they take a more active part in shaping the culture of their team and organization. They don't just shrug their shoulders with resignation at the antics of the crazy; they do something about this whenever they can. This does not mean they subject themselves to a toxic environment. Like my young friend above, they know when it's time to move on.

Of course, this presupposes that they are developing intrinsic self-worth and not just performance-driven self-esteem. In management circles, this distinction is not always very clear. I would like to put forward five solid reasons why any organization—small or large—benefits when people pay attention to this distinction and consciously develop self-worth.

First of all, *performance* improves when people ditch the baggage of endless self-evaluation. We discussed this already in Shift #4, from self-evaluation to usefulness. While occasional self-assessment can be beneficial, ever-present self-evaluation feeds narcissism and insecurity. When we release ourselves from the burden of what anyone thinks of us (including ourselves), we are free to get on with the job. In short, done is better than perfect.

Second, as already noted in chapter 5, *resilience* and energy improve. When professionals have self-worth, they bounce back more swiftly from setbacks and disappointments. Given that professional life is frequently tough and unfair, this is rather important.

Third, *teamwork* gets better. Many of the principal enemies to good teamwork are insecurity, trying to prove oneself, self-preoccupation, and an incessant drive to be "interesting." With self-worth comes a calm sense of self-assurance, valuing oneself rather than proving oneself (Shift #6) and being "interested" in the wider context around you (Shift #7). Just think of how much shorter meetings would be if each person only spoke when they really had something to say!

The fourth benefit comes as a result of the first three: people are better able to spot *opportunity* when they have self-worth and energy. Because they are more interested in the world around them—out of the cycle of proving themselves or trying to be "right," which consumes so much of their energy—they can see where real needs are and where improvements would be useful. For example, they can spot opportunities to reduce cost, increase quality, and meet customer needs. They can partner with clients, rather than just be their servants (a topic explored further in chapter 13). Why? Because their attention is on the world around them, not on their own reflection in the mirror.

Finally, they are more *creative*. Some of this flows from the previous points, but most significantly this great benefit comes from releasing the inner critic. Creativity is one of the casualties of our contemporary culture of assessment. If people are afraid of making mistakes (and hence getting a negative review) it's hard for them to be creative. Even when such reviews are not given by the boss, they are often given by the inner tyrant of self-esteem.

Taken together, these five benefits constitute powerful reasons for any business or organization to pay attention to self-worth, not only to its glamorous cousin, self-esteem. Whatever its role in shaping leaders, self-worth plays a very significant role in shaping followers and middle-managers, and hence in the choice of leaders that they elect in a democracy or find acceptable and credible in a business. When individual self-worth is low, people easily buy into charismatic heroes peddling a myth. If, on the other hand, the self-worth of a follower is high, they will ask questions. They are less likely to be persuaded by showman tactics, nor do they need to take shelter under the umbrella of other people's beliefs. They can think for themselves and trust in their own values.

Winners and Self-Worth

It takes self-worth to question the Winners, and so they often go unchallenged. Most Winners tend to be outwardly confident, so we could conclude that most have high self-esteem as well. It's worth pointing out that I've not been able to find any solid empirical basis for a statistical link between self-esteem and leadership. Nevertheless, I think it's reasonable to assume that those who make it into leadership somehow possess an above-average degree of self-esteem.

But what about self-worth, as we now understand this term? I see considerable evidence that many confident leaders who may well score high on self-esteem do not necessarily score high on self-worth. This explains many things that are otherwise hard to fathom, for example:

- their incessant need for praise and validation;
- their need to be right;
- their behavior as a control-freak or micro-manager;
- their insatiable demand for money, power, and status;
- their emotional outbursts and difficulty controlling compulsions;
- their extreme narcissism;
- their unhappy personal relationships.

It's hard to believe that many of these people have low self-esteem, but it's very easy to believe that many may have low self-worth. The confident—even aggressive—exterior is the mask behind which they can hide their own demons.

Maintaining this mask day in, day out is a constant struggle, one which you can often see etched on their faces. Every hour, they are proving themselves and therefore (to paraphrase author Rollo May) fighting on someone else's conviction rather than their own.

I hope that this link between leadership and self-worth will be properly researched; to date, I have only anecdotal evidence plus a few decades of personal experience. At times, I shudder to think of the damage done by leaders with low self-worth, of the daily nightmare that many people have to endure by serving under them.

Victims of sexual harassment by leaders in all walks of life will be all too familiar with this. What drives people to abuse power in this way? I'm sure the full explanation is complex, but I'm equally certain that the need to prove themselves via sexual conquest is certain to feature in that explanation. Particularly when abuse is repeated, we may be certain that low self-worth is a big part of the emptiness within, driving these so-called Winners to exert power over others.

To compound the problem, abusers tend to choose victims with low self-worth, too. This tendency is well documented in the case of sexual exploitation of children. It's often those in care, aching for love and affection, who become the targets of abusers. Low self-worth magnifies their vulnerability, and manipulators have a natural talent for finding people with low self-worth.

There are many less extreme, mundane ways in which low self-worth influences the world of work every day. We have the endless talkers who see every interaction as an opportunity to prove themselves, treating others as passengers in their eternal ego trip. We have those leaders who are so withdrawn and ice cold that working for them feels inhuman. We have the micro-managers who leave others with no room for growth. We have the chronically insecure and mistrustful, whose suspicion and paranoia poisons any hope of building trust.

Leaders with Self-Worth

I am not claiming that all Winners in leadership positions fit this "high self-esteem/low self-worth" profile. If they did, the world would indeed be a poor place. If Nelson Mandela survived twenty-seven years in captivity, he almost certainly did so because of high sense of innate self-worth. Leaders like Winston Churchill, Richard Branson, and Barack Obama would generally be credited with high self-worth. Many of Churchill's legendary quotes come straight out of his innate sense of self-worth, for example, "Success is the ability to go from one failure to another with no loss of enthusiasm."

Self-worth raises the game, both for leaders and followers. If we had more self-worth in the world, perhaps we would choose better leaders to begin with. If more and more people valued themselves, they would probably make better choices about who they looked up to and admired—in politics, in business, and in the arts.

Dare we hope that one day we will stop rewarding narcissistic attention-seekers and greedy bosses who rule by fear? If intrinsic self-worth could grow, replacing self-obsessed self-esteem in workplaces and in politics, perhaps we would stop rewarding superficial qualities and start rewarding people who really contributed.

Imagine what a difference this could make. We would not only seek leaders with more permanent values, but we would also make better choices in our personal lives as well. Flamboyant performers might still be tolerated as entertainment but would no longer be entrusted with leadership roles. Self-serving managers would be replaced by those whose focus was on nurturing contribution in the wider organization rather than serving the needs of their own ego.

Perhaps the greatest favor we could do for the world is to raise our own sense of innate self-worth and educate our children to do likewise. The choices that many make today have their roots in a deep lack of worthiness, manifested by an endless need to prove themselves before the ever-present god of self-esteem. In the era of Homo Globalis, it is harder than ever for many to find significance. If only they could access a sense of intrinsic worth, they would no longer need to take refuge in the tyranny of saviors. They would find worth within, rather than outsourcing their worthiness to what they "need to do" or "need to have."

The benefits of self-worth, therefore, go far beyond the benefits to an individual. When you access your innate sense of value, you also perform a service to the people around you. You make better choices. You are no longer seduced by illusion. As a true friend to yourself, you can lead or follow unencumbered by the burden of proving anything to anybody. Even to you.

Don't Quit

When things go wrong as they sometimes will,
When the road you're trudging seems all up hill,
When the funds are low and the debts are high
And you want to smile, but you have to sigh,
When care is pressing you down a bit,
Rest if you must, but don't you quit.

Life is strange with its twists and turns
As every one of us sometimes learns
And many a failure comes about
When he might have won had he stuck it out;
Don't give up though the pace seems slow—
You may succeed with another blow.

Success is failure turned inside out—
The silver tint of the clouds of doubt,
And you never can tell just how close you are,
It may be near when it seems so far;
So stick to the fight when you're hardest hit—
It's when things seem worst that you must not quit.

JOHN GREENLEAF WHITTIER

(13)

Money:
Charging for Your Worth

*"If you really put a small value upon yourself,
rest assured that the world will not raise your price."*

UNKNOWN

GIVEN THAT MY day job for the past two decades has been filled with coaching sessions on subjects of value and negotiation, I could hardly write a book on self-worth and leave out this very significant topic. If it's of no interest to you, dear reader, then feel free to turn to the next chapter. For many readers, however, any discussion of self-worth sooner or later has to grapple with the thorny question of how we negotiate our value in the marketplace.

The link between self-worth and charging for what your services are worth is surely an obvious one. If we are going to ask for money for our services, it helps to believe we are worth it. As a client once memorably put it, "You cannot charge a fee if you cannot get the words out."

In order to explore this subject, we need to understand some typical patterns of conversation and relationship-building at work. Just as business is often built upon relationships, relationships are built by conversations. To use a metaphor from chemistry, if relationships are the molecules of business, then conversations are the principal atoms from which these molecules are constructed.

A word here about terminology. It's worth noting that some of the professionals with whom I work are not charging "fees," they are charging premium prices for high-quality technical solutions. In this chapter, I use the terms "price" and "fee" interchangeably, as I also do with "customer" and "client." I will leave it up to the reader to choose whether the word "fee," "price," "salary," or "remuneration" is most appropriate for them.

There is another reason, too, for drawing examples from the world of "client and professional." This is where the gap between "low" and "high" fees (or prices) is most vivid. I regularly encounter professionals who charge five times what their "cheapest" competitors charge. It's not uncommon for the gap to be tenfold or even more. For example, a keynote speaker at an international conference will probably charge ten times more than others on the same platform, if indeed the latter are paid at all.

Why the gap? How can one professional convince a buyer they are worth it, while others struggle to convince that same buyer, even when they are available at a fraction of the cost? How is such value determined?

Forget qualifications, charisma, experience, or even supply and demand. I can give you examples by the dozen of eminently qualified professionals being passed over in favor of lesser-qualified mortals at double the price. Many of the latter are far-from-charismatic extroverts: indeed, they are just as often more introverted than rabid networkers or super-confident individuals.

Before we come back to self-worth, we first need to understand the mindset of value-centered professionals who can charge a premium because of the high value of what they deliver. It matters little whether they are self-employed or working in larger organizations, whether they are highly qualified thought-leaders or in humble support roles. As we will see shortly, what matters is that they possess some key characteristics that set them apart from the majority of their peers.

So how is it possible that some people can charge premium fees, even in a market where the average is often less than half the price? How can they get those words out? Are they simply a different species from the rest of us? Or are they just lucky opportunists?

Context versus Content

Most of the time, the answer to these questions is "none of the above." Those who command premium prices are ordinary mortals like you and me. What distinguishes high-value professionals from their cheaper competitors is their superior grasp of the client *context*, rather than any characteristic of their personality or expertise or *content*. Let's take an example.

Suppose your consulting practice has a requirement for some PR expertise. Two companies are pitching to you this afternoon. Both have colorful success stories. Each company claims a wide network of journalists and opinion influencers. You believe both of them can probably get the press-mentions you are looking for. Both claim extensive expertise in social media, as well as traditional channels to market.

However, one of them brings you some niche-specific insights, suggesting how you can magnify the effect of your PR project by linking it to your current events and also some leadership conferences you are already involved in. They ask intelligent questions about what's driving your PR investment at this stage of your development. They show you some pitfalls to avoid, for example failing to respond quickly enough to comments on LinkedIn. They emphasize what you need to do in order to guarantee the success of the campaign and avoid the pitfalls that others have fallen into. Which company will you give the job to, even if they are more expensive?

What generally distinguishes premium professionals is their superior grasp of the client world. They are not simply knowledgeable about *their* field of expertise. They can apply that knowledge to *your* world, *your* opportunities, and *your* risks. Their superior grasp of *your* world is precisely what makes them valuable.

If this is true, why doesn't everyone become an expert in the world of their clients? This mystery puzzled me for many years, even before I wrote the ebook *Hidden Value* back in 2006. It has always amazed me how many professionals are preoccupied by their own expertise (content) and fail to develop any fluency in the client world (context). I believe that less than 10 per cent are really fluent in the client world. (Some of my colleagues at my company VCO Global believe this to be less than 2 per cent.)

Today, I see a large part of this problem in terms of self-worth. *You have to be fundamentally okay with yourself to drop all self-preoccupation and step fully into the client world.* The better PR professional above is not preoccupied with demonstrating their credibility to you. Precisely because they believe in their own worth, they are free to explore your world: your opportunities, your risks, your strengths, your pitfalls. Having sufficient self-worth, they can turn their minds to your essential questions. That's probably why you trust them.

The Importance of Discovery Questions

For this PR professional to gain that level of trust with you, they will need to be skilled at asking discovery questions. I dealt with this topic more fully in my previous book *The Courage to Ask*. In short, the ability to ask questions and make requests can be regarded as a foundational skill of most business development.

Author and management consultant Peter Drucker used to call this the art of naive questioning. He would regularly preface his discovery questions with "May I ask a naive question?" In this way, he paved the way for asking the very questions that others were afraid, or simply forgot, to ask.

"Naive questions" aren't just any old questions. Effective discovery questions are those that focus on the context of the project, not solely on the content of the work to be done. Examples might include:

- "Why is this project important right now?"
- "Who will be judging this a success, and how?" (Or "How will you know this has been successful?")
- "What have you tried already?" (Or "What's the history of this issue?")
- "What do you see as the key risks that you want to reduce?"
- "What other developments are going on that relate to this project?"

You can find a full list of discovery questions on the Self-Worth Academy website at SelfWorthAcademy.com.

It takes a modicum of self-worth, as well as courage, to ask these questions. This is particularly true in today's hurried business environment, where buyers often resist the needs-discovery process. Some are too impatient: they just tell you to read the spec. Others have consciously engineered a procurement process that explicitly limits your involvement pre-quotation. Quite a few of today's savvy buyers are determined to prevent scope creep.

This all means that you generally need to "make space" for discovery questions. For example, you may have to explain the risk of drawing up any proposal until certain crucial facts are established. Not only will this take certain skill on your part, it will also entail a degree of self-worth. You will need to believe in your right to explore.

Of particular importance are those questions that relate to "Why?"—not just to "What?" and to "How?" Going back to the example of the PR professional above, your project with them will look very different if you are driven by a) a fight for survival, perhaps following the departure of a key player from your firm; or b) an opportunity for growth because of specific marketplace developments; or c) building on some recent success stories involving a celebrity; or d) building up the firm for your offspring to inherit. Your purpose will influence your budget, your choice of partner, and your whole approach. If your PR partner shares an interest in your purpose, you will certainly value them more.

Service-Centered Disadvantage

The influence of self-worth can surface in other ways, too. Many knowledgeable service-focused professionals suffer a disadvantage because of their fear of asking "Why" questions or of pushing back on client requirements. When a prospect demands a proposal by tomorrow, they drop everything to fulfill that request. Before an engagement even begins, they are interacting with the client as a *servant* rather than as a professional *partner*.

This has consequences, not just for the fees they can charge but often for the dynamics of the entire relationship. If you start out as a servant, it's very difficult to build a partnership relationship later on. The client will just keep telling you what they need, when they need it, as well as how much they are willing to pay. One day, they will tell you that you have been replaced by someone just marginally cheaper.

Whenever I ask someone where they wish things had been different, the answer is usually "At the very first meeting." Invariably this is about some question they wished they had asked before giving away a solution or spending costly time and effort with the wrong person.

So why didn't they ask those vital questions up front? Sometimes this is a skills issue—in other words, not knowing which questions to ask. But very often, it's a feeling of being rushed along by the buyer, who may be dangling a carrot, a stick, and quite frequently both.

Why did they allow themselves to be rushed along? Given their vast experience as experts in the field, why do so many established professionals bow to client pressure to send that quotation by tomorrow afternoon? This is often the crux of the problem.

Rooted in Self-Worth

People often see negotiation as about being able to hold a position, possibly via compelling arguments. In my experience, negotiation begins much earlier, with the ability to ask great questions that allow you to gather the raw material for your subsequent proposals and pricing. You find out what the client's underlying drivers are, you discover the risks and pitfalls that they are worried about, you uncover previous history with other suppliers like you, you explore options and budget, you find out how they will judge success.

At its simplest, when asked for that price or quotation, you need to be able to say, "Sure. To help me do that, may I ask a few questions first?" Sometimes we will have to go further, for example, pointing out the risks of embarking on the wrong approach, illustrated by the appropriate horror story. Having spent many years training and coaching professionals to ask value-centered questions (and even having written a book on the subject), I sometimes wish I could have appreciated years earlier just how vital the roots of intrinsic self-worth are. Without those roots, the professional will always be driven back to the need for client approval. They will be a hostage to every changing whim and requirement of the client and will often feel used.

No matter how well a professional understands the questions or can rehearse these in a safe context, it takes that inner foundation of self-worth to really get started. Paradoxically, once they do so, self-worth can be nourished and grown through the daily practice of Shift #7 (from being interesting to being interested)—becoming interested in the contexts of prospective clients—and Shift #4 (from self-evaluation to usefulness)—focusing on value-based solutions for them. Thereby, a virtuous circle gets created, where self-worth drives value-centered exploration and vice versa. At this point, the practice of professional life becomes quite energizing. Each day is a fresh discovery, because every client context is different.

As a professional becomes a master of different client contexts, all the while honing and crafting their own quality *approach* rooted in self-worth, over time they develop a real professional identity. They can confidently discuss the rationale behind their specific approach: the "why" as well as the "what" needs to be done. They can stay loyal to this approach, explaining the risks when clients want to cut corners, usually driven by hurry or cost. They are credible professionals not just because of their expertise or qualifications but because of their focus on usefulness.

One of the most delightful examples of how effective this focus can be came from Mei-Yin Teo, who runs a dog training school in Brussels. Mei emailed me shortly after participating in the one of the Self-Worth Safaris:

Hi John, I just wanted to thank you for your Self-Worth Safari. It was certainly a worthwhile journey. I had many insights, in particular being "useful" in the session on Work. As I am starting a new dog training business, I always tried to prove to my clients how much I know; now I go into each meeting thinking, "How can I be valuable instead of proving how valuable I am?" I connect with the dog and owners and really try to see things from their point of view. It was a shift that has made a world of difference that helps me relate to the owners better, and the dogs respond to me differently too. Thanks for that!

I was particularly delighted to read that the dogs respond differently, too. I wonder how much pain our animal friends have suffered over the years, because of the incessant need that many humans have to prove things to themselves? When we go into meetings with the intention of being useful, rather than proving anything, this changes all manner of relationships. Even with dogs.

You as Partner versus Servant

When focused on usefulness, you won't just be bringing solutions, you will be getting a buyer to think differently about their problems. You will be tailoring your approach to be of maximum service to each specific situation.

Service is not the same as servitude. When hooked on client approval, it's all too easy to slip into servitude. In that setting, a professional is just there to do the client's bidding, and self-worth often suffers as a result.

You will want to challenge your buyer graciously and respectfully, and to learn this skill if you don't already have it. This is the art of value-centered selling at its finest.

Some of the many ways in which we can be useful to clients and prospects are by:

- bringing them insights from our wider experience, tailored for their context;
- alerting them to risks or pitfalls to avoid;
- encouraging them to rethink future plans, to create more benefit or reduce operational cost;
- devising ways to make their life easier or eliminate hassle;
- enabling them to be more agile in their market;
- speeding up processes to improve efficiency;
- reducing waste;
- improving their planning, decision-making, or controls;
- supporting them to stay ahead via better product or service design;
- improving their marketing, sales, or pricing;
- attracting or retaining the right people;
- developing people to do all of the above.

The following diagram attempts to summarize the key steps in a value-centered selling process. In each step, the goal is to produce value for the client, even before any sale is agreed. This is what distinguishes a trustworthy professional: the day-to-day focus on usefulness to the end customer.

As a result of practicing incisive discovery questioning, of reframing customer requirements (rather than just meeting customer requirements), there is now every probability that you have become your customer's trusted partner. Therefore, you are now in a good position to discuss options and budget with them. You can share what other clients have done and warn them of the consequences of inadequate investment. You can quote fees and prices that may well be higher than others. Of course they are! You have demonstrated a superior quality approach.

The entire approach focuses on your usefulness, not your self-evaluation. You are there to focus on their world, their problems, their opportunities. This is how you raise the value of your work. This is the art of value-centered selling, which thrives when rooted in the rich soil of self-worth.

(If you would find it useful to learn more about value-centered business development, or VCO's seven-step approach to value-centered pricing and selling, there are various resources available in the Work section of the Self-Worth Academy's website.)

Money

When it comes to money
It's kinda funny
How people see things differently

For some it's evil
A weapon lethal
In the hands of others, invariably

Some see a reserve
Or a reward deserved
After a long hard slog, pursued faithfully

For others it seems
More a distant dream
That future castle on the hill

For the lucky it might
Even be an innate right
Abundant evidence of goodwill

But for many it's more
A body aching and sore
From too many hours on the treadmill

Whatever the tale
Money will prevail
To value products and services rendered

So the question is less
About money I guess
Than the value of what has been tendered

So instead of complaining
We can start contemplating
How to be a bit more value-centered

Boundaries and Self-Worth

*"Healthy boundaries are not walls.
They are the gates and fences that allow you
to enjoy the beauty of your own garden."*

LYDIA HALL

ONE OF THE recurring issues discussed in my coaching work is the difficulty that many clients have setting boundaries with their clients, colleagues, and partners in the business world. For some people, this will be the problem of over-servicing clients or bosses, worrying too much about pleasing them, and hence going far beyond what they are paid to do. For others, it will be difficulties making requests.

As we saw in chapter 5, these difficulties are compounded when self-worth is low. Setting a boundary with a problematic client or boss is never easy, but it's borderline impossible if you don't believe you deserve to do so.

To make matters worse, the specific problems of low self-worth are often not understood by the person advising you to set the boundary! Those fortunate people who somehow inherited a calm sense of self-assurance don't always understand why you might be struggling. They advise you on the techniques of boundary setting, without necessarily dealing with the critical dimension of worthiness. For example, they rehearse with you what to *say* to the client but ignore the difficulty you may have around asking for space in that client's busy agenda. Do you feel entitled to raise the issue in the first place?

Heritage

I did not hear about the concept of boundaries until I was well into my thirties. It seemed somehow odd, luxurious, even artificial. The idea that you could not only claim your own private psychological space, but also tell people how they might treat you, had no cultural or societal precedent in my upbringing.

Having spent five years of my adolescence in a boarding school, I certainly understood the need for private space. I always seemed to be in search of it. Going to a bathroom cubicle was often the only way to find a few moments of privacy in an environment where you were constantly surrounded by other boys. A locked door was about the only form of boundary you could rely on.

As for informing people about how they might treat you... well, in a boarding school, you don't make the rules. Over time, you learn which rules you can safely bend (such as smoking or talking quietly during study) and which ones you really need to follow. You learn many other things, such as adaptability and self-reliance. But you don't learn to make rules.

Or at least I didn't. As a young boy, I was largely compliant with rules. Later, in university, I developed a rebellious streak, but even then only when it was relatively safe to do so. In my early life, I was not a risk-taker. From institutions of school and church, as well as from family values, I internalized a belief system around being "nice," friendly, and kind to others. And not being demanding. Not exactly a mindset that was conducive to defining rules.

I have no regrets about that. Even if I could, I would not swap my family upbringing for anything that I've seen since. Whatever might have been missing, we were lucky to know real kindness and love.

Nevertheless, it was a heritage that came with low self-worth and certainly not any real sense of entitlement. Home, school, and church generally viewed entitlement with deep suspicion and it was quickly met with either overt suppression or at least sarcastic humor. Any sense of deserving—if allowed to exist at all—at least had to be earned.

Deserving

The idea that you can claim personal space or instruct others on how they can treat you presupposes that you have some innate sense of entitlement in the first place. My problem was I simply did not. Not because I was mistreated or abused in any way, but because the rural, Irish Catholic culture of my upbringing was one of survival, not deserving.

Many years later, I would hear that same lack of entitlement illustrated in a story about two teenagers visiting the doctor. One is middle class so she sees the doctor as her peer. She asks questions and seeks clarification if she doesn't understand something. She does not feel that she needs to rush the appointment, even if the doctor appears hurried. The other teenager comes from a working-class background and therefore is out of her comfort zone. She sees that doctor as someone above her, so she simply answers the doctor's questions. She does her best to fit with the doctor's schedule, even if she leaves the consulting room with unanswered questions of her own. From a very early age, a sense of entitlement (or lack thereof) starts to define how we engage with the world.

Entitlement is often inherited from family and culture. From our earliest years, we hear our parents talking and from this we learn our place in the world. We learn which rules we must follow and which ones we can get around or even break.

From the perspective of my rural/peasant upbringing, it's always been so obvious to me that most of the literature of self-love and self-compassion comes straight from an educated middle class. Such things are always more apparent to the outsider. Ask any immigrant. Furthermore, there is a cultural component: most of these notions are Anglo-American in origin. Being myself a relative newcomer to this "self-deserving" space, I cannot help but notice that the cultural (and class-based) foundations on which these notions rest are often transparent to those who grew up in privileged environments. The concept of "deserving" is literally dripping in a cultural identity. If you grew up feeling entitled to it, "deserving" is a given, like the air you breathe. But if you didn't, it can be hard to acquire a sense of deserving, and even then, you always wonder if it's "for real."

Self-love and self-compassion are wonderful practices but both presuppose a sense of self-worth to begin with. The same is true of boundary setting.

Let's say you want to set a boundary about being yelled at. You want to ensure that people treat you with respect and don't shout at you, whether it's a boss, a friend, a client, or a public official. Many people would like to establish such a boundary, but some really struggle to do so.

Do you feel entitled to set that boundary? Do you feel that you deserve not to be shouted at? Or do you make excuses, such as "everyone gets angry from time to time," or "that's just the way he is," or even "that's what I have to put up with"?

Essential Foundations

To practice boundary setting, you have to know you are worth it. There must be a kernel of entitlement to the sense that you *deserve* this space or respect. This is the deeper issue faced by many with insufficient boundaries: a fundamental lack of self-worth. Once self-worth is established, they are in a position to set boundaries and also practice other forms of self-compassion.

A few years ago, I worked with a recently appointed partner in a law firm. Steve got in touch initially for some help with communication skills; he felt he was not "measuring up" in partner meetings. In addition, he was under constant stress and was sleeping badly. After he'd spent a decade working hard to get to partner level, it no longer seemed to be the promised land that he expected.

Steve readily admitted that he had weak boundaries. Since his earliest years, he saw his role in life as a problem-solver. Indeed, this was precisely what drew him to a legal career in the first place. The issue was that Steve often felt the need to solve other people's problems as well as his own and his clients, and this meant that he and his team were constantly being "dumped upon." Clients were delighted with Steve because they often got service that went far beyond the brief they were paying for. Colleagues were happy with Steve because he would bail them out when they needed him.

Much the same was happening in his private life. Steve's wife suffered from alternating bouts of depression and anxiety so, during the work day, Steve would regularly receive calls that often started with words like "I need to talk to you." Friends also had a habit of inviting themselves over on weekends, particularly when they needed a bit of free legal advice.

Intellectually, Steve had a good grasp of boundary setting. However, having attempted to practice this several times in his career and in his personal life, he felt he frequently failed to do so successfully. His self-esteem suffered. Steve had a constant feeling of vulnerability, and this often kept him "on alert" and unable to sleep.

Instead of starting with the issues of workload and communication, I invited Steve to look more closely at his identity as a problem-solver. Why was this so important? What other possible identities might there be that perhaps better fit his current role as a leader and as a professional?

Week by week, Steve began to see that he would have to change the entire foundation of his professional identity. Being a problem-solver might have been all very well in early career, but Steve realized that being a leader is more than just making people happy, sometimes it's about making them think. Or letting them grow by solving their own problems.

As is so often the case, life sometimes lends a hand. In Steve's case, this took the form of a significant business-development challenge. It became necessary for the entire firm to reposition its services in a very changed UK marketplace, and this provided a context in which Steve could reinvent himself, to assert his self-worth and start protecting his boundaries.

To do so, however, Steve first had to practice the seven Safari shifts and develop an intrinsic sense of his own value. Changing his identity from Problem Solver to a Development Leader required a significant leap in unconditional self-worth. Once Steve grasped this, both mentally and emotionally, it was not too hard to do some boundary setting. Steve already knew how to do things like say no; he just needed to believe he was worth it.

The shift from proving oneself to valuing oneself (Shift #6) particularly resonated with Steve. He realized that he had spent years proving himself—not just in his career but also in his personal relationships. Realizing that he did not need to do so was a big revelation.

Chicken and Egg

Just as basic self-worth is essential for boundaries, it's equally true to say that boundaries are also important for self-worth. For example, if I cannot say no to a colleague who wants to dump work on me, then my relationship with myself will invariably suffer. So which comes first, the chicken or the egg?

If I fail to set boundaries with partners, colleagues, and family, does my self-worth suffer? Certainly, my self-esteem will be impacted. I will almost certainly think less of myself. But what about intrinsic self-worth? After all, we now know that we can have intrinsic self-worth—and be a good friend to ourselves— even on those days in which we allow ourselves to be dumped on by that manipulative boss or colleague.

In short, it depends. If I occasionally miss setting a boundary, which with hindsight (or even foresight) I "should" have set, then my self-worth is probably not impacted. In all probability, I can laugh off the incident and see it for the exception that it is. However, if this is happening all the time, or worse still, if self-worth is low to begin with, then the absence of boundaries is indeed likely to damage self-worth.

Conversely, the practice of boundaries is a great way to build self-worth. I'm reminded of a quote from Brené Brown: "The most compassionate people are also the most boundaried." This comes as no surprise. The ability to be compassionate extends to ourselves as well as to others. Without boundaries, colleagues

Boundaries

will dump on you, ex-partners will continue to invade your space, and that narcissistic friend will continue to manipulate.

Setting boundaries is a great way of practicing Shift #2, moving from conditional self-esteem to the expression of self-worth. Asking people not to shout, saying no to last-minute requests or to work outside your scope, ceasing to gossip about others, setting time limits on complaining conversations—each of these is a tangible expression of self-worth.

It's often easier to make these requests as expressions of our own needs, rather than as a critique of other people or as a judgment about them. It's also more effective. As Marshall Rosenberg vividly illustrated in his book *Nonviolent Communication*, judgments of others rarely help to create insights or improve relationships. We stand a much better chance of being heard when we communicate our own needs, instead of expressing a critique of other people's attitudes or behavior.

Each time we set a boundary, self-worth is nourished and strengthened. Each little fence and gate contribute to the security and prosperity of our own garden. Our boundaries are not high walls to keep people out or to segregate ourselves in cozy luxury. They simply define the space in which we can fully be ourselves.

Practice: Boundary Check

This practice can take thirty to sixty minutes, so make sure to allocate time to do it. Answer the following questions on paper, thinking about your life over the last three months.

1. Are your plans constantly interrupted by the need to solve other people's problems? Give examples.

2. Do you "blow up" when things get to be too much?

3. Is your sleep interrupted by other people's problems or feelings of insecurity about "what's going to happen next"?

4. Are you constantly having to justify, explain, or defend yourself, even in your head?

5. Do you often feel vaguely annoyed that somehow you are being taken advantage of?

6. Romantically, do you "fall for" problematic people, perhaps faster than you think you should?

7. Are you being contacted by people from your past, such as ex-lovers, who you prefer would leave you alone?

8. Do you often feel that others are responsible for your unhappiness?

9. Are you being repeatedly contacted by certain adults (for example, siblings, grown children, parents, friends) who expect you to solve their problems or bail them out?

10. Do some people invade your physical space, for example, touching you in ways that you find uncomfortable?

11. Do other people blame you for their emotional states?

12. Do you often feel that it is not safe to share your political, social, or spiritual views?

13. Do other people frequently interrupt, ignore, or "talk over" your contribution?

14. Do you find yourself an unwilling passenger in someone else's ego trip?

Taken individually, there are explanations for each of the statements above, other than boundaries. For example, a person with intact boundaries might well lie awake at night worrying about the health of a loved one. However, if you find yourself agreeing with more than half of the statements above, then it might be time to check those gates and fences.

A Self-Worth Approach to Setting Boundaries

From a self-worth perspective, before we consider setting a boundary, it helps to get clear about why we are doing so. It's worth summing this up in a phrase or mantra, as we discussed back in the first terrain in the very beginning of this book. This mantra might be:

- "Because I'm worth it."
- "I have a right to take care of myself (and so do they)."
- "I have a right to my own space (as they have, too)."

Why is this important? Remember it's often not the boundary setting that is difficult: it's our own sense of deserving. When we get crystal clear about that, the boundary issue becomes easier to manage.

The boundaries that most people need to set are as follows:

- **Physical:** what are the limits you have for your personal space, body, and touch? For example, no touching without permission. Each person is entitled to their own space and access to their own body, without justification.

- **Emotional:** separating your emotions (and responsibility for them) from someone else's, for example, accepting/giving advice, blaming, or accepting blame. Each person is always entitled to feel what they feel.

- **Mental:** are you able to share your thoughts, values, spiritual beliefs, and opinions, as well as listen to those of others comfortably?

- **Social:** you are entitled to choose your friends and to pursue your own social activities. So are others.

- **Time:** you are entitled to time and space for yourself. As are other people.

- **Purpose:** you are entitled to choose what gives your life purpose and meaning, and you are also entitled to change your mind about that. So are other people.

Note that with each boundary, there is also respect for the other's boundary. For example, if I am entitled to my political views, so are they. For a person with low self-worth, this is often an equally significant challenge, frequently because they would like to manage other people's opinions about them. Personally, it took me many years of maturity to realize that "other people's opinions of me were none of my business."

Once we are clear about the boundary we need to set, it can often be helpful share it with a good friend to get their perspective and enlist their support. As already noted, when setting a boundary, it's usually wise to express the boundary in terms of taking care of our own needs, not in any way judging another person or their behavior. But above all, it's important not to judge yourself for your boundary-setting performance: your efforts to do so, whether well executed or not, are a credit to your self-worth.

Ongoing Development

In my later adult years, I find I need to continually re-educate myself about boundaries. It sometimes takes me weeks of reflection to set a boundary, limits that others seem to be able to set in a matter of minutes. Perhaps they grew up with a better sense of entitlement, or maybe it's just personality based and they possess more self-assurance. Whatever the reason, it often takes me more time for reflection in order to do it.

For example, I have particular difficulty with those boundaries where I need to withdraw support (whether time, financial, emotional, work-related, or personal) that somehow has morphed into some form of dependence. The added complication is that the people involved are usually people who I like. As a result, it's particularly difficult to set a limit that, in my heart and soul, I know I should have set months earlier. I see how they are struggling. Therefore, I tend to procrastinate, hoping that the problem will solve itself with time. It usually doesn't. Indeed, the very opposite usually happens and dependence increases.

The setting of a boundary often feels "selfish." The challenge is to see that my real underlying motivation is usually an effort to prove myself worthy in the first place. Once I see that, I can usually let that expectation go, and then the boundary gets easier to define.

The types of boundaries we need change with time. My responsibilities toward my now-adult children are not the same as they were when they were kids. My work responsibilities are different than they were a decade ago. Therefore, even as I write the conclusion of this chapter, I reflect that boundaries are a work in progress. It's an ongoing development.

Deserving

Get your body movin'
Live in reality, not illusion
Don't let a thousand threads tie you down

Whatever they say or do
Be a loyal friend to you
And don't waste a single hour in a frown

Hold your boundaries with grace
When they try to invade your space
That space is yours; you have every right

To your wishes and your time
To your music and your wine
To make mistakes and learn from hindsight

Even if you've lost a loved one
Or never found that special someone
Or still wonder where your destiny might be

Each day is a beginning
Another chance at winning
By being interested and useful and we'll see

That when your work is over
And you're pushing up the clover
At least you are happy to leave behind

A world that's slightly better
For your presence, lesser or greater,
A memory of you as warm and kind.

(15)

Imposter Syndrome

"The fundamental cause of trouble in the world today is that the stupid are cocksure while the intelligent are full of doubt."

BERTRAND RUSSELL

SITTING ON THIS flight to China, I feel like a bit of a fraud writing about imposter syndrome (IS). After all, I first heard the term only a year ago, despite the fact that the term "imposter phenomenon" (IP) has been out there since 1978. Apparently, it was then coined by the psychologists Pauline Clance and Suzanne A. Imes to refer to people who feel like a fraud no matter how many successes they have chalked up in their careers.

People with imposter syndrome live with the constant insecurity that they will be found out. No matter how solid their track record of achievements, they tend to dismiss their success as luck, timing, or being in the right place at the right time. They live with a perpetual feeling that their success is undeserved and that it will melt away at any moment. Hence the word "imposter."

Many famous people have owned up to this phenomenon, such as Emma Watson, Natalie Portman, and Sheryl Sandberg.

While women seem to find IS easier to talk about than men do, artists like Tom Hanks and Neil Gaiman have owned up to IS, too.

It's worth noting that imposter syndrome has nothing to do with reality. Many of the self-confessed sufferers are clearly very successful in their careers. It's a feeling that they live with that does not seem to have anything to do with facts.

Who am I to write about this? What can I possibly add to the volume of pages already written on the subject? I write these words with no hint of irony. Perhaps I'm just flashing my ID as a card-carrying member of the IS Club. Even here, it seems I need to prove a sense of belonging.

Effects of IS

It's the third time I've flown to China to work with this team and each time I assume it's the last. Deep down, I'm still astonished that they have not seen through my limitations already. What more have I got to give them? Surely, they know much more about doing business in Asia than I do. No matter how much I prepare, there is that nagging sense of insecurity that I will be found out this time. No matter how positive the feedback is from the last event, or how concrete the evidence coming back to me that these value-centered approaches to sales are working in Asia, I still tend to ascribe this to the talents of the sales team or luck or management intervention or just about anything else.

Welcome to a typical week in the IS world. Others might tell you about their feelings of being over-promoted in their careers or of landing roles because of their looks or of being fortunate with family connections or resources or any of a hundred ways that would discount their own success.

It's a bit like the story of the two drunks crossing a bridge on a moonlit night. Looking down at the reflection of the moon

in the water, one drunk says to the other, "How on earth did we ever get up here?" Living with IS is a bit like that.

Limits of the Self-Esteem Approach

It will come as no surprise that much of the advice popularly meted out to imposter syndrome sufferers comes from the self-esteem school of thought. In the next paragraph, I include a brief selection. Notice how each of the measures reinforces that performance-based mindset.

- Keep a log of your successes, much as an athlete keeps a trophy cabinet. Refer to your "glory file" when you doubt your abilities.

- When people ask you to explain your success, avoid referring to external factors. Instead, refer to internal factors, such as your diligent preparation or your passion for the subject.

- Accept that you had at least some role in your own successes.

- Stop comparing yourself with others. Each person's contribution is unique.

- Affirm your right to be successful. Nobody belongs here more than you, and so on.

- Journal your stream of consciousness so that you can see how silly it is.

- Get comfortable with rejection.

- Take action. Any action is better than none.

All of these measures have a certain plausibility. For those people whose attack of imposter syndrome is fleeting and atypical, these actions may well work. For example, a confident career professional may have a passing attack of IS after some negative feedback from a boss or a rejection by a client. If their sense of self is well rooted, this may be just a temporary squall in an otherwise sunny climate of self-esteem. For people like that, the measures above may be quite effective.

However, for others, such tips and tricks miss the mark entirely. I know, because I am one such person. My issues do not lie in a cognitive forgetfulness of success (nor even in my right to be successful) but in a gut-level doubt about whether such success has been *deserved* in the first place. Just as with the subject of boundaries, we are back to "deserving" again.

A performance-based approach to IS has all the same limits as a performance-based approach to self-esteem. It's good as far as it goes, but it just does not go far enough. Something deeper is needed, something that goes beyond the realm of conditional (and fluctuating) performance and gets down to the underlying belly level of insecurity. It's not just enough to change the source of the validation from external factors to internal merit; what's needed is an unconditional relationship with the self that goes deeper than the level of all assessments—even the so-called positive ones.

For people like me, the real issue of IS does not lie in the relationship with success, it lies in the relationship with myself. If I have a deeper relationship with myself, my roots go downwards toward an intrinsic sense of worth, not outward toward an extrinsic search for validation, not even in a conditional and often fleeting reputation with myself.

A Self-Worth Approach to IS

The self-worth approach to IS might sound a bit paradoxical. Instead of trying to find the solution via a new concept of success, I invite clients suffering from IS to stop thinking about themselves entirely and instead develop a new relationship with the world around them, particularly in the workplace or the market in which they want to position themselves.

Continuing the metaphor above, we don't start by tinkering with the roots, we start by cultivating the ground. In self-worth, as in agriculture, this produces better results.

For example, suppose that Anne feels like a fraud. She's probably super-intelligent, as IS people often are. She's adored by her clients and colleagues and has sufficient self-awareness to be able to report this to me factually, in all sincerity. Yet every Sunday evening, Anne dreads the week ahead, scared that this is the week in which it will all come tumbling down around her.

Being no stranger to personal development, Anne has read all the tips above and many more. On her better days, she can even practice them, at least well enough to counter-balance the endless gnawing insecurity that has been her constant companion since her days at school and university.

But on other days, the inner anxiety simply does not allow her to even open her "glory file." She dreads the next presentation to her boss or the next review with a client. The pipeline seems woefully inadequate to feed the successful business unit that Anne has built up around her. Is this the week that it all comes crashing down?

At times like this, Anne can find occasional relief in mindfulness practice or meditation or exercise. However, as soon as the mat is rolled up, the awful reality is often waiting for her again, poised to ambush her confidence to deal with the world.

When working with someone like Anne, I often begin by inviting her to notice the frequency of her self-assessments (Shift #1). In this exercise, even positive assessments are problematic, because what is being practiced via both positive and negative judgments is a conditional relationship with herself. As you might expect, we also work on Shifts #2 (from condition to expression) and #3 (from self-reproach to self-acceptance), so that Anne starts to understand self-worth in terms of self-acceptance, even on those days when her insecurity about herself is high.

From Self-Evaluation to Usefulness

It is often with Shift #4 (from self-evaluation to usefulness) that the big breakthrough occurs for IS sufferers. While freedom from self-evaluation is welcomed by most professionals (once they understand what that really means), for IS sufferers it's like being released from a narrow stall into a large open green field.

At first, moving toward an identity based on usefulness instead of success may sound like wordplay. But this shift is a fundamental game changer. It spells release from the narrow confines of performance-based anxiety.

Suppose that Anne could go to work on Monday, permanently freed from the need to prove herself, and just focus on usefulness. What might happen as a result? We'll put aside for a moment the process of getting to that happy place and simply visualize what it might look like in practice.

As she opens her emails on Monday morning, she notices a message from her boss expressing dissatisfaction with her draft slides for the next management meeting. Last week, she would have read this email during the weekend, in her ever-present anxiety to stay on top of things. As a result, her weekend would have been ruined by this negative feedback. Today, she still experiences a tightening feeling in her stomach, but now she can move past that and simply be curious about how the boss's expectations have evolved and what needs to be changed.

She hasn't time to deal with that immediately, because she is pitching to a new client in a half-hour. Last week, this would have spun her into a state of panic, due to her lack of preparation. This week, she decides to focus the pitch on discussing the pros and cons of possible project approaches with the client, rather than coming up with a single solution that she would then have to defend to impress the client. Her objective for the meeting is to be of maximum usefulness to help her client choose the best approach, whether they want to work with her team or not.

In the meeting, the client quizzes Anne about some technical aspects of one of these approaches. This is exactly the drilling that Anne usually dreaded and became flustered in attempting to answer. This week, she calmly explains that she was not recommending any specific solution yet and that there were a few questions she needs answers to first.

When the client expresses surprise at this, she explains some of the risks inherent in diving into any one solution, until the full challenge of future operation is understood. She holds her ground and repeats her questions.

After the meeting, she's greeted by a tearful team member who has been on the receiving end of a blistering critique from her boss. Last week, she would have felt obliged to cover for her colleague to deal with the crisis. This week, she expresses her wish to be helpful but that this will have to be later in the afternoon.

It's not even lunchtime yet and Anne still has many issues to deal with. We don't yet know whether her new client, her boss, or her colleague will be happy with her by close of the business day. But something important has already happened: Anne's capacity to deal with problems has been enhanced by an attitude of usefulness, irrespective of how others are evaluating her (or how she's evaluating herself).

If you are in any doubt about the difference this makes, ask yourself this question: which Anne would you like to employ?

The old Anne that was self-obsessed about her ratings and credibility or the new Anne that is focused on the key business objectives? When you consider the question from both the client's and employer's points of view, the answer is rather obvious.

Shame and Guilt

Back at the beginning of the book, we introduced two closely related feelings, both of which will be familiar to IS sufferers: guilt and shame. Let's recap Brené Brown's definitions that make a distinction between these two corrosive cousins:

Guilt: I've done something I shouldn't. The act was bad. Guilt is about the *action*.

Shame: I've done something I shouldn't or not done something I should. I am bad. Shame is about *me*, not the action or inaction.

If Anne suffered from a deep or traumatic experience of shame, she would probably be unable to make the shift above. Indeed, she might not be able to do that job in the first place. But either way, she would almost certainly need therapeutic help, well beyond the scope of this book.

One of the products of shame is a deep sense of unworthiness, often surfacing as imposter syndrome. Needless to say, this will undermine self-worth. Even without the extremes of trauma, most human beings will grapple with some shame-related issues at some point in their lives.

So how do you deal with shame-related issues? Brené Brown is clear about one approach: sharing our experiences with another empathetic person. She sums this up succinctly: "Empathy's the antidote to shame. The two most powerful words when we're in struggle: me too." By sharing, we discover we are not alone. With the support of others, we can connect with intrinsic self-worth, leaving behind the endless imperative of proving ourselves only to gain a temporary measure of conditional self-esteem.

Yin and Yang

The more we drop our self-concerns, the more room we have to be useful. We create space in which we can be curious, helpful, creative, and, as a result, successful. We become less concerned by rejection, criticism, and the unfair judgments of others because we are no longer defining our very identities by their expectations of us. Not even by our own expectations of ourselves. No matter what is going on, we can always return to "usefulness."

Furthermore, this approach builds trust. Somehow other people can tell when your intention is usefulness, rather than self-obsession. Even when your questions or solutions are judged to be insufficient in their eyes, they are more likely to retain the relationship with you because they respect you for being trustworthy. Even when the approach "fails," our intention remains intact.

Paradoxically, this is one of the most solid ways for IS sufferers to build self-worth. Instead of redefining their relationship with success, they successfully redefine their relationship with themselves. By seeing the world through the lens of usefulness, they gain a different perspective on their own strengths.

The self-esteem approaches call for the afflicted to redefine their relationship with failure, for example, to see failures as stepping-stones to learning or to success. A self-worth approach calls us to a deeper relationship with ourselves, where neither success nor failure are defining characteristics. With this sense of freedom, we can pursue our aspirations with a fresh sense of lightness and joy. In the words of Edgar Z. Friedenberg, "What we must decide is *how* we are valuable rather than how valuable we are."

Imposter's Haiku

Yellow sun rises.
Is this the day when I get
Finally found out?

(16)

Humor and Self-Worth

"It is more fitting for a man to laugh
at life than to lament over it."

SENECA

A S YOU'VE READ the preceding chapters, you may have
noticed a little humor surfacing here and there during
the course of the Safari. One of the hallmarks of the
Safari groups is the sound of laughter, not directed at anyone in
particular but at the paradoxical and often comic situations that
arise when living on the basis of proving things to ourselves.

Humor is a valuable form of insight. Moments of comedy
and laughter give us perspective and allow us to see life from
fresh angles. If we can approach ourselves with a certain comic
lightness, we can often see with clarity some of those ridiculous
burdens that are unconsciously weighing us down. Laughter can
be restorative.

But there is a deeper rationale behind the humor. In the con-
text of self-worth, laughter is not just an accidental by-product
of some dry developmental process; it's an essential part of the
adventure. Why? In order to fully appreciate this, it helps to
understand a little more about the nature of humor itself.

A Very Brief Philosophy of Humor

Humor has not been given a particularly kind treatment from philosophers. For the most part, laughter has been ignored or even treated as an unfortunate habit to be repressed. Starting with the Greeks, Plato regarded laughter as an emotion that overrides rational self-control, which was no more appreciated in ancient Greece than at a modern-day funeral. In the *Republic*, he says that the Guardians of the state should avoid laughter, "for ordinarily when one abandons himself to violent laughter, his condition provokes a violent reaction." In *Laws*, Plato even advocates giving strict fines to those who cause damage to others through laughter. How would your third-party insurance policy read in those days?

While Aristotle considered wit to be a valuable part of conversation, he nevertheless agreed with his teacher Plato that laughter was not to be encouraged. Wit, he says, is "educated insolence." It's a sobering thought that most of my friends would probably have ended up in prison in the Republic. Enjoying Monty Python would have been regarded as sedition and rebellion.

This antipathy toward humor was not confined to the ancient Greeks. The rejection of laughter and humor continued right through the Middle Ages, particularly in the Christian monastic tradition. Even Descartes, who in so many ways smashed through the walls of medieval thinking with his famous "*Cogito, ergo sum,*" shared this antipathy to laughter. Studying philosophy during those centuries was a serious business.

One wonders how happy these philosophers were. We know that Descartes suffered ill-health for most of his life and spent days and weeks confined to his room alone. No wonder his writings are peppered with images of flickering fires. In all probability these were often his sole companions. As for Socrates, his views on marriage give us a hefty clue about his state of happiness: "By all means, marry. If you get a good wife, you will be happy. If you get a bad one, you will be a philosopher." The lovelorn Kierkegaard struggled with depression from his childhood until his death at the age of forty-two, writing in one of his journals: "I am in the profoundest sense an unhappy individuality, riveted from the beginning to one or another suffering bordering on madness . . ."

Oh dear. Taken together, our philosophic tradition does not give much credit to laughter and humor, even to happiness. It's really only in the twentieth century that we start to get a different view. The French writer Henri Bergson was one of the first to write an entire book on humor: *Le Rire: Essai sur la signification du comique* (*Laughter: An Essay on the Meaning of the Comic*). Now who says the French don't have a sense of humor?

Bergson noted that the comic is a peculiarly human phenomenon. Of particular interest to us students of self-worth, he also described how laughter requires a certain detachment from sensibility and emotion. This theme of detachment is also echoed in the work of the late Umberto Eco, who devoted a significant part of his writing (both fiction and nonfiction) to a deeper understanding of laughter and humor.

As poetically expressed by Umberto Eco, man is laughed into existence and his defining trait that connects him to the divine is not intellect or spirit: it is laughter. Although we are very close to animals in terms of playfulness, Eco argues (like Bergson) that what we have (and that they do not) are comic feelings and a sense of humor. In a later work, "The Comic and the Rule," Eco goes on to describe how humor helps us to see previously unseen "social rules." When we laugh, we are liberated from the rule or, as Bergson had earlier described this, from the rigidity of life.

Liberation

....

When it comes to self-worth, laughter is not just about fresh perspective; it is also about liberation. When we laugh at ourselves, we do more than just *see* those burdens of expectation that have often weighed us down for years. In a moment of hilarity, we can also *free* ourselves from those burdens.

When I first tried to describe the distinction between self-worth and self-esteem to Monika Majvaldova, whom I'd just met on a scuba-diving trip in the Philippines, the example I used stayed with her precisely because of its comic element. In an effort to get past the rules of language (not to mention the differences in our mother tongues), I said something like "self-esteem is walking down the street as if you owned it; self-worth is walking down the street and not caring who owns it." (I introduced you to this distinction at the beginning of this book.)

Monika laughed heartily—as she still does—at this image. In a brief moment, we broke through the confines of different languages and inherited imperatives about self-belief. Through laughter, two distinct frames of reference were laid bare. Even now, I can imagine Umberto Eco smiling somewhere in the shadows of the hanging wetsuits in that diving resort in Malapascua. As he would have seen it, a "rule" had been broken.

When we laugh at ourselves, we experience that sense of elusive (almost mystical) liberation that so much of Eco's writings try to capture. It's for this reason that I love comic sketches like Dylan Moran's mockery of "potential." On the surface, it's cruel: "Potential is like your bank balance: you always have less than you think. It's potential ... leave it! You will only mess it up!" Yet somehow, we also sense that Moran is being kind to us. By exposing those endless imperatives that we pursue (at the gym or yoga or chasing potential), we experience a moment of liberation, of laughter at ourselves.

Self-esteem, being the new orthodoxy that it is, may well frown at Moran's levity. For example, his rebel views may be given a serious cultural treatment, probably explained as a trademark Celtic antipathy toward self-improvement. If self-esteem is the new religion, self-mockery is probably as taboo in some circles as loud belly-laughter ever was in a medieval monastery or in Plato's Republic.

Law-makers have always been wary of comics. Recall that Plato advocated strict fines for those who caused damage through laughter. So we should not be too surprised if self-deprecating humor is resisted by many. Laughter at ourselves is a rebellious act in the orthodox church of self-esteem. Expect fines and penalties.

Humor comes in many shades. We are speaking here of light-hearted humor that encourages us not to take ourselves too seriously. It's important to contrast this with bitter or sarcastic put-downs, which are often the voices of critical parents still living in our minds. To be genuinely liberating, there needs to be underlying kindness toward the human subject, a kindness which you can usually find in the attitude of great comics like Billy Connolly or Eddie Izzard.

Laughing with a Friend

The British philosopher Bertrand Russell once said that "one of the symptoms of an approaching nervous breakdown is the belief that one's work is terribly important." Much the same might be said of self-esteem. For several decades, we have been slaving for a better reputation with ourselves—better looks, more achievement, keeping fit, optimal work-life balance, not to mention changing the world—but is all this really making us happier?

We are in the midst of an entire industry peddling a "better version of you" message. For good reason: it's the way that an increasing number of people make their living. If you subtracted from the workforce all the people teaching yoga, giving therapy and coaching sessions, doing beauty treatments, offering experiences around the world, selling inspirational courses and books, doing personal branding, teaching you how to be a better communicator, dancer, performer, and leader, then society would end up with a lot of unemployment. There are now far more people selling "better versions of you" than there are selling bread.

This book explicitly swims against that tide. The message here is almost the direct opposite: you can be a friend to yourself today, with no preconditions. You do not have to change at all. Whatever your education, weight, intellect, age, or relationship status, you can be loyal to you right now. Even before you embark on any qualifications, jobs, adventures, or new careers, you are okay already. Fundamentally, there are no shoulds; there is nothing to be proven.

When rooted in real self-worth, we can, of course, chase these pursuits to our heart's content. This book is not advocating that we abandon self-esteem, just that we don't plant our friendship with ourselves in this shallow soil. When rooted in a deep unconditional friendship with ourselves, we naturally want to pursue love, achievement, learning, and health. Whatever the outcome, we can still be happy. Through summer and winter, those deep inner roots of a loyal friendship keep us alive and thriving.

Laughter is an art that helps us to see and experience our real self-worth. By laughing at the imperatives that rule our lives, we can liberate ourselves from them. We are laughing with a friend. In this uniquely human state of humor, we can indeed laugh with the gods on Mount Olympus. Because we are worth it. We belong there.

The Mystery of Aimhirgín

I am the wind that breathes over the sea
I am a wave of the ocean
I am the murmur of the wave

I am the ox of the seven combats
I am the vulture upon the rocks
I am a beam of the sun
I am a tall green plant

I am a wild boar in valor
I am a salmon in the water
I am a lake on the plain

I am a word of science
I am the death-point of the battle spear
I am the God who kindles in the head of man the fire of thought

Who is it that casts light over the hosting on the mountain top?
Who is it that announces the ages of the moon?
Who teaches the place where couches the sun?
Who?
If it be not I?

ANCIENT CELTIC POEM, ORIGINS UNKNOWN

Coming Home

"The privilege of a lifetime is being who you are."

JOSEPH CAMPBELL

ONE SUNDAY MORNING in April, early in my own Self-Worth Safari, I went for my usual weekend run in the Forêt de Soignes near Brussels, where I was then living. The sun was shining and white clouds were scuttling across a spring sky. A light April breeze was rustling early green leaves, the birds were singing, and I felt an extraordinary thrill of new growth and adventure. Though I knew these pathways from years of training for the "20 km de Bruxelles," I was suddenly seeing them with new eyes. I felt like a horse that had been shut in all winter and was suddenly galloping through fresh pastures.

Objectively, nothing was outwardly different from a month earlier. I was still a bit overweight and well behind where I wanted to be in terms of fitness and physical ability. In my work life, I was still unsure of my future direction. Several projects were well behind schedule. I knew a couple of friends were disappointed by my recent unavailability and I regretted that. In so many ways, I was not meeting my expectations. My reputation with myself was as tarnished as ever.

But deep inside, something significant had shifted. There was a real feeling of having at last come home to myself. Behind all those self-assessments and doubts and uncertainties, I had discovered the possibility of being a real friend to John, irrespective of whether he lived up to his expectations of himself or not. As I ran, I felt immense joy and freedom that had nothing to do with fitness targets or pace. I could marvel at the morning light through the trees even if I wasn't sharing them with anyone else. I was experiencing all this with a true friend: myself.

My joy in that moment was undiminished by the knowledge that my awareness was incomplete. On the contrary, I was thrilled by the certainty that there would be much more to learn. I was filled with conviction that I had just tasted an appetizer for a homecoming banquet that lay ahead. Later on, I would read about how an infant is born with this worldview, which no doubt explains the endless wonder of childhood. In the words of the poet Patrick Kavanagh, "And the newness that was in every stale thing / When we looked at it as children..."

Along the way, a sense of wonder gets obscured by necessity: by the rigors of schooling, the expectations and judgments of parents and other kids, the hard knocks that armor our exterior defenses. An inner tyrant of ego grows out of the imperatives of self-esteem, constantly seeking and setting new conditions that need to be fulfilled in order to think well of ourselves. Over the course of half a century, I had internalized these attitudes, expectations, and imperatives. The workhorse had grown accustomed to the plow and the stable, rigors imposed every bit as much by his own imperatives as by the farmer's whip.

On this April morning, however, the horse had finally discovered an open field. So I ran, not to fulfill a task or the dictates of self-esteem but for the sheer thrill of running. With all the excitement of a child, I realized that school was long over and that, from now on, nothing *had* to happen. I could really be happy with myself, just as I was.

This was my homecoming. It happened suddenly, dramatically, in the space of a Sunday morning. In a moment, I had a defining experience of self-worth that felt as if I had at last come home to myself. I've since spoken to many others who report their own defining, belly-level self-worth experiences, such as when criticized by a friend or when simply resting on a couch.

Other people report more gradual experiences of self-worth, but even they often describe defining moments. Whether yours is sudden or gradual, my hope is that you, too, experience a real sense of coming home to yourself.

I cannot possibly know what calls you to forge a new relationship with you. In my own case, it was in part personal loss and in part empathy for the struggles I saw around me. Others find their way to the Self-Worth Safari via other routes. Sometimes the call is just a whisper, as in Carl Sandburg's beautiful poem "Calls," with which I close here as a song to celebrate whatever calls you home to you.

Calls
BECAUSE I have called to you
as the flame flamingo calls,
or the want of a spotted hawk
is called—
    because in the dusk
the warblers shoot the running
waters of short songs to the
homecoming warblers—
    because
the cry here is wing to wing
and song to song—

    I am waiting,
waiting with the flame flamingo,
the spotted hawk, the running water
warbler—
    waiting for you.

Conclusion

Continuing the Adventure

"We have a plan. What could possibly go wrong?"

SPIKE MILLIGAN

YOU ARE NOW in possession of a valuable foundation for both happiness and effectiveness. Self-worth is not just a skill or a toolkit. It is an experience and a philosophy of life. Once a person fully grasps the shift from self-esteem to self-worth as a basis of living, this tends to change their entire thinking about themselves, their careers, their relationships, and their plans for the future. Not surprisingly, they often wish to share this insight with loved ones, colleagues, and friends.

This book is the textbook for the Self-Worth Safari, which started in the autumn of 2017 and to date has run in five countries, with about 120 participants so far. By the time you are reading this, hopefully many more people have experienced the adventure of discovering a whole new relationship with themselves.

Right from the start, many voyagers expressed the wish to stay in touch with each other and some firm friendships have grown up between Safari "alumni." To support this, the

Self-Worth Academy has created a community structure so that people can "step into the self-worth conversation" in whatever way is of most interest to them. For example, some want to learn and share about self-worth in the context of leadership, others in the context of business, still others in the context of relationships, and so on. Quite a few are interested in related topics of mindfulness, self-compassion, self-love, and living authentically.

People come to the Self-Worth Safari for various reasons. Some find their way there through pain or loss. The losses are not always personal. Loss of meaning can be just as painful as loss of a special person. Others find that, having striven for success for years and finally achieved it, it does not taste as sweet as they imagined that it would.

For others, it's a nagging feeling of insecurity. Even with outward success, many people are haunted by a feeling of not being good enough, of somehow not living up to an imaginary standard, or of losing what defines their identity.

Sometimes it's an event, perhaps a big birthday or a school reunion, that triggers a new wave of questioning about life and who one is in it. Perhaps it's a redundancy or loss of a business that somehow defined a person for years. Or the kids have left home and now... who am I?

The most vulnerable times are often the times of *transition*. From school to college, from education to employment, from relationship to living alone, from one country to another, from one career to the next, from employment to self-employment, from busy home to empty nest: these are the periods when self-worth is called into question. These can be lonely times, too. We are often surrounded by people telling us what we "need to do." Even loving parents and friends can unwittingly reinforce a conditional sense of self-esteem, rather than support our intrinsic sense of self-worth.

If you would like to connect with other people who are also interested in developing self-worth, see SelfWorthAcademy.com.

Safari Groups

Safari groups are made up of participants who take the Self-Worth Safari together. Most of the Self-Worth Safari groups run over a six- to eight-week period, though some take place over a single weekend. Some groups run online, others are city groups that meet up face-to-face.

The purpose of working with others is twofold. First, we experience what we are reading at a slower pace. It's one thing to allow your brain to conceptually glide across the page, absorbing ideas. It's entirely another to slow down and feel these phenomena in your body, to really see the habit of negative self-reproach, for example. We can only change by experience, not by ideation.

The second reason is best explained by what I now call the "Paradox of Self-Worth." Sustainable self-worth sometimes needs to be kick-started from the outside; thereafter, it can usually sustain itself. It's like a motor that needs a battery to get going.

In a group setting on the Safari, we learn to develop unconditional self-worth together. Reading provides a good introduction to the concepts, and group work supports putting these into practice in our lives in a very real way.

For some, joining the Safari has been a celebration of the self-worth they already have. Equipped now with a better awareness of self-worth, they find they benefit from deepening and nurturing a sense of friendship with themselves. Perhaps they have been applying this well in personal relationships, but now they want to apply self-worth in their career as well. Or perhaps they have been successful in work but attempts at home have not yet proved so successful.

If you would like to know more about the upcoming program of Safari groups, please see SelfWorthAcademy.com.

Licensing the Program

As we got together and shared our experiences, a number of people expressed the wish to be trained as Self-Worth Safari facilitators, so that they could integrate the program into their work. These range from professionals in leadership and management development, in education, in personal growth, as well as professionals working in project management, and in business development.

While some of the above professionals are in established businesses, others are transitioning from previous careers. Sometimes, training as a Safari facilitator is part of their own self-worth adventure—finding a more meaningful career because they are "worth it." Contrary to many misconceptions, such a shift does not always happen because a previous job or business is not working. On the contrary, it's often because it's been at times a bit too successful, consuming much of a person's energy and even their identity. Supporting the self-worth of others offers both a fresh pasture as well as meaningful work.

There are so many fields in which self-worth is relevant. At the time of writing, the number of areas to which self-worth applies seems to be growing by the week. These range from recently appointed managers, professionals in project management, women in leadership positions, sales professionals, career coaching, mindfulness work, presentation skills, the long-term unemployed, leadership development, solopreneurs, and young people everywhere. Not to mention all the variations of all the above fields by language and culture. Plus a host of personal applications, such as weight loss, coping with a breakup, not finding a partner, or feeling "lost in life." Self-worth is the key to liberation on so many fronts.

People who choose to license the program come from many walks of life. Some are trainers, wishing to add a dimension of self-worth to their skills transfer. Others are coaches or therapists working on a one-to-one basis with clients and seeing the relevance of self-worth in just about every session. Some are in leadership development, tackling the challenges of feedback and managing change. Others have an education background and see specific challenges faced by millennials. A few are themselves in career transition and, having experienced what self-worth has done for them, would like to pass on this experience to other people.

When people license the Self-Worth Safari, they are trained to incorporate the materials into their own work: whether this is in management development, personal coaching, or sales training. Some licensees are also invited to host Self-Worth Academy events and webinars, which enables their services to be visible to a wide international audience.

If licensing the program is of interest, please email me at John@SelfWorthAcademy.com. I have a particular wish to support facilitators working with young people. Looking back at my own life between the ages of eighteen and thirty, awareness of intrinsic self-worth would have saved me a lot of angst. Having someone to talk to about self-worth would have been invaluable.

The Self-Worth Academy

The Self-Worth Academy is a global network of people who are interested in promoting self-worth as a foundation for life and work. The purpose of the Self-Worth Academy is to encourage a fresh understanding of self-worth in professional and personal life; in education and in leadership. In doing so, we actively connect self-worth professionals with each other to share their gifts and insights.

We also want to create a learning space for further exploration of self-worth: sharing research and approaches, healthy debate, and also a place where new people can come to experience a taste of what self-worth is all about. Self-Worth Safari facilitators range from professionals in leadership development to education to professionals working in project management and in business development.

This book is just a beginning. Much has yet to be discovered about unconditional self-worth. In contrast to self-esteem, which has been researched and studied for decades, intrinsic self-worth has seen very little of the limelight.

We should not be too surprised. Self-esteem itself was only "discovered" about a century ago and the presence or absence of self-esteem is much more readily perceived than that of self-worth. In contrast to the audible sound (or even the high-pitched shout) of self-esteem, self-worth is a soft whisper—one that is often distinguishable only in those moments when we are out of our comfort zone and when our relationship with ourselves is therefore called into question.

We hope to meet you some day on the self-worth adventure. In the meantime, we wish you a warm and supportive friendship with yourself. No matter what happens—even when you do not live up to your own expectations of yourself—you are worth it.

Acknowledgments

"Any time you see a turtle up on top of
a fence post, you know he had some help."

ALEX HALEY

I COULD NOT HAVE written this book even a decade ear-
lier. It's taken me a long time to realize how fundamental
self-worth is to all that is worthwhile in life. In a real sense,
the volume you are holding has been wrested from the grip of
upbringing and history. It has survived the guerrilla tactics of
various poltergeists, some of whom are still alive, often tak-
ing the form of psychologists and academics. Some of these
voices are those in my head, suggesting I find something else to
write about.

Like any adventure, this book nearly came to an untimely end
on more than one occasion, mainly due to my own self-doubt.
Who am I (in other words, not being a psychologist) to write a
book on self-worth? Why not at least wait another year, until
more people have experienced the Safari?

These nagging questions haunted me throughout the writ-
ing, on countless planes and trains as well as along seashores,
forest trails, and cityscapes after dark. The ghosts of dead

relatives would fall into step beside me, asking me whether it would not be better to turn my attention to "real-world" issues, such as poverty, disempowerment, equal rights, or the creation of opportunity in today's uncertain economy. Why focus on this chimerical image called the self?

Without the support of close friends and colleagues, this volume would certainly never have seen the light of day. With hindsight, I see I was really fortunate to meet some like-minded voyagers early in my travels. Claudia Vettore added the mindfulness perspective during a memorable visit to Ortigia in May 2017, and together we ran a London Safari in September and a weekend Safari in Sicily in October of that year. Monika Majvaldova brought her deep experience of Head+Heart® leadership from the Czech Republic and organized one of the first Safari groups in Prague in October 2017. In Belgium, An van de Steen added the bodywork exercises from her specific skills of mind/body connection and was also my co-host for the Brussels Safari group that same year. My sincere thanks to each of you.

Starting with the three people above, each month has brought a new practitioner to the Self-Worth Academy, focusing on specific aspects of self-worth with leadership, young professionals, and the unemployed. I would like to particularly mention the contribution of Alison Spackman, who has constructed the self-worth survey on SelfWorthAcademy.com. Thanks also to Cathy Bennett, Kath Gigg, Stuart Webb, Sonja Wekema, Diana Petkovics, Irene Ciuci, Joana Pancada, Charlotte Wells, and Clarinda Cuppage for their feedback, as well as to my colleagues at the Self-Worth Academy.

The Sesimbra Safari in Portugal was particularly instructive, both in highlighting the strengths of the approach but also some of the weaknesses in the Safari experience that needed improvement. Some of these amendments have been incorporated into this book. I'm particularly fortunate to share the journey with a host of courageous souls who came on the Safari during its first years when we were together "building the bridge while still walking on it."

As ever, I am indebted to my own support team. Pam Harris and Colette Kwong Hing have been my loyal co-workers for more than fifteen years. Claire Marshall, Amanda Mulder, Madalena Banha, Isabel Lima, and Barbara Monteiro joined us in 2018 to contribute their skills and help prepare the launch of the Academy. My continuing thanks to all of you, in particular for your honest and authentic feedback.

I could never have survived the tough times without the support of my friends: Andrea Rees, Patrice Van de Walle and Wendy Towers, Laura Vesajoki, Jenni Joy, Jonathan Clarke, Anthea Smyth, Shubham Bagdia, Angelika Poltz, Gaëlle Tournade, Gina van Hoof, Michael Myerscough, and many fellow travelers on the road of happy destiny around Porte de Hal in Brussels and, later on, the Rockers in Lisboa and Estoril. You know who you are.

When it came to preparing the text for publication, I'm particularly grateful for the talents of my editor Kendra Ward, copy editor Crissy Calhoun, project manager Rony Ganon, and the entire team at Page Two for guiding us through the minefield of publishing.

My life has been enriched beyond measure by the hundreds of people with whom I've worked over the past two decades: whether as coach, mentor, or consultant. No words can express my appreciation of their trust. This book could never have been written without the privilege of sharing their experiences of living and working, which hopefully has been woven into some of these pages. I have learned at least as much from them as they may have from me.

It has been my good fortune to have always felt valued by a loving family: my mother, Annie, and my father, Michael, now both deceased; my brothers in the United States and in Ireland; my son, Harry, and my daughter, Jane. As time goes on, I know how lucky I've been to be part of a family where I am valued for who I am, rather than for what I've done or possessed. If only everyone was so fortunate, the world would indeed be a happier place.

The adventure continues to be thrilling, as I hope it will be for our fellow travelers, too.

Appendix A

The Self-Worth Quiz

"This revolutionary act of treating ourselves tenderly
can begin to undo the aversive messages of a lifetime."

TARA BRACH

TO GET THE best value from this section, it's a good idea to start with the quiz contained in chapter 1 of this book. Please take the time to write your answers there, or in a journal, before proceeding further. The distinction between self-worth and self-esteem is a vital one to understand. Looking at each statement, determine whether it's one of self-worth or of self-esteem. Please note that your self-worth does not depend on getting the "right" answers!

Answers

1. If I could only find meaningful work, I would feel so much better about myself. *By placing conditions on how we feel about ourselves, we are operating in the realm of self-esteem.*

2. I am grateful for my good health. *Laudable . . . but it's still self-esteem. You can have self-worth even if your health is not good. Indeed, that's exactly when you need it most.*

3. I deserve to be happy. *You do. This is self-worth.*

4. I am so proud of my children. *Congratulations! But this is self-esteem, as well as esteeming them.*

5. I believe in always doing my best. *Good. This is self-worth in action. As long as you don't make self-worth contingent on the results of doing your best. Because then you'd be back in self-esteem mode.*

6. I want to be a good friend to myself. *This is a classic statement of self-worth.*

7. A healthy lifestyle is essential to a good relationship with myself. *If you choose so, then it is. In any case, this is a statement of self-esteem.*

8. I have value because I am loved by God. (Or, the Universe supports me.) *These are spiritual beliefs, which are your choice. If you want to make them essential to self-esteem, you may. These can be valid paths to self-worth, too. However, wouldn't you agree that even non-spiritual people can have self-worth?*

9. I choose to take responsibility for my own well-being. *Good. Both self-worth and self-esteem in action.*

10. Good time-management is essential for self-care. *It probably is, but it's not essential for self-worth.*

11. I live for my family. *Laudable. But problematic for self-worth. What if one of them disappoints you? Although service to others is noble (see chapter 11), living for others can be a classic manifestation of co-dependence, which is nearly always the*

result of low self-worth. Why not live for yourself, first and foremost? Why make your life's meaning contingent on family?

12. One of the benefits of a new relationship with myself is the freedom to contribute. *It is. Self-worth in action.*

13. I must live with integrity. It's essential that I can trust myself. *Most people would agree that trusting oneself is essential for self-esteem. However, I would argue that an addict seeking recovery can still have self-worth, even when they might still struggle to trust themselves.*

14. I must remove all negativity from my life. *Followers of positive psychology may be tempted to say this is essential for self-worth. However, I disagree. Embracing the shadow sides of life, such as loneliness, sadness, grief, or loss of purpose is often an essential part of the self-worth journey. By trying to kill "bad" emotions, we can kill all emotions.*

15. I sometimes feel very lonely. *This does not stop you from experiencing self-worth. Indeed, many of us have found loneliness (or rejection) to be a path toward a deeper friendship with ourselves.*

You can access a full list of downloadable resources and other checklists on SelfWorthAcademy.com.

Appendix B

Checklist: 24 Things That Do Not Define Your Self-Worth

"Your time is limited, so don't waste
it living someone else's life."

STEVE JOBS

WHILE SAFARI VOYAGERS lived the self-worth adventure, many began to notice how the world around them frequently seeks to "hook" their relationship with themselves to a variety of extrinsic factors, such as how they look or how they spend their free time. It seems that our education, our culture, and our economy continue to subtly introduce "shoulds" into our lives, no doubt to cultivate the very hunger that their products and services are designed to satisfy. Or perhaps just to validate other people's choices. The effect is the same.

Therefore, we need to keep vigilant. It's easy for a host of extrinsic dependencies to sneak in under the radar, pretending to be essential for your optimum relationship with you. Businesses and educational establishments are particularly adept at the "Ideal You" message. But you may also hear the same refrain from friends, colleagues, and people you meet on the personal-development circuit.

The following checklist is included as a reminder of topics already covered and it's provided as a handy reference point, should you feel that you are being snared by any of those self-esteem dependencies again. Summing up, your self-worth does *not* depend on:

1. Whether you have a defined purpose in your life.
2. Your relationship status.
3. Your level of education.
4. Your home or who else is there, or even if you have one.
5. Your job or career.
6. How you look—your weight or appearance.
7. Your income or net worth or business success. Your net worth is not your self-worth.
8. Whether you are sticking to a diet or exercise regime.
9. Whether you have been rejected by a romantic partner recently or in the past.
10. Whether you have been rejected for a job or a promotion recently or in the past.
11. Your relationship with your parents.
12. Whether you have children or how they have turned out.
13. Your relationship with your children or siblings.
14. The number or quality of your sexual experiences.
15. Whether you feel happy or depressed or anxious or even angry.
16. Your lifestyle, vacations, car, technology, or size of your home.
17. Whether you have friends or feel lonely.
18. Whether you got through your task list today; whether you feel you are achieving or not.
19. Your social media profile/score/followers.

20. Whether you do dance, sport, yoga, or anything else.
21. Whether you are up to date on current affairs, fashion, culture, or technology.
22. Whether you missed an opportunity—for example, a career, an investment, or even a life partner.
23. Whether you are a published author or won acclaim as an artist or performer.
24. Other people's opinions of you, no matter who they may be.

No doubt you can add a few items of your own to this list. Each time you do so, you sever another thread that ties down your self-worth. With each snip, you open up another fragment in the frontier of freedom.

About John Niland

JOHN NILAND IS best known as a conference speaker and coach with VCO Global (VCO-Global.com), focusing on supporting professionals to raise the value of their work and create opportunity through better dialogue with their customers and marketplace.

John graduated in philosophy only to discover that his native Ireland had limited requirements for philosophers in the 1980s and that supply greatly exceeded demand. He hurriedly cross-trained into computer science and lived in disguise as a systems analyst/project leader for fifteen years, managing large pan-European projects for fast-moving consumer goods, retail, and petrochemical organizations until even the money could not induce him to continue. He then set up his own systems company and soon discovered how little he knew about managing people. The real learning began: how to develop business *with* people rather than *for* them.

Since 2000, John has been coaching others to achieve success, with increasing misgivings about the value of this, until he discovered a passion for supporting those who wish to contribute rather than just to win and hence produce some real value: both social and economic. With trademark humor, he's a popular speaker at professional conferences on raising the value of work, value-centered selling, and negotiation.

In parallel, John is one of the co-founders of the European Forum of Independent Professionals, reflecting nineteen years of coaching more than 600 professionals to create more value in their work. His books include *The Courage to Ask* (co-authored with Kate Daly) and the ebooks *Hidden Value* and *Opportunity Conversations* (all available on VCO-Global.com). John is passionate about raising the value of professional services and inspiring contributors to find meaning in work.

He currently lives in both Lisbon and London and still talks about settling down someday.

SelfWorthAcademy.com